THE CITY & GUILDS TEXTBOOK

LEVEL 3 AWARD IN

EDUCATION

AND TRAINING

C000285931

THE CITY & GUILDS TEXTBOOK

LEVEL 3 AWARD IN
EDUCATION
AND TRAINING

AMANDA TURNER

JOANNE WHITING

About City & Guilds

City & Guilds is the UK's leading provider of vocational qualifications, offering over 500 awards across a wide range of industries, and progressing from entry level to the highest levels of professional achievement. With over 8500 centres in 100 countries, City & Guilds is recognised by employers worldwide for providing qualifications that offer proof of the skills they need to get the job done.

Equal opportunities

City & Guilds fully supports the principle of equal opportunities and we are committed to satisfying this principle in all our activities and published material. A copy of our equal opportunities policy statement is available on the City & Guilds website.

First edition 2014
Reprinted 2016
Reprinted 2017
ISBN 978 0 85193 294 1

Commissioning Editor Tom Guy
Development Editor James Hobbs
Production Editor Natalie Griffith

Text and cover design by Select Typesetters Ltd
Typeset by Integra Software Services Pvt., Ltd
Printed in the UK by Cambrian Printers Ltd

British Library Cataloguing in Publication Data

A catalogue record is available from the British Library.

Publications

For information about or to order City & Guilds support materials, contact 0844 543 0000 or centresupport@cityandguilds.com. You can find more information about the materials we have available at www.cityandguilds.com/publications.

Every effort has been made to ensure that the information contained in this publication is true and correct at the time of going to press. However, City & Guilds' products and services are subject to continuous development and improvement and the right is reserved to change products and services from time to time. City & Guilds cannot accept liability for loss or damage arising from the use of information in this publication.

City & Guilds
1 Giltspur Street
London EC1A 9DD
T 0844 543 0033
www.cityandguilds.com
publishingfeedback@cityandguilds.com

CONTENTS

ACKNOWLEDGEMENTS

City & Guilds would like to sincerely thank the following.

For invaluable education and training expertise
Helen Handyside, Donna Latimer

Further thanks
Charmain Campbell

Picture credits
Every effort has been made to acknowledge all copyright holders as below and the publishers will, if notified, correct any errors in future editions.

Bedford College: p162; **Cambridge Regional College**: p267; **Canterbury College**: p136; **Eastleigh College**: pp24, 178, 338; © **Educationphotos.co.uk**: pp1, 20, 57, 65, 173, 193, 199, 202, 216, 253, 258, 314, back cover; **Science Photo Library**: © Mauro Fermariello/Science Photo Library p40; © Ria Novosti/Science Photo Library p39; **Shutterstock**: © AjFile p60; © Ammentorp Photography p334; © Andresr pp161, 181, 311; © Andrey Eremin p282; © auremar pp62, 91, 92; © baranq p181; © Brian Goodman p138; © Champion studio p273; © Christian Wilkinson p26; © Claudia Fernandes p101; © Constantine Pankin p11; © Diego Cervo p4; © EM Karuna p336; © eurobanks p134; © Goodluz pp97, 212, 218, 237, front cover; © Guy Shapira p89; © Ilja Dubovskis p276; © IMG_191 LLC p308; © Juan He p324; © kedrov p186; © Konstantin Chagin p167; © lightpoet pp99, 295; © Lisa F. Young p42; © Little_Desire p247; © Monkey Business Images pp22, 45, 54, 215, 222, 225, 284, 286, 320; © ollyy pp12, 280; © Paul Aniszewski p51; © Pichugin Dmitry p298; © Pressmaster pp118, 119; © Rido p184; © Robert Kneschke pp40, 209, 339; © S_L p302; © SnowWhiteimages p131; © spotmatik p121; © Stankevich p348; © Stokkete p306; © Syda Productions p146; © Sylvie Bouchard p332; © takayuki p29; © Tribalium p18; © VisibleMind p299; © wavebreakmedia pp171, 261, 307, 331, 339; © wongwean p336

It is funny how I can write a book but I have found writing the acknowledgment the hardest part. I have had so much support, guidance, love and encouragement from so many people it is impossible to list everyone. So a sincere thank you goes to all my colleagues, friends and family who made this book possible. Finally, a special thanks to all my learners over the years who have provided me with the opportunity to do what I love – teach.

Amanda Turner

Special thanks to Tom Guy, James Hobbs and Charmain Campbell at City & Guilds for their guidance and patience during the writing of this book, and also to Amanda for halving the load and doubling the enjoyment. I would like to thank my colleagues in the teaching training team at Eastleigh College, Hampshire for sharing their experiences and ideas; Ida Halton, Dick Cervantes and Sofie Van der Veen. Also, to my friends Myra, Jane, Julie and Kylee for providing me with such wonderful memories of those early teaching days and all my learners of the past 15 years, from whom I have learnt so much. Most importantly my grateful thanks to my husband Neil and to George and Emily for their encouragement and love.

Jo Whiting

ABOUT THE AUTHORS

Joanne Whiting has worked in further and higher education for over 15 years and holds a BA (Hons) Degree in Education. She started her teaching career delivering anatomy and physiology courses part time within the beauty department. She quickly moved to a full-time position and taught NVQs from Level 1 to Level 4. She was the lead Internal Quality Assurer within the beauty department before moving to teacher training in 2003.

She has also worked as an Advanced Practitioner and been part of Eastleigh College's Observation Team and Quality Review Board.

She is an experienced teacher who has been teaching and managing courses from City & Guilds for over 15 years. She now works full time as the course manager for teacher training at Eastleigh College. In addition Joanne works in partnership with the University of Portsmouth delivering the Post Graduate Certificate in Education (PGCE) course.

Joanne lives near Southampton, Hampshire with her family.

Amanda Turner is a full-time lecturer in teacher training at the College of West Anglia, in Norfolk and has been delivering education and training in further and higher education since 1996. Amanda holds an MA in Education, a PGCE and a BA (Hons) in Art Education.

In her current role she draws from years of experience of teaching learners with special educational needs, including challenging behaviour and specific learning difficulties and disabilities. However, over the past three years, it is the success stories from the trainee teachers that continue to provide new inspiration.

Amanda is a member of the Quality Team at the College of West Anglia. Through bespoke training, individual support and observation, she uses previous management and teaching experience in support of a whole-organisation approach to teaching, learning and assessment.

Amanda has presented at conferences both locally and nationally and continues to conduct research into developing inclusive practices within teaching; particular interests include barriers to learning and differentiation strategies.

FOREWORD

After the surprise of being approached by City & Guilds to write a book to support the 6502 Level 3 Award in Education and Training, we realised that this was a great opportunity to use our years of teaching teachers to create a book that would be a useful, practical guide for all new teachers/trainers.

As practising teacher trainers we feel that there is a real need for a colourful, easy-to-read book which is full of lots of useful tips and ideas yet still contains the theory that underpins great teaching and learning.

We wanted the book to be as visual as possible and we hope that the many diagrams, tables and pictures will help you to remember and understand the main principles of teaching and learning to help develop your teaching. We have also included guidance on how to make your teaching interesting, fun and inspiring.

We have both learnt so much from the hundreds of learners that we have taught over the years and we would like to thank them for all the ideas and examples of good practice that have found their way into this book.

Amanda and Joanne

INTRODUCTION

This book has been designed to help you acquire the skills and knowledge needed to teach in an effective and motivating way. It is aimed at anyone who:

- works or wants to work as a teacher/trainer in the further education and skills sector
- is not yet in a teaching role, or who has just started a teaching role
- wants a short qualification to help with any career choices
- has already achieved appropriate Learning and Development units that can be carried forward into this qualification
- teaches or trains as part of their role or who wants to understand the basic principles of teaching.

It offers examples of good practice and covers the basic skills that a new teacher/trainer will need in order to teach professionally. This book has been written against the criteria for the level 3 Award in Education and Training (6502) from City & Guilds.

Each unit relates to the qualification units that make up the Award in Education and Training. Within each unit the outcomes from each qualification unit have been used as section headings for easy reference. In this book you will cover:

- Understanding the roles, responsibilities and relationships in education and training
- Understanding and using inclusive approaches in education and training
- Facilitating learning and development for individuals
- Facilitating learning and development in groups
- Understanding assessment in education and training
- Understanding the principles and practices of assessment.

The level 3 Award in Understanding the Principles and Practices of Assessment (unit 301), which is part of the 6317 suite, is embedded in this qualification and will assist anyone who also intends to complete the TAQA assessor's award.

Each unit starts with an introduction which lists the key aspects that will be covered along with the learning outcomes for each qualification unit. Within each unit the learning outcomes have been used as section headings to allow information to be found easily. This can be used for reference or to assist with linking the teaching theory to assignments needed for the Award in Education and Training.

There are tip boxes offering practical advice and word focus boxes to help with unfamiliar words or phrases. Activities and tasks have also been included to help you relate the new information to your own teaching.

At the end of each unit there is a summary which concentrates on the main learning points. An assignment focus has also been included to help you to plan and structure your assignment.

A unit on helpful information, suggestions and tips has also been included to help you to:

- write a reflective learning journal
- reference your work
- prepare for your micro-teach and
- study, structure and present your work.

There is also a unit containing further sources of information which includes websites, reading lists and references. This book will provide good practical advice for anyone who is planning to enter the exciting and challenging world of teaching.

UNIT 301

Understanding roles,
responsibilities and relationships
in education and training

INTRODUCTION

It is vital for a teacher to understand their role and responsibilities within lifelong learning. This is a professional role that requires the teacher to be aware of the demands and challenges ahead of them. The role of a teacher is a varied one that requires the teacher to have many skills. This is both part of the appeal and the challenge of the job. One of the most important roles of a teacher is to provide a safe and happy environment in which learners can learn. This unit provides information on how this can be best achieved and will offer some examples in best practice for setting ground rules and respect for others.

The professional relationships between teacher and learners and the teacher and other professionals in lifelong learning are also considered. There are professional boundaries that must be in place in order to promote a positive and enabling learning experience for *all* learners. Learners might have a variety of individual needs from physical disabilities to different learning needs. These needs are recognised in this unit which will provide some practical tips and guidance for a teacher to try with their own group of learners.

Another key aspect of this unit is to consider the responsibility a teacher has to promote equality and to value diversity. An all-inclusive learning environment needs to be created so that each individual learner feels both valued and included. Examples of how resources might have to be adapted are also given.

A teacher must also be aware of the many rules, regulations and important key aspects of legislation that must be adhered to. This unit will summarise information on the main legislative requirements set by government, awarding organisations and learning providers.

Some of the aspects covered include:

- key aspects of legislation
- the roles and responsibilities of a teacher
- how to make learners feel valued
- the difference between equality and diversity
- how to produce inclusive resources
- the importance of getting to know learners
- how to motivate learners
- meeting the needs of learners with disabilities and/or learning difficulties
- the importance of icebreakers
- identifying professional boundaries
- the points of referral available to a teacher
- why ground rules are important.

In Unit 301 you will cover the following learning outcomes:

LO1: Understand the teaching role and responsibilities in education and training
LO2: Understand ways to maintain a safe and supportive learning environment
LO3: Understand the relationship between teachers and other professionals in education and training

ROLES AND RESPONSIBILITIES IN LIFELONG LEARNING

LO1.1 Explain own roles and responsibilities in lifelong learning

One of a teacher's responsibilities is to be supportive towards their learners

The teacher's role

Teachers assume many varied roles, some of which are more obvious than others. **Roles** are functions a teacher might willingly or voluntarily take on while a responsibility is something the teacher must do as part of their job. A job description will list the key responsibilities of a teacher but there are many other roles that a teacher might have to adopt to be professional. Each role will bring with it its own various responsibilities. One of the main responsibilities of a teacher is to encourage learners to want to learn and to achieve their goals.

Roles are 'nouns' (job titles), while responsibilities are what a teacher needs to do to accomplish the role

“ ”

The fundamental teaching role is one of facilitating learning by providing expertise, managing resources and encouraging learners to help themselves to attain their goals.

(Walklin, 1990, page 245)

SOME IMPORTANT ROLES TO BE CONSIDERED

Administrator and record keeper
A teacher is responsible for completing all paperwork required by their own organisation and for the awarding organisation. All records need to be accurate and kept up to date.

Assessor
A teacher will need to check that learners are making progress and meeting their own individual goals.

Communicator
A teacher must be able to pass on their knowledge in a clear and understandable way. They need to build a rapport with their learners and ensure that learners communicate with each other. They also require good listening skills and display open, relaxed body language.

Counsellor and coach
A teacher must act as a counsellor or guide in a professional, fair, non-judgmental and objective way. It is important for a teacher to know when to refer learners to more professional help if needed.

Facilitator
At times a teacher will need to allow learners to learn independently and 'get on with it' while observing from a distance and helping to direct learners only when needed.

Health and Safety Officer
A teacher is responsible for the health and safety of their learners. They need to ensure that the learning environment is a safe place in which learners can learn.

Helper and supporter
A teacher must identify the individual needs of each learner and offer help and support where they can. They might need to refer the learner to the relevant person and must be aware of professional boundaries.

Interviewer
A teacher might have to interview future learners to check that it is the correct course for the learner and that all the entry criteria have been met. At this stage they will also identify if any other support needs to be provided and answer any queries that the learner might have regarding the course.

Market researcher
A teacher needs to keep up to date with any changes within their subject area and should be aware of any changes to the qualification that they are teaching.

Mentor
A teacher will act as a role model and someone to whom the learner can go to for support and guidance.

Monitor and evaluator
A teacher must regularly check that learning is taking place and identify what changes are needed to help improve their own teaching.

Motivator and team leader
A teacher should have a passion for the subject that they teach and lead by example.

Organiser and planner
Teachers must be well organised and have good time-management skills. They need to make sure that they are well prepared and ready for each session. They should plan to deliver each session using a variety of teaching methods and provide suitable resources.

Personal tutor
Sometimes learners can have several teachers teaching them on the same course. One teacher will act as the personal tutor for the group and be responsible for the well-being of these learners. This will involve giving learners information and guidance on a wide range of issues and knowing when to refer them to other professionals for help.

Publicity and promotional materials officer
Most courses, full and part time, will run only if a minimum number of people have enrolled onto the course. Sometimes it is in the teacher's best interest to promote and advertise the course. This might include attending open evening events and taster days.

Special needs and multicultural practitioner
A teacher must promote equality for all of their learners, regardless of age, sex, religion or culture.

Reflective practitioner
It is important that a teacher keeps up to date with any new developments. They also need to evaluate sessions, learning programmes and identifying their own continuing professional development needs (CPD).

Subject knowledge expert
A teacher should have a sound, up-to-date knowledge of their subject matter. They should be able to share examples from their own experiences and background with their learners, where appropriate, as this will help gain the confidence and respect of learners.

Teacher
A teacher should be able to impart knowledge in a clear and understandable way and regularly assess what their learners have learnt.

(Adapted from a list by Walkin, 1990, pages 245–246)

The roles of a teacher appear never ending. Walklin (1990, page 246) established some of the roles of a teacher as: change agent and innovator; counsellor and coach; helper and supporter; implementer; monitor and evaluator; motivator and team leader; needs identifier and advisor; organiser and planner; staff developer; teaching and learning media expert and, finally, tutor.

Teaching effectively is not the only skill needed by a teacher. These varied roles each bring with them new challenges and skills that might have to be learnt. A teacher must be able to adapt to ever-changing circumstances. The skills, qualities and characteristics that a teacher requires to fulfil these roles will help them to deal with the many varied responsibilities that they face.

When you study a list like this, it might seem that the number of skills a teacher is expected to possess to fulfil these roles is overwhelming. A teacher will have some natural talents, and will already have acquired skills which will make some of these roles easier, but there will also be some roles that do not come so easily to some people. It is possible that new skills might have to be learnt to enable a teacher to perform their job effectively.

It is important that a teacher takes all their roles seriously in order to become the facilitator of their learner's learning. Teachers need to be confident, knowledgeable, motivational, and passionate about their subject and to provide their learners with the best possible learning experience. It is important that they remain professional yet approachable at all times. The more a teacher knows about their learners the more this will increase their understanding of a learner's possible needs and enable support strategies to be put in place. Learners look up to their teachers, so it is important that teachers also recognise the impact that they have on their learners' lives.

❝❞

We have to show a genuine interest in our students if we want them to respond well to us.

(Minton, 2005, page 91)

Responsibilities

The responsibilities that a teacher has are more specific than their roles. It is the responsibility of the teacher to ensure that both the needs of the learner and the organisation are met. It used to be that the responsibility of a teacher was simply to impart knowledge (to teach). However, the responsibilities have been increased so that a teacher should now aim to motivate their learners to *want* to learn.

To teach effectively there are lots of other responsibilities that need to be fulfilled

- Abide with the rules of the organisation and all legislation and codes of practice
- Plan and prepare sessions
- Make sessions as varied and interesting as possible
- Plan and use a range of assessment methods
- Keep up to date with any changes within the subject area/industry
- Mark all work and return to learners in a timely fashion
- Get to know their learners and identify any individual needs
- Make sure that support is in place for all learners from as early as possible
- Prepare and use a range of resources
- Respect diversity
- Include one-to-one tutorials with learners
- Set achievable targets with learners
- Be aware of learners' learning styles
- Identify any barriers that a learner may have towards their learning
- Correspond with other interested parties, eg employers, parents
- Keep records and all paperwork up to date
- Be professional at all times
- Be honest and trustworthy
- Not judge or make assumptions about learners
- Be a good role model
- Negotiate clear ground rules and enforce them
- Create a good rapport with learners and between learners

ACTIVITY

Make a list of the roles and responsibilities that you will need in order to teach within your chosen subject area. Tick all the ones that you think that you are capable of and then consider how to gain the skills needed for the ones you don't.

❝❞

As with any area of work, teachers must work within the boundaries of the law and professional values. There are a vast number of laws, directives and professional ethics; they are constantly changing or being updated.

(Wilson, 2009, page 18)

It is a teacher's responsibility to keep acquainted and up to date with the relevant legal and regulatory requirements and codes of practice, in order to conduct themselves in a professional way. This also enables the teacher to provide an environment that is both safe and conducive to learning. The welfare of learners, colleagues and their own well-being should be a foremost concern before any teaching takes place.

The teaching cycle

A teacher needs to structure their teaching in a logical order. The teaching cycle (sometimes referred to as the training cycle) will help and encourage teachers to plan their sessions in a supportive way. The teaching cycle helps teachers and learners to identify what is required by looking at the individual needs of the learner. This information can then be used to help make any changes in the design and planning of the session or course to help and fully support the learner.

These changes can then be implemented in a variety of ways (see Teaching methods, page 56). A teacher will then assess and evaluate the progress that is being made and check that learning is taking place.

This cycle is a continuous process which can be joined at any stage.

Identify the need

Design

Implement

Assess and evaluate

The teaching cycle

LEGISLATION AND REGULATION

LO1.2 Summarise key aspects of legislation, regulatory requirements and codes of practice relating to own role and responsibilities

There are many Acts, regulations, codes of practice and rules that a teacher must follow. This unit will outline the differences between these and list the main ones that will affect the teaching profession. Each subject area might have additional legislation, so it is important that a teacher must ensure that they are fully updated with any new developments or changes.

What's the difference?

Acts of Parliament
An Act is a law passed by Government. Therefore if an Act is broken it will mean there has been a breach in the law and possibly severe consequences will follow. An Act describes how a law must be followed.

Regulations
A regulation sets out general principles made under an Act. Both Acts and regulations are law and must be followed.

Codes of Practice
A code gives practical guidance on how to comply with the legal requirements of specific regulations. These are normally set by professional bodies.

Byelaws

Byelaws are laws made by local councils and affect only their local area.

Rules

Rules can be set by any organisation or individual. They might include or make reference to guidelines or procedures that need to be followed.

All learners are individuals with different backgrounds and needs

Equality Act (2010)

The Equality Act came into force in October 2010 and replaced all previous equality legislation in England, Scotland and Wales: namely the Race Relations Act (1976), the Disability Discrimination Act (1995), the Sex Discrimination Act (1975), the Equal Pay Act (1963), the Employment Equality (Age) Regulations (2006), the Civil Partnership Act (2004), the Employment Equality (Religion or Belief) Regulations (2003).

It brings together different aspects of discrimination under one piece of legislation. It is a teacher's responsibility to include activities that help learners embrace diversity and create an atmosphere of tolerance, friendliness and respect. A teacher must challenge any forms of antisocial behaviour such as bullying, offensive language and/ or discrimination.

The same characteristics are still protected but they are now called 'protected characteristics' (PCs). These include:

- Age
- Disability
- Gender
- Gender reassignment
- Race

- Religion or belief
- Sex
- Sexual orientation
- Marriage and civil partnership
- Pregnancy and maternity.

Discrimination

■ **Disability discrimination**

All learners must be able to fully participate in their learning. Learners should be asked if they have any disabilities before the start of a course and if a learner declares a disability then it is a teacher's responsibility to ensure that the organisation is aware of it and to assist in addressing the needs of that learner.

■ **Race relations**

Teachers are not allowed to discriminate on the grounds of nationality, race, colour or ethnic origins. All learners should be encouraged, by the teacher, to work together and value the differences that they might bring to the group.

■ **Sex discrimination**

Any person regardless of their sex or marital status will be treated equally. Courses should be made available to all learners.

Data Protection Act (1998)

This Act regulates the processing of personal information that is held on paper or electronically. All personal information must be stored securely and used only for the specific purpose for which it was collected. Data must not be disclosed to other parties without the consent of the individual. A teacher must ensure that they keep all personal information up to date and that it is not kept longer than necessary. This Act also enables individuals to request access to records held about them.

A teacher must take particular care if they need to take records outside their organisation, for example visiting work placements or delivering a course in a variety of locations. It is essential that personal information is handled in a professional way and particular attention must be given to the confidentiality and privacy of learners. A teacher should:

- never disclose or discuss the personal circumstances of any learners with anyone outside the organisation, and only with relevant individuals within it
- establish good practices for secure management of documents containing personal information, at all times
- always use secure password protection to restrict access to computerised records.

The Data Protection Act (1998) is mandatory. *All* organisations that hold or process personal data *must* comply.

CLASSROOM MANAGEMENT

In the teaching environment it is important that any learner information, enrolment forms and assessment paperwork is kept in a secure place and not left in classrooms where other learners may have access to the personal information of others.

Copyright, Designs and Patents Act (1988)

This Act states that if anyone copies, adapts and distributes material from any book, journal or from the internet, they must acknowledge the original author. Teachers should also ensure that learners reference everything that they submit, if the work includes another person's published work.

Teachers must adhere to this Act while reproducing material for teaching and need to make sure that learners are aware of it. Organisations can also purchase a licence to enable photocopying small amounts of information and usually have a member of staff to provide guidance on this.

The detail of copyright law is complex, but it means that unless resources are either over a certain age, or clearly marked 'photocopiable' or 'copyright free', then permission may be needed and their use acknowledged. Special conditions apply to sound recordings and media clips, particularly if these are intended for use with e-learners, and teachers should consider this if they think that it is applicable to their work.

It is also important to check with your organisation on its and your responsibilities on the ownership of any papers you produce to use with learners; sometimes this will be shared rights, but it can be on behalf of and therefore the property of the organisation.

HANDY HINT

By joining a professional body you will receive regular magazines that will help you to keep up to date with any changes in legislation for your subject area.

Freedom of Information Act (2000)

This gives the right to the learners to ask for any personal or general information that is held about them. A teacher's responsibility is to facilitate this need and to ensure that any personal data is kept confidential. This Act also requires public authorities to publish some information about their organisation and to provide certain information to the public on request.

Children Act (2004)

This Act promotes the safety and well-being of children up to 19 years of age or older if assessed as vulnerable, for example those brought up in care. It requires teachers to enforce these values and to provide a safe learning environment for learners. If a teacher believes that any of their learners are at risk then they should report this to their line manager and document any incident.

The Act also takes into account **Every Child Matters (ECM)** which has five outcomes

- Be healthy
- Stay safe
- Enjoy and achieve
- Make a positive contribution
- Achieve economic well-being

A teacher should embed these outcomes by ensuring that the teaching environment is comfortable and safe; for example, taking note of any sharp edges, broken furniture, and loose electrical wires. They should report their findings to the relevant person within their organisation so that the problem can be fixed.

Regular breaks should also be provided to enable learners to relax and have access to water and food to keep themselves healthy and refreshed.

HANDY HINT

Go to www.hse.gov.uk/education for up to date information on legislation and health and safety.

Education and Skills Act (2008)

This Act was passed in response to the government's concern that too many adults do not possess basic skills for life such as English, mathematics and ICT.

Learners are entitled to feel safe, protected and healthy within their learning environment. It is the responsibility of both the organisation and the teacher to provide such an environment.

Health and Safety at Work etc Act (1974) (HASAWA)

The HASAWA requires teachers to provide a safe and healthy environment for themselves and for their learners. For example, for courses that deal with hazardous or electrical material they must ensure that learners have the correct clothing to protect them and that electrical equipment is inspected regularly. Risk assessments must be carried out as necessary and documented appropriately. Teachers should check for any hazards before teaching; for example checking for any trailing cables that learners could trip over. Classrooms should be left in a safe and tidy order ready for the next class and any broken or faulty equipment should be reported to the relevant person.

In a workplace situation this typically means:

- ensuring that for face-to-face delivery a teacher would know where the fire exits are located, the evacuation procedures and how to contact a first-aider if needed
- performing risk analysis either formally or informally when working with learners in unfamiliar surroundings
- ensuring that particular procedures are followed in specialist environments for example; computer rooms, workshops and labs. This will help to maintain safety and prevent accidents or danger to both the teacher and the learner
- following reporting procedures if accidents or incidents should occur.

(HSE, nd)

Safeguarding Vulnerable Groups Act (2006)

This Act introduced a vetting and barring scheme for working with vulnerable adults. Teachers need to have a Disclosure and Barring Services (DBS) check to work with children or vulnerable adults. This has replaced the Criminal Records Bureau (CRB) check.

Human Rights Act (1998)

This Act deals with people's basic rights, including the right to education.

REGULATORY REQUIREMENTS

Control of Substances Hazardous to Health (COSHH) Regulations (2002)

These regulations deal specifically with the use of hazardous material. They require teachers to provide a safe and healthy environment. For example, for courses that deal with hazardous substances they must ensure that learners are fully aware of the safety procedures to follow and what action to take in case of a breach of these procedures.

Adult social care legislation

This is currently under review in response to population changes, the economic climate and public expectation in relation to the protection of vulnerable adults. Codes of conduct and practice guidance are prevalent in this sector owing to the risks of negligence under the general duty of care. A teacher will need to ensure learners understand the main legislative framework and signpost learners to their employers for guidance.

Code of Professional Practice (2008)

This was developed by the Institute for Learning and outlines the code of conduct for teachers.

Teachers have a duty of care towards their learners and to take preventative measures to protect them from harm. This can be achieved by the teacher behaving professionally and responsibly with colleagues, learners and others. At all times a teacher must ensure that they respect the rights of learners, embrace diversity and never discriminate against anyone, at any level. Both organisations and individuals have a general duty of care towards others and if this is not enforced then they could be found guilty of negligence.

There might also be regulatory requirements linked to subject areas. Membership of a professional body would enable a teacher to stay up to date with changes to their subject area by attending annual conferences and training days. It is also important for teachers to keep themselves up to date with any changes in legislation.

ACTIVITY

Can you think of any other legislation that is specific to your subject area? Make a note of each one in the table below. One has been done for you.

Legislation	Key points
The Electricity at Work Regulations	All electrical equipment must be portable appliance tested (PAT) annually. All equipment must be used correctly by the teacher and learners.

EQUALITY AND DIVERSITY

LO1.3 Explain ways to promote equality and value diversity

Teachers should value the differences between their learners

Teachers need to be aware that each new group of learners will bring with them new challenges and something different from the previous group of learners. In the same way that each group of learners will be different so are the individuals who make up each group. The UK is a multicultural society and the range of cultures, nationalities, religious beliefs, abilities and sexual orientation is wider than ever before.

Under the Equality Act (2010) it is law that all learners are given the same opportunities to be able to learn. All learners have to be treated fairly and with respect. Any personal views or beliefs that a teacher may have must not be allowed into the classroom. A teacher must be professional at all times and value the differences that individuals bring to the group.

A teacher must never discriminate but should realise that it is their responsibility to create a fair, happy and all-inclusive environment in which their learners can feel comfortable. It is also the teacher's responsibility to make sure that everyone feels that they belong and that their views and opinions are valued and indeed sought after. Learners need to be encouraged by the teacher to work together and support each other.

CLASSROOM MANAGEMENT

Taking the time to encourage learners to get to know each other is time well spent as it will help to create a happy learning environment. It is quite often the smaller, simple things that a teacher might do that can make such a positive difference to how a learner might feel.

TEN TOP TIPS ON HOW TO MAKE ALL LEARNERS FEEL VALUED

1   Learn their names (see page 77 for some tips on this). You should know all your learners' names by the third session (on longer courses).

2   Use their names (see page 77). If a name is difficult to pronounce then make a point of learning it. The more a teacher uses a learner's name, then the quicker other learners in the group will learn it. This could make a huge difference to how quickly a person feels that they are part of the group.

3   Get to know your learners. Use relevant examples in your teaching that will mean something to them.

4   Include everyone and don't exclude.

5   Display open body language and give all learners an equal amount of eye contact.

6   Smile and encourage everyone's ideas throughout the session.

7   Thank all learners for their contribution to the lesson.

8   Use praise and actively encourage learners to speak and join in with the session.

9   Make time for learners to talk with you.

10 Show you care. Look interested.

A teacher should plan to include these points in every session they deliver. The positive outcome will be that learners will feel valued, included and happy.

Remember: happy learners learn more

What are equality and diversity?

Equality
This means treating all learners fairly and giving them an equal opportunity to learn. This does not mean treating all learners the same.

Diversity
Diversity means valuing the differences that learners have.

Inclusion
Inclusion is to include all learners and not to exclude anyone.

Differentiation
This is the teaching approaches and methods the teacher uses to ensure that all learners learn well, despite their many differences.

It is a teacher's responsibility to promote equality and diversity within their teaching by promoting a positive and enabling experience for a diverse range of learners.

A teacher should ask themselves the following questions when planning and delivering their sessions:

Planning stage

- Do all planning documents take into consideration the individual needs of the learner?
- Is there clear evidence of initial assessment on the scheme of learning and in lesson plans?
- Are independent learning plans (ILPs) going to be used?
- Is the learning environment suitable for all individuals in this group of learners?
- Have the sessions been planned to include a range of activities?
- Have the learning styles of the learners been taken into consideration?
- Are learners given the opportunity to discuss additional support at the beginning and throughout the course?
- Are the assessment methods that are planned fair and free from discrimination against any learner?
- Are resources prepared so that all learners can access the information easily?
- Have resources been adapted to make it easier for all learners to learn?
- Are people from diverse socioeconomic and cultural backgrounds and people with disabilities visible in course materials?

Delivery

- Have ground rules with learners been set at the start of the course?
- Are simple terminology and plain English used so that everyone understands?
- Have any reference to religious/cultural words been avoided? For example winter and spring break should be used instead of Christmas and Easter holidays.
- Is appropriate, non-discriminatory and sensitive language used?
- Will inappropriate use of language be challenged?
- Is diversity included within teaching – making reference and using examples from a variety of cultures, religions and traditions?
- Are prejudice and stereotyping challenged in the classroom?
- Are discussion and comments within the learning environment managed to ensure learner language is appropriate and non-discriminatory?

A teacher uses a PowerPoint presentation that has been adapted to suit her learners

Always allow time to check the background colour of your PowerPoint on the screen in your classroom. It will normally be a shade or two lighter than on your computer screen. You might have to adjust it before the session starts.

How to produce inclusive handouts and PowerPoint slides
At the start of any course a teacher should find out if an individual learner has any particular needs. Petty (2009, page 560) states that 'Inclusion, diversity, entitlement, differentiation, ensuring equal opportunities and personalised learning all require teachers to treat students as individuals.' It is a teacher's responsibility to adapt any resources that they use to suit all learners. Some learners might need a handout that is produced in a larger font or the background colour on a PowerPoint changed. These are easy things to change and the rest of the learners might not even notice. A teacher needs to make sure that they make themselves available at the start of the course so that learners are able to talk in confidence about their needs.

- Leave lots of space and make sure that there is not too much text or information on each page. Printing on both sides of the paper means there is more space but less paper is needed.
- Use a clear font. Arial, Gill Sans, Century Gothic and Comic Sans are better than most as they are clear and easy to read. Teachers should ask individual learners which font they prefer. Comic Sans contains the letter a in its true form of 'a' instead of 'a'. Learners with dyslexia will recognise the shape and format of this widely used letter more easily. Learners may have specific needs if they are dyslexic or have a visual impairment.

- Use point 12 for text or bigger if a learner requests it. It is not appropriate to enlarge using the photocopier as this will distort the letters and make them hard to read.
- Avoid using jargon and be careful to use plain, simple English. However the gentle introduction of any subject-specific language should be encouraged.
- For learners who have a visual impairment, any pictures, charts or symbols must be explained in text format, so learners can access them.
- Some learners find it easier to read from coloured paper than white paper. Black on pale yellow paper is particularly good. A teacher should check with the learner. There will also be a cost implication that a teacher has to take into account. Some organisations invest in coloured overlays.
- Avoid dark-coloured or fluorescent paper which can be hard to read.
- Use pictures to aid the understanding and meaning of the text. Pictures are especially useful for deaf learners who think and communicate visually.

CLASSROOM MANAGEMENT

A teacher needs to make sure that they make themselves available at the start of the course so that learners are able to talk in confidence about their needs.

We might look the same but we are all individuals

ACTIVITY

Imagine that you are teaching a group of 12 to 17-year-old boys. They are all white, British and they have all grown up in the same town and attended the same school. But even with so many things in common there will still be many factors that will make each of them different. A teacher needs to take into consideration all of these factors as each individual boy will have his own needs. How many things can you think of?

ACTIVITY

Now imagine that you are teaching a group of 12 17- to 25-year-olds. There is a mix of male and female learners from a range of ethnic backgrounds. Two learners have learning difficulties and one learner is partially sighted. What extra factors do you need to consider? Add these to your original list.

GETTING TO KNOW YOUR LEARNERS

LO1.4 Explain why it is important to identify and meet individual learner needs

❝❞

Good teacher–student relationships are based on mutual respect.

(Petty, 2009, page 98)

Babies are born with an inbuilt need to satisfy curiosity and to find out about their surroundings. This intrinsic need requires each individual to gather information, and make sense of what is going on, and this need for learning is with a person throughout their lives. It might be as simple as learning to cook so that they can feed their children or it could be as complex as an intricate mathematical theory. A teacher has a key role in this and should strive to encourage learners to be happy, confident and independent individuals.

A teacher should make it a priority to get to know their learners as soon as possible. Close liaison with the administration team, and being involved in the enrolment process, means that information about individual learners can be made available to the teacher at an early stage. When this is not possible, a teacher can benefit from reading their learner's application form. During the first session some initial assessment and icebreaker activities (see page 30) are also a good way to get to know learners. People attend courses and want to learn for all sorts of reasons. Understanding why a learner has enrolled on a particular course will help the teacher to get to know them and help to identify any learning or physical needs that a learner may have. It will also help the teacher to adjust and plan future sessions.

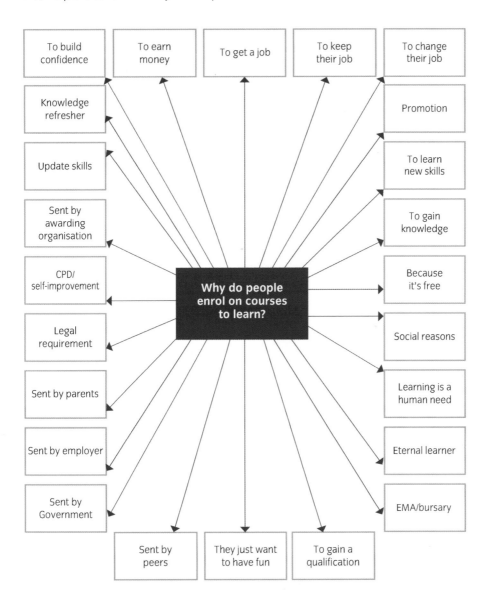

Motivation

How to motivate learners

Once a teacher knows some of the reasons why a learner has joined their course then they can plan to put strategies in place to help and support them. A teacher will potentially have in front of them a combination of all of these learners. A teacher needs to be able to motivate everyone in their class despite each learner's different reasons for being there. It is important that a teacher does this from the very first session. This might seem like an impossible task but there are some strategies that can be used which will help to motivate *all* learners.

Smile – this is the best first impression you can make

First impressions

Learners will need only a few seconds to start forming an opinion about their new teacher. In this short time opinions about appearance, body language, mannerisms and dress sense will start to build up. A teacher should plan to impress and gain their learners' confidence as soon as possible by making sure that they are:

- on time
- prepared with all resources ready and to hand
- smiling
- welcoming learners
- looking clean, presentable and dressed appropriately
- looking calm and organised
- feeling confident
- ensuring the room is prepared for the learners (layout)
- friendly yet professional
- using simple, clear language
- using friendly introductions.

A teacher should build on this good start and use it to begin creating a rapport with their learners. Throughout the course there are several ways that a teacher is able to help build confidence and help to motivate learners:

- Let learners know that they are making progress and that they are on target to completing the course.
- Make time for each learner.
- If you say that you are going to do something, then do it.
- Allow learners to have regular breaks.
- Build a good rapport with learners.
- Praise and encourage learners throughout the course.
- Take time to explain things carefully.
- Don't rush.
- Encourage learners to ask questions.
- Present information clearly and logically.
- Make reference to previous and future learning.
- Avoid jargon.
- Check learning throughout the session.
- Include some study skills.
- Allow time for learners to practise their skills.
- Encourage peer support.
- Set individual targets for learners.
- Display SMART objectives.

When a teacher acts in this professional way learners will have more confidence in their teacher and this in itself will help them to feel motivated. They will appreciate that time has been taken to organise and prepare the session.

ACTIVITY

Think of the best teacher who taught you and analyse why they were so good.

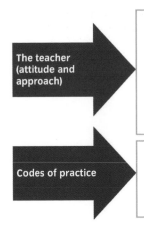

The teacher (attitude and approach)

- Recognises and rewards success.
- Praise is personal, specific and genuine.
- Friendly and approachable, but without needing to be 'liked' or a 'friend'.
- Appearing confident and in control, even when you don't feel like it.
- Own the room. First and foremost it is your space!
- Layout – move furniture (if possible) so that it is your space that will work for you, your teaching strategies and gives you access to everyone.

Codes of practice

- Clear, negotiated guidelines for acceptable behaviour.
- Agree sanctions that are do-able and stick to them.
- Insist on silence and get everyone's attention before dishing out instructions.
- Make sure your instructions are clear and simple.

The delivery

- Good planning (both short term and long term) leads to motivated and engaged learners.
- Communicate aims to learners at the start; link to previous lesson and check learning at the end.
- Use a starter activity to provide focus.
- Chunk lessons to ensure that the time in the classroom is fast paced and varied. This can be achieved by adopting a range of teaching and learning approaches that use resources in an imaginative way.
- Use timed activities and do not interrupt the 'flow' of a lesson with impromptu notices or additional information. This may be an opportunity for learners to become distracted and off task.
- Be prepared to be flexible within the delivery and responsive to unforeseen circumstances. Have extension tasks ready. These do not need to take long to plan and could be simple questions or summarising a discussion.
- Enjoy the lesson and listen to your learners. Allow time for ideas to be processed and developed.

Maslow (1908–1970)

Abraham Maslow studied motivation and created a hierarchy of basic needs. This states that the lower-level basic needs have to be satisfied before progress on to the higher levels is possible. Once these needs have been reasonably satisfied, then it is possible to reach the highest level, which Maslow called self-actualisation. Robertson, as cited by Reece and Walker (2004, page 79), applied each level of the hierarchy to the classroom and teaching (see next page). When learners feel safe, comfortable and that they 'fit in' or 'belong' then they are more likely, with some encouragement from the teacher, to learn more effectively and therefore reach their full potential (self-actualisation).

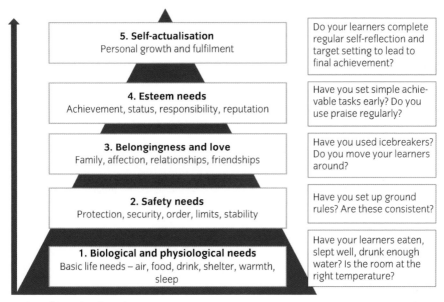

5. Self-actualisation Personal growth and fulfilment	Do your learners complete regular self-reflection and target setting to lead to final achievement?
4. Esteem needs Achievement, status, responsibility, reputation	Have you set simple achievable tasks early? Do you use praise regularly?
3. Belongingness and love Family, affection, relationships, friendships	Have you used icebreakers? Do you move your learners around?
2. Safety needs Protection, security, order, limits, stability	Have you set up ground rules? Are these consistent?
1. Biological and physiological needs Basic life needs – air, food, drink, shelter, warmth, sleep	Have your learners eaten, slept well, drunk enough water? Is the room at the right temperature?

Maslow's hierarchy of needs

Intrinsically motivated learners will perform well because they are willing and eager to learn. They see their learning experience as something meaningful and they are motivated to do well.

HANDY HINT

The opposite to **intrinsic motivation** is **extrinsic motivation**.

HANDY HINT

Remember: the higher up the pyramid you want to get, the more important the lower levels are to your success or failure.

Barriers to learning

There are many factors that might prevent learning or hinder someone from feeling motivated. Feelings of inadequacy or self-doubt might stop someone from even enquiring about a course. These barriers to learning for adults may be self-imposed or might result from past learning experiences.

Intrinsic motivation is an internal desire to perform a particular task; learners will do certain activities because it gives them pleasure, interests them or develops a particular skill

Extrinsic motivation is caused by factors external to the individual learner and unrelated to the task they are performing. Examples include money, good grades, and other rewards

Ensuring equal opportunities within the organisation and within the teaching in your centre will start turning some of the barriers to learning into positive learning messages. Good communication with learners is the key (see page 153).

It is important that a teacher is able to recognise the barriers that a learner may have and put strategies in place to help motivate them. Francis and Gould (2009, page 36) recognise that 'Each time we meet a new group of lifelong learners, the only certainty that we can rely on is that they will all have their own particular needs, characteristics and peculiarities.' A teacher needs to make the time to get to know their learners as quickly as possible because some barriers will not have presented themselves on application forms or at interview. The quicker that a teacher can gain the trust of the learner then the more likely it will be that the learner might divulge their concerns or worries. In the table below are the most common barriers to learning that an adult learner may have, along with the reason why they might have that barrier.

 CLASSROOM MANAGEMENT

A teacher needs to make the time to get to know their learners as quickly as possible because some barriers will not have presented themselves on application forms or at interview.

Barrier	Reason
The teacher	An uninspiring and uninterested teacher will have a very negative effect on a learner.
The learner's attitude	A learner who is not motivated and has a poor attitude will hinder their own learning.
Past learning experience	Many adults had a hard time at school and so they are wary about re-entering a learning environment, especially if the centre is based in a traditional learning institution.
Time	Adults are often restricted to particular times when they can learn. A fixed timetable can effectively prohibit some adults from learning.
Fear	Many people are still fearful of using a computer. They might not understand how to use it or they could be worried about looking silly because they do not have the required computer skills. They could have a fear of failure, especially if they are returning to formal education after a long gap. They might also have a fear of meeting new people.
Childcare	Many adults will find it too difficult or too expensive to arrange childcare.

Costs	Costs are a significant barrier to learning. There may be a number of reasons for this: lack of control over money, lack of access to a personal income, or not having enough money to spare for learning when household needs are the first priority.
Literacy, language and accessibility	Learners who need help with literacy or whose first language is not English may need extra support; this may include translation of course material and publicity materials.
Disability	Learners who have a disability might need special arrangements to help them learn.
Location	For some learners location could be a problem. They may have no means of reaching the centre, or they may feel uncomfortable in the area where the centre is located. In rural areas learners may need help with transport.
Personal and social needs	Many learners are hampered by deep-seated feelings of inferiority generated by social conditions and expectations.
No motivation	Some learners have been pressed into attending and really don't want to be there. They tend to be the 'I-don't-want-to-learn' participant.
Poor health	The learner might miss some sessions through ill health.
Poor facilities and resources	The room could be too hot or cold, too dark or overcrowded. Resources might be lacking, out of date or of a poor quality.
Bad relations	There could be a 'personality clash' between teacher and learner or between learner and learner. The teacher should not allow a 'personality clash' to develop.
Age	A learner might feel that they are getting too old to learn.
Other responsibilities	Families, careers and social commitments could prevent or hinder attendance and learning.

Icebreakers

An icebreaker activity will help learners to relax and develop a bond at the start of the course. The quicker a teacher can help their learners to get to know each other and communicate the easier their job will be. It is the responsibility of the teacher to try to create a happy learning environment for their learners to learn in. There are lots of icebreaker activities to choose from. A teacher must choose carefully as an inappropriate icebreaker might annoy and demotivate learners. However if the right one is chosen then it will provide the course with an excellent start.

EXAMPLES

- Put learners into pairs; make sure that they are paired with someone whom they don't know (split up friends). Agree some questions with the whole group and write them on the board. Your name, what town you live in, why you are on the course and a fun question like an interesting fact or the name of your first record/CD/download. Allow learners about ten minutes to find out this information about each other and then ask for a volunteer to start and get each pair to introduce their partner. This works well as people would normally prefer to talk about someone else rather than themselves.
- Each learner is given a list and they have to mingle with the rest of the group and find someone to match everything on the list: a jogger, a dog owner, a Leo … When they have found someone who matches the criteria they add their name against it so that they are learning each other's names. As before there could be some amusing categories to introduce a bit of fun at the start of the course.
- Pass around a pad of sticky notes and ask learners to tear off as many sticky notes as they want (everyone has to take at least one). Don't tell them what it is for. Ask each learner to write a fact about themselves onto each sticky note. Then go around the room and invite everyone to share their name and facts with the rest of the group.

There are many more icebreaker activities to choose from. Be mindful of the age and ability of your learners when choosing which one to use. The key to a successful icebreaker is to make it fun and useful, so that people start to get to know each other.

Irrespective of the approach to icebreakers, the outcome should be to help learners relax, enjoy the activity and get to know each other. Icebreaker activities can be useful tools to create an atmosphere of equality and embrace diversity. They can be used to help retain attention, keep motivation high and help the group to work together.

The other reason for using an icebreaker is so that the teacher can assess who they have in their group. A teacher can get much useful information about their new learners from observing the icebreaker activity.

❝❞

Used with care and in a non-threatening way, icebreakers may establish a group identity in an hour rather than weeks or months.

(Reece and Walker, 2004, page 134)

What to look for

Things that a teacher should observe during the icebreaker activity include the following.

- Who volunteered to go first? This is normally the louder more confident learner or – quite the opposite – the person who wants to get it over and done with!
- Who spoke clearly and loudly?
- Who seemed quite relaxed and happy to speak?
- Who was really nervous?
- Who was funny?
- Who was serious?

A teacher should be observant and look at the body language of each learner.

- Who stood up to speak?
- Who spoke to the floor?
- Who fiddled with their pen?
- Who gave eye contact to their peers?

Planning and delivery
One-to-one tutorials, small-group support, clear communication, inclusive activities, active differentiation, peer support, consider layout of the room

Resources
Tape recorders, loop systems, specialised software, enlarged handouts, note takers/scribes, learning support assistants

Accessibility
Car parking, wide doors, lifts, external ramps, internal ramps, adjustable desks, automatic doors

Meeting the needs of learners with disabilities and/or learning difficulties

The initial barrier faced by many learners with physical disabilities is access. The above diagram lists some of the main considerations of a teacher regarding accessibility, resources, planning and delivery. A teacher should discuss with all learners who have disabilities or learning difficulties the best options for them. Their personal preferences will need to be taken into consideration.

HANDY HINT

Don't assume anything – not all learners with dyslexia prefer yellow as a background colour on handouts or in a PowerPoint. Ask each individual what the best colour is for them. It is good to offer handouts in a range of colours if possible.

Learners who are deaf or partially hearing

Some people may have been born deaf, while others may have become deaf either gradually or suddenly. For the majority of the population hearing impairment tends to be acquired as they get older.

People who become deaf before they learn to speak may have difficulty in speaking clearly. People who are born profoundly deaf will probably have learnt to use sign language (British Sign Language) which is a language in its own right.

A teacher working alongside a signer

Technology can enhance deaf people's access to language. For example:

- email and text messaging on mobile phone or a Minicom
- hearing aids which help to amplify sound
- loops – which can be either a permanent fixture in a room or a portable loop which can be set up in any suitable room.

Practical tips

- Make sure that learners can see who is speaking.
- Ensure that everyone speaks clearly, at a natural speed using clear language.
- Do not talk and gesture or demonstrate at the same time.
- Make sure that background noise is kept to a minimum (a carpeted room absorbs sound).
- Plan to give learners a rest from lip-reading as it is tiring.
- Provide handouts in advance as they are helpful in complementing spoken instructions.
- Include pictures and diagrams to make it as visual as possible.
- Take care not to speak while writing on a board or chart.
- Include subtitles on any video clips.
- Always address the deaf person and not the interpreter.

Partially sighted learners are provided with specialist IT resources

Learners who are blind or partially sighted

Some people may be born blind or with partial sight, but the majority of people tend to acquire a visual impairment later in life. The needs of learners who are partially sighted will vary depending upon the level of their sight problem. Some learners may need information in other formats, such as Braille, or via some speech software.

There are different technologies that can be used via the computer, including different voice recognition software packages, Braille keyboard and electronic note-taking devices.

Practical tips

- Consider seating and lighting.
- Explain the layout of the room to the learner.
- Be aware that too much light can be a hindrance, many learners who are partially sighted cannot tolerate bright light.
- Produce resources in advance so that they can be put into Braille, modified print or audio tape.
- Use Arial font at point size 14, black print on plain yellow or white paper (although learners may have individual preferences).
- Some learners might prefer using a voice recorder.

HANDY HINT

Awarding organisations produce assessment guidelines for people who are blind or partially sighted. Examination arrangements could include extra time, readers or scribes for written assessments, or a separate room.

Dyslexia

Dyslexia affects around 10% of the population, nearly half of whom experience severe difficulties in processing written language. Learners with dyslexia can often cope well with a range of complex tasks, such as solving complicated problems in electronics or design, yet find difficulties with simple tasks such as reading and spelling, following instructions or finding their way around.

Most learners with dyslexia tend to think holistically rather than step-by-step. It is good to show them the whole picture first before the detailed parts. They learn best from direct experience and they like to make personal connections to help them remember things. The use of colour, humour, stories and images will also assist their learning.

Dyslexia affects 10% of the population

Practical tips

- Use coloured paper for handouts and add a coloured background to PowerPoints.
- Coloured overlays may be helpful.
- Encourage computer-generated work so that learners are able to use the spell-check function.
- Use appropriate teaching strategies.
- Encourage learners to use visual representations such as mind maps.

A range of other difficulties

These include:

- dysgraphia – handwriting difficulties
- dyspraxia – poor motor coordination or 'clumsiness'
- dyscalculia – difficulties with calculation/maths.

Mental health problems

Learners with mental health problems may experience more anxiety about learning than other learners. They could be taking medication that affects their memory and concentration. The most common mental health problems you are likely to encounter are depression, anxiety and stress. It is possible that their attendance, punctuality and behaviour might be affected, which in turn could have an effect on their learning. They might find it difficult to participate in new activities so they may need more reassurance in order to build their confidence.

Practical tips

- Establish good rapport with the learner and give plenty of encouragement.
- Deal sensitively with personal information and focus on what is required to help the learner.
- Be aware that anxiety hides a learner's true potential and it might take time for the learner to relax.
- Use praise to encourage them and help them to feel more confident.
- Be clear on the extent of your role and when to refer on to other professionals and counsellors.
- Encourage a supportive environment especially for learners who may find social interaction difficult.

ACTIVITY

Think about the words, phrases and expressions that you use when teaching. Cover the left-hand side of this chart below and see if you can write down the correct language that a teacher should use.

A guide to preferred words and phrases

There are often concerns around the appropriate terminology to use when addressing disabled people. Below is a guide to the appropriate use of language.

Use	Do not use
'People/learners with …' (eg diabetes)	The adjective as a noun 'the disabled', 'a diabetic'
Adjective, eg 'dyslexic person' or 'disabled person'	'persons'
'learners with learning difficulties and/or disabilities' (as a general term)	'people suffering from' or 'people afflicted with' (implying victim role) 'SEN' or 'special educational needs'
'disabled person'	'cripple(d)' 'invalid' 'handicap'
'person with a learning difficulty'	'SEN' or 'ESN' 'mentally handicapped' 'person with a mental age of …' 'retarded'
'wheelchair user'	'wheelchair bound'
'person with partial sight' 'blind person' 'partially sighted person'	'visually handicapped person'
'deaf' or 'deafened' 'hard of hearing' 'person with partial hearing'	'deaf and dumb' 'deaf–mute'

'person without speech'	'dumb'
'person with mental health difficulties' 'a mental health service user'	'psychiatrically disturbed person' 'mental patient' 'sufferer'
'person with autistic spectrum disorders'	'autistic people'
'toilet/facilities that are accessible'	'disabled toilets'
'non-disabled' or 'not disabled'	'normal' which implies that disability is abnormal

GROUND RULES

LO2.1 Explain ways to maintain a safe and supportive learning environment

LO2.2 Explain why it is important to promote appropriate behaviour and respect for others

❝❞

... people like structure. Establishing and implementing appropriate rules and routines is part of providing structure.

(Scales, 2008, page 240)

Rules are everywhere. Setting and enforcing ground rules within the classroom could make the difference between learners learning to their full potential or achieving way below what is required. Calling it a classroom charter rather than using the word 'rules' might make the whole process a lot more positive.

A teacher facilitates as a group of learners create a classroom charter

CLASSROOM MANAGEMENT

G ood classroom management

R espect is needed

O wnership of rules can be achieved if the learners are involved in setting the ground rules

U nderstanding of where the boundaries have been set

N egotiate with learners, standards and sanctions

D iscourage unacceptable behaviour

R esponsibility of their own behaviour is given to the learners

U nderstanding of other learners' needs is encouraged

L imits are realised by everyone

E veryday practical needs are met

S afety and security in the classroom are established

CLASSROOM MANAGEMENT

Setting clear ground rules with learners will enable good classroom management, ensure respect, help to create a feeling of safety and security in the classroom as well as meeting practical needs.

There are common ground rules that apply to all ages of learners; for instance, being prepared for the session and turning off mobile phones. There are also rules specific to the learners' age range. Younger learners might need slightly different rules from older learners. The course subject will also determine certain rules; for instance a hairdressing learner might be allowed to have some background music playing while they are cutting hair. However, music would not normally be played during a maths session. Some learners might prefer to wear headphones when they are working independently and as long as there is no 'sound leakage' that might disturb other learners this could make a difference to the way in which they learn.

It is a teacher's responsibility to set ground rules at the start of the course. Some rules will be non-negotiable; for example a no-smoking policy will be in place for all buildings. These are normally set by the organisation that the teacher works for or may be a legal requirment. However a teacher might have room for negotiation in other areas, such as what time learners may take their break.

HANDY HINT

Remember, prevention is better than cure.

How to set ground rules

A teacher could state the rules at the start of the course or learners could be encouraged to set their own rules. Allowing learners to do this will encourage them to work as a group at the beginning of the course. Learners have to work together to create a set of rules which everyone has been able to contribute to. The teacher should stand back and facilitate this exercise, although some suitable suggestions might be needed. This method gives the learners ownership of the rules and they are more likely to abide by them. It is a good idea to get one of the learners to act as a scribe and record everything before *all* the learners sign it. It can be displayed on the wall or kept by the teacher and produced later in the course, if needed.

CLASSROOM MANAGEMENT

As the teacher you also need to abide by the rules. One rule that is normally set by the learners is to start on time. You could ask to add 'If you are here on time, I will finish on time' …

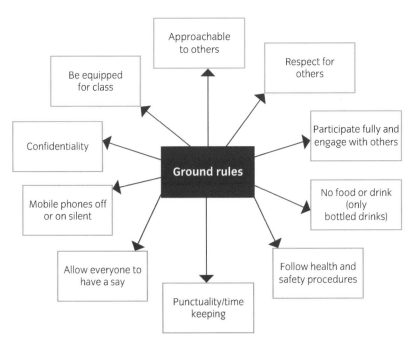

An example of ground rules as set by an adult group of teacher trainees (adapted from Daines et al., 2006, page 46)

However the rules are set it is important that some rules are non-negotiable. For example, there must be zero tolerance for any form of bullying, bad language or threatening behaviour. Sanctions must also be agreed and enforced otherwise they might not be taken seriously and this would mean that there is little point in setting the rules in the first place. Gravells (2012, page 93) goes on to say 'we could also refer to the ground rules when they are not broken as a positive reinforcement of good behaviour'.

HANDY HINT

Remember that whenever rules are set – they will be tested.

ACTIVITY

Make a list of the ground rules that you feel are important for learners to consider at the start of their course.

The teacher as a role model

A teacher is in the position to demonstrate good behaviour to their learners and lead by example. A teacher who is disorganised, late and disrespectful will soon lose respect from their learners. Learners will look towards their teacher to promote the appropriate behaviour and set the standard for good behaviour.

A teacher who looks pleased to be in the classroom and displays a positive attitude will promote a happy learning environment. It is also important for a teacher to demonstrate equality and embrace diversity. Learners should be inspired by the teacher to use the correct language and behave in a respectful way to their peers, regardless of any differences that they may have.

It is also important to explain to learners that there are professional boundaries and rules that a teacher will have to work within. Gravells (2008, page 11) states that you will have professional boundaries within which to work and it is important not to over step these.

It is important to promote a happy learning environment whilst maintaining professional boundaries

PROFESSIONALISM

LO3.1 Explain the boundaries between the teaching role and other professional roles

LO3.2 Describe points of referral to meet the needs of learners

LO3.3 Explain how own role involves working with other professionals

It is crucial that, in order for a teacher to have a clear idea about their roles and responsibilities, professional and personal boundaries are set which will help to maintain professional standards.

In this context a boundary is a limit on the extent of involvement.

(Francis and Gould, 2009, page 12)

All teachers should act in a professional way with everyone they meet – including their learners, colleagues, parents, employers and other professionals. Being professional in this context means that a teacher will act in a competent and ethical way and that they will be trustworthy, reliable and committed. Teachers should strive to put their learners first and to be supportive and approachable at all times. Teachers should also keep up to date with their own professional development to enable them to offer the most up-to-date information to their learners.

Boundaries

Being an effective teacher includes helping learners to identify matters that have an effect on their well-being and ability to learn. Support can then be provided by the teacher as well as information to help address any issues or problems. It is difficult for a teacher to carry out all of these roles and responsibilities by themselves.

Boundaries that a teacher needs to consider include:

- time constraints
- teaching within their subject
- keeping within their job role
- safeguarding
- confidentiality and
- personal relationships.

Wilson (2009, page 23) states that:

> **❝❞**
>
> Knowing the boundaries of the teacher's role is essential to an effective learning environment. It is also important for the teacher to realise that there are some aspects of the learner's expectations that are far beyond the role of the teacher.

Points of referral

A teacher is required to act in a professional way and realise when their learners would benefit from other professional help. Some of these professionals may work within the same organisation and others may work for external organisations. A teacher should always try to direct learners towards the most appropriate and best possible help available.

Internal (same organisation)
- Line manager, other teaching staff, support staff, information and guidance staff, administrators, technicians, finance staff, learning support assistants, security guards, technicians, IT support, counsellors, librarians, student reps, chaplaincy (all and non-faith), special needs assistants, career advisors and staff providing off-curriculum activities.

External (outside organisations)
- Previous teachers, parents, employers, social workers, probation officers, Alcoholics Anonymous, counsellors, GPs, childcare, Talk to Frank, Childline, National Debtline, Jobcentre, church, Victim Support, NHS Direct, awarding organisations, and external quality advisors.

Professional boundaries

All of the above can prove to be the useful referral points that might help in providing additional support to learners. There are professional boundaries to consider and it is vital that a teacher is aware of these. Sometimes an inexperienced teacher might be tempted to overstep these boundaries in order to help a learner. The golden rule is to let each professional do their job, refer to each other when needed and for everyone to work within the limits of their roles.

If a teacher offers the wrong help or works outside their boundaries then this potentially could do more harm than good. It is the responsibility of the teacher to be aware of the internal and external support mechanisms and point learners in the right direction when more qualified help is needed, especially when the problem extends beyond the classroom. For example, if a learner has a concern about their health, including suffering from anxiety, fear and depression, then they should be referred to a counsellor, internally or externally, or to their GP.

Wilson (2009, page 23) states 'the teacher should always consider the interests of the learner as paramount' and this includes knowing when to use the expertise of other professionals.

Remember also that learners don't just have emotional, physical or social needs; some learners may need to be referred to employers or Job Centres for their professional needs.

Communicating with other professionals

Communication with any of the above should always be both professional and confidential. The language that is used should also be professional, polite and appropriate. The correct terminology should be used as this will help to forge respect between each profession. Records should be kept of conversations and meetings in case these are needed as evidence in the future.

There is a whole range of people that a teacher might have to liaise and work with and it is important that good, professional relationships are established. Everyone should work together to form a strong professional team with the best interests of learners at heart. These may include other teachers, employers, school personnel, administrators, government officials, the police, counsellors, social services, the prison service and many others.

Communicating with stakeholders

A teacher might also need to communicate with a number of other people who have a vested interest in their learners. These may include parents, employers, government officials, awarding organisations, or funding councils; and as Wilson (2009, page 4) indicates, 'the student population is ever changing, bringing new demands on teachers.'

ACTIVITY

Find out what internal support is available for learners within your organisation.

UNIT SUMMARY

This unit aims to make a teacher think about their own role and responsibilities towards learners and other professionals. It provides examples of good practice that will help them to make a confident and professional start to their teaching.

This unit has concentrated on some of the key legislative requirements that a teacher needs to follow, as well as the many roles and responsibilities that come with the job. It has looked at the ways a teacher can promote equality and value the diversity that each new group of learners will bring with them. It has identified the needs that individual learners may have and explains how these needs can be met. It is important that a teacher acts in a professional way and that they understand the boundaries between the teaching role and other professional roles. This has been explored along with the points of referral, both internal and external, that are available to a teacher.

The first priority for a teacher is to make sure that their learners are safe. Ways of providing a safe and supportive environment to help promote a positive and enabling learning experience have also been considered. One of the key elements in this unit has been to look at ways to promote appropriate behaviour and respect for others and it has looked at the many things a teacher needs to consider at the start of a course. This includes, most importantly, the benefit of building a good rapport with learners, the importance of setting ground rules and recognising any barriers to learning that a learner may have.

Suggested websites have also been included along with a book list to assist you with any further research (see References, further reading and other useful sources).

A group of learners working together

ASSIGNMENT FOCUS

This unit provides you with information to enable you to understand the role and responsibilities of a teacher in the lifelong learning sector and the relationship between different professionals in lifelong learning. It includes responsibility for maintaining a safe and supportive learning environment for learners.

The learning outcomes will be assessed by a piece of written work, such as an assignment. You will need to cover all of the following assessment criteria in order to evidence your knowledge and understanding successfully.

Assessment criteria

1.1 Explain own roles and responsibilities in education and training

1.2 Summarise key aspects of legislation, regulatory requirements and codes of practice relating to own role and responsibilities

1.3 Explain ways to promote equality and value diversity

1.4 Explain why it is important to identify and meet individual learner needs

2.1 Explain ways to maintain a safe and supportive learning environment

2.2 Explain why it is important to promote appropriate behaviour and respect for others

3.1 Explain how the teaching role involves working with other professionals

3.2 Explain the boundaries between the teaching role and other professional roles

3.3 Describe points of referral to meet the individual needs of learners

Tips

You might want to consider the following when planning your assignment:

- What are the main legal requirements for teachers?
- Are there any specific legislative requirements that affect your subject area?
- Explore the main roles of a teacher.
- What are the roles and responsibilities that you have within your own subject area?
- Discuss the importance of making learners feel valued.
- Explain the importance of promoting equality and diversity within your teaching at both the planning and delivery stage.
- State examples of how you can adapt your resources to make them more inclusive.

- Consider the reasons why learners learn.
- Discuss strategies for how you will motivate learners.
- Consider why making a first impression is so important.
- Identify any barriers to learning that your learners may have and give examples of how you will overcome these.
- Give examples of icebreaker activities suitable for your subject area and learners.
- State how you can meet the needs of learners with disabilities and learning difficulties.
- Discuss some of the boundaries that you will need to be aware of as a teacher.
- Explore who you could refer learners to – both inside and outside your organisation.
- Discuss ways to establish ground rules with your learners.

UNIT 302

Understanding and using inclusive teaching and learning approaches in education and training

INTRODUCTION

An inclusive approach to teaching is one in which a teacher recognises that all learners are individuals and this informs all aspects of planning and delivering the subject. There are many factors to think about when trying to take an inclusive approach that enables all learners to participate and succeed.

It is important that the teacher has knowledge and understanding about the different ways in which learners learn and the different strategies that can be used to deliver the subject. Another important aspect to consider is the environment where the learning will be taking place. Within any learning environment there could be a number of barriers that might prevent or hinder the learning process for the learners. The learners too may have barriers that prevent them from learning. An important part of the role of the teacher is to recognise this and look at ways to break down such barriers so that everyone is given an equal opportunity to succeed. Finally, all learners should be treated as individuals and therefore information should be gathered to enable a **personalised approach** to learning.

Personalised approach is one in which a teacher plans how they are going to deliver sessions based on individual need. Often used when working with learners who have learning difficulties

Although there are numerous benefits to both learner and teacher, taking an inclusive approach can also present challenges. This unit explores strategies and approaches to teaching and learning and how these can be used to meet the needs of learners. It also explores ways to create a positive and engaging learning environment that motivates learners.

The information given will also support the delivery of the practical element of the course: the micro-teach. Some of the aspects covered include:

- barriers that prevent learning from taking place
- teaching methods used that are effective and suitable
- learning theory and strategies to provide an inclusive experience
- creating a positive learning environment and the use of ground rules to motivate and engage learners
- developing resources and using assessment and feedback to meet the needs of learners
- ways to help learners develop and practice their functional skills.

This unit focuses on understanding and using inclusive teaching and learning, but there is additional information in other units that will also be helpful.

In Unit 302 you will cover the following learning outcomes:

LO1: Understand inclusive teaching and learning approaches in education and training
LO2: Understand ways to create an inclusive teaching and learning environment
LO3: Be able to plan inclusive teaching and learning
LO4: Be able to deliver inclusive teaching and learning
LO5: Be able to evaluate the delivery of inclusive teaching and learning

DELIVERY BASED ON THE INDIVIDUAL

LO1.1 Describe features of inclusive learning

What is inclusive learning?

Inclusive practice is about adapting what is being delivered to make learning accessible to everyone regardless of ability, special educational need (SEN) or any other barrier that might exist. When planning to meet the needs of everyone in the group it is essential that the teacher has as much information about each individual as possible. This is something that will be gathered through the application, interview and induction stage. However, not all learners disclose all or indeed any learning difficulties from the outset. It is common for learners to disclose information on a voluntary basis throughout the duration of the course.

As discussed by Powell and Tummons (2011), a truly inclusive curriculum takes into account the needs of all learners. This ensures that everyone has been provided with the best opportunity for them to learn and achieve. However, there are different constraints that can make this difficult and not always achievable.

Inclusive practice is where a teacher uses a range of strategies and approaches when planning in order to teach everyone regardless of barriers.

> **❝❞**
>
> More often than not, when faced with the reality of such things as limited resources and little time, a compromise is reached, a trade-off between being as inclusive in our approaches as possible and what is actually achievable.
>
> (Powell and Tummons, 2011, page 9)

Although this is the case, it is still crucial that as professionals all teachers strive toward making their sessions as inclusive as possible. Each teacher needs to develop teaching styles with which they are comfortable but which give variety. There is also the need to add variety to keep learners interested. Some teachers work to a premise of changing the activity or teaching method every 12 to 15 minutes!

Potential needs, barriers and challenges

Most teaching roles will involve an element of giving suitable advice and guidance to learners about their chosen programme of study. The teacher will need to consider and ensure that both the choice of learning aim and the methods and modes of study are appropriate. By remaining impartial, and by keeping the interests of the learner always in mind, it is possible for the teacher to consider all options according to *individual needs*. Initial assessment encompasses all of this and more.

Type of course	Types of initial assessment	Assessment method used
Practical vocational course	Practical skills	Observation
	English and maths skills	Online diagnostic test Short written exercise Question and answer Self-disclosure of SEN/ESOL
	Prior experience	Question and answer Application form Evidence of qualifications
	Attitude and approach	Interview and observation during induction or 'taster day' Team exercise
Theoretical course	Ability to apply concepts	Short written exercise
	English and maths skills	Online diagnostic test Question and answer Self-disclosure of SEN/ESOL
	Prior knowledge	Question and answer Application form Evidence of qualifications
	Attitude and approach	Interview and observation during induction or 'taster day'
Short or one-day course	English and maths skills	Online diagnostic test Question and answer Short question paper exercise Self-disclosure of SEN/ESOL
	Prior knowledge and experience	Question and answer Application form Evidence of qualifications Workplace records
	Attitude and approach	Interview and observation during induction or 'taster day'

Depending on the subject and level of the course it is sometimes necessary for the teacher to develop their own assessment tools or use existing initial assessment 'tools'. Some examples of these are given in the table. The results of these assessments may lead to referring the learner to additional support or to another level of the same course. The results will also provide more information to help the teacher when planning how to deliver the course to make sure that all learners' needs have been catered for.

When specific additional learner needs are identified, the teacher could refer the learner to specialist support within the organisation if possible.

This image illustrates how a one-to-one meeting with a learner can be productive if the learner brings along examples of work. This provides a good starting point for the discussion, including around any barriers that may exist.

Teaching one to one

Examples of potential needs, barriers and challenges

Learning difficulties and disabilities	Wider influences
Disabilities (physical)	Lack of confidence or motivation
Learning difficulties (dyslexia; dyscalculia; dyspraxia)	Lack of social skills
Behavioural difficulties (ADHD)	Lack of resources or personal/work/ home circumstances
Limited basic skills (low literacy and/or numeracy)	Lack of support
Mixed ability (spiky profile for literacy)	Poor self-discipline
Culture and language barriers (ESOL)	Environment
Emotional or psychological difficulties	Family commitments
Mental health illness	Peer pressure
Mobility problems	Poor attendance
Hearing or visual impairment	Access to or fear of technology
	Transport issues
	Faith and religion
	Age

	Fears (change; previous negative experiences)
	Financial
	Bullying (either in person or cyber)
	Childcare arrangements
	Housing problems

(Adapted from Gravells, 2011, page 45)

ACTIVITY

Write a list of some of the types of barriers to learning that you have experienced during your own teaching. Consider what you did with this information. How did it help you when doing your planning?

How do learners learn?

'Flexible learning' in this context is used to describe the wide range of teaching and learning styles and methods that are available for teachers to use with individuals and groups. It may be a one-day course, or a module/unit in a longer programme, but there is always a need to provide learning opportunities to everyone in a variety of ways. Learners do not all learn in the same way, so in any group of learners the teacher will need to enable learning *for all* by offering different methods which enable them all to learn.

Learning styles

The theory that underpins most modern approaches to adult learning puts forward the idea that differences in the way that individuals learn *best* can be broadly categorised as 'learning styles'. A popular learning styles theory is based on the acronym VARK:

Visual

Aural

Read/write

Kinaesthetic.

It argues that there are learning (and teaching) preferences and that it is necessary to recognise that each person in a learning environment will naturally gravitate towards one or more of these particular styles of learning.

For example, consider a beginner's class in family history.

- **Visual** learners will like to watch footage from case studies and have a model to follow: they will start to create mind maps and other visual organisers.
- **Auditory** learners will want to listen to presentations and enter into discussions and debates about the topic.

- **Read/write** learners will prefer to read documents, research independently, use subject-specific software and have time to write about all the pros and cons.
- **Kinaesthetic** learners will prefer hands-on practical work and real-life experiences.

When teaching a group of learners there could be similar proportions of these four learning styles in the room. This means that the teacher will need to offer teaching methods to suit all four types. But this is not as daunting as it sounds. Every learner should be given an opportunity to learn in their preferred style, during the lesson, at some point. The teacher can also use what they know about learners' styles to form effective groups. There are different questionnaires available online that will provide the teacher and the learner with more information about their own learning styles. Once these strengths and weaknesses are identified in the learners, the teacher will be able to see how best to support them.

The image below shows how learners are working on a practical element using a simulated task.

How do teachers teach?

There are several choices to make when teaching a subject and at the planning stage it is important to consider how the subject will be delivered. What teaching method or strategy will be the most successful?

Teaching is about trying to engage the learner in the subject so that **deep learning** takes place, rather than surface or rote learning. Deep learning takes place when a learner is actively thinking about a session and they are taking part, engaging with the subject, rather than letting the learning just happen to them.

Deep learning
is a type of learning that will last over a period of time because the learner has understood and made sense of the information

This type of learning happens best when the learning is directed by the learner and not the teacher. The best teaching methods that allow this to happen are the ones where the learners are *doing* something.

Teacher-centred	**TEACHING**	Learner-centred

Passive	**LEARNING**	Active

Active versus passive learning

This table illustrates the difference between an active and a passive learner. Some learners are comfortable taking a passive role. It may take time to switch learners on to learning, but by doing so the learning will last a lifetime or at least the enthusiasm will.

Passive learner: Learning is something done to me by the teacher	**Active learner:** Learning is something I must do to myself
Focused on: ■ Likely negative outcomes ■ The impossibility of getting it perfect	**Focused on:** ■ The positive ■ The process ■ Improvement
Mindset: disempowered	**Mindset: empowered**
Success or failure depends on factors beyond my control: ■ How good the teacher is ■ The resources ■ My intelligence ■ My talent for the subject	Success or failure depends on me: ■ I need to check my understanding ■ I need to find the right resources ■ I need to find the gaps in my learning ■ I need to take control and responsibility
So if I don't learn: ■ The teacher is at fault ■ The resources are at fault ■ I'm stupid and lack ability	

Either way, I should quit the course	So if I don't learn:
	 ■ I need to try harder
	 ■ Or change my strategy:
	   ■ Try another book
	   ■ Ask a friend for help
	   ■ Talk to the teacher

Approach: defeatist, fatalistic, despairing	Either way, I am likely to succeed if I take control of my learning
	Approach: adaptive, responsive, self-believing

Learner characteristics

Features of inclusive learning

■ All learners are individual, learn in different ways and may have barriers that restrict their learning.

- Teachers have to identify barriers in terms of learning difficulties and disabilities, as well as social, financial and motivational factors.
- It is important to look for ways to remove barriers, such as adapting the learning environment, delivery, resources and/or providing individual support.

Putting the teaching cycle into practice

As discussed in Unit 301, the role of the teacher is a diverse one and many factors need to be considered in order for learning to take place. It is important that the teaching cycle should be followed for all sessions.

Each aspect of the teaching cycle has been expanded below to develop some of the main points to consider in the teaching role. It is how these all work together holistically that should result in excellent teaching. One point is no more important than another.

The teacher has as much **initial information** about each learner as possible and is kept up to date about any changes. If possible this information should be tracked on an individual learning plan (ILP) with involvement from the learner.

The teacher **reflects** on the lesson, as it is progressing and afterwards. This provides an opportunity for changes and improvements, as well as considering individual learner need on a regular basis.

The teacher works within a **supportive team** and a holistic approach to all the sessions is considered.

Clear, appropriate **assessment strategies** are used effectively to measure the learning that is taking place within every lesson.

Lessons are **planned** and link to both previous lessons and future lessons.

There is a **flexible approach** taken within the lesson, which is varied and thought provoking. This may include researching the topic and creating resources.

Careful consideration is made about the **teaching environment**.

Layout, individual needs and **group dynamics** are thought about and the room adapted as necessary.

The teacher uses **clarity of communication** and is aware of all aspects of both verbal and nonverbal communication. Their use of language is focused and accessible to everyone.

A **supportive, positive relationship** is developed between the teacher and the learners. There is mutual respect and high expectations which are underpinned with praise and a clear code of behaviour.

The teacher has genuine **enjoyment and pleasure** from teaching. The lessons are engaging, learners are valued and inclusive, differentiated strategies are adopted which are appropriate to the learners.

Initial assessment · Planning · Delivery · Assessment · Evaluation

The teaching cycle

Rate yourself out of 5 (5 being the highest) in terms of how confident you are about your own knowledge and ability for each of the eleven points. Take the three that you scored the lowest in and make a list about what you plan to do to improve this area of your teaching.

TEACHING METHODS (STRATEGIES)

LO1.2 Compare the strengths and limitations of teaching and learning approaches used in own area of specialism in relation to meeting individual learner needs

When planning the strategies or methods to use to deliver the subject, the teacher will consider the following:

- Is it a practical or theoretical subject?
- How good is their own subject knowledge (and confidence)?
- What room or environment is available to use? Can it be seen before the session?
- Are the resources already available? If so, what are they like?
- How much time is allowed for the session?
- Is there any ICT available to support the subject?
- Are you aware of any special requirements/needs of the learners? How can these be accommodated? Is there any additional learning support (ALS) available?

There are several different strategies or methods available to use. The table provides an introduction to some of the most widely used. Note that more information about these and other types of methods can be found in Units 304 and 305/306.

Teaching strategies (methods)	Suited to what?	Things to consider	Differentiation strategies
PowerPoint presentations or lecture style delivery	Passive learning Theory subjects Large-group delivery Information gathering	Low or short attention spans can result in poor behaviour or low attainment of knowledge and lack of understanding of the subject	Provide handouts of the presentation Ask learners to move to a position where they can see/hear Check learning with directed questions
Case studies or written tasks – can be individual, paired or small-group activity	Active learning Theory or practical subjects Small-group delivery Learning through problem solving and experiential learning Visual and auditory	Learner confidence and literacy ability can result in lack of engagement Peer rivalry can also affect participation	Provide key words or images and questions or clues to support the task Provide regular verbal guidance

Teaching strategies (methods)	Suited to what?	Things to consider	Differentiation strategies
Learners are given a topic; they may work together to prepare a presentation. Materials are checked by the teacher before the presentation	Active learning

Theory or practical subjects

Small-group delivery

Practical 'hands-on' task | Learner ownership and possible peer rivalry will need to be managed | Put more able learners with less able learners.

Break topic up into smaller parts. Provide a self-assessment checklist |
| Teacher-led whole-class discussion. Teacher asks learners a question, then volunteers (nominates) learners to give an answer | Passive learning can become active and can take place in any location

Auditory | Excludes the non-confident learners.

Could encourage the group to create something tangible, such as a mind map or display of Post-it® notes | Could split the group into smaller groups

Could provide the questions in advance and allow time to consider the answers |
| Practical tasks (in the workplace or workshop) | Active learning

Smaller groups | Limited to resources

Clear communication and boundaries as health and safety need to be considered | Pair learners according to ability

Keep a record of what everyone has achieved so that each practical session can be tailored to new activities |
| Facilitating individual activity using past paper exam questions or Gapped handouts | Passive

Individual activity | Learner ability (additional support may be needed) | Adapt by giving questions orally, and give learners option to write answers down

Could be done in pairs Check each others' work |
| Role play | Active

Small group activity | Resources available including space

Clear guidelines and support during and after the task | By offering some learners to opt out

Provide information about the different roles in a variety of formats – supported with visual images and objects |
| Practical demonstration led by the teacher | Fairly passive

Can be larger-group activity

Suited to practical tasks | Resources available

Health and safety considerations

Clear guidelines | Provide simple written instructions for learners to follow

Ask questions throughout to check understanding

Provide opportunities for learners to 'have a go' |

By using a range of these methods across all the sessions all of the different learning styles will be catered for. This means that all of the learners in the group should have been able to participate in some aspect of the session and this also should increase their motivation and engagement with the learning process.

HANDY HINT

If you want to take a break from a PowerPoint presentation during the session, but don't want to turn off the projector, press 'W' on the keyboard and the screen will turn white. Press 'B' and it will turn black. Just press any key to return back to the presentation. This will help you and your learners focus on the discussion without any visual distractions.

TEACHING AND LEARNING THEORY

Delivery based on level

Theory suggests that learners learn information in different ways, whether they are visual, auditory, kinaesthetic or read/write (VARK). However, another aspect to think about when planning the teaching and learning is what level or amount of learning do the learners need to achieve?

- How much information and knowledge should learners learn in the session?
- What level should the information and knowledge be pitched at?
- What practical skill level should they be able to demonstrate?

Bloom's taxonomy
There are three domains:

- **psychomotor**: about learning a skill
- **cognitive**: about learning knowledge
- **affective**: about beliefs and attitudes.

It is useful to consider your teaching in terms of Bloom's psychomotor domain (cited in Scales, 2008, page 104). This provides the teacher with a clear structure to different stages of learning a practical skill.

Bloom's taxonomy: the psychomotor domain

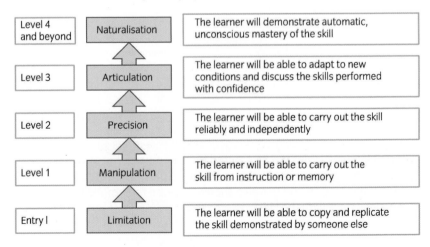

The **psychomotor domain** is based on learning practical skills. It is important that each stage that a learner goes through is considered and tasks are set that are easy in the beginning and build up over a period of time.

Psychomotor domain
is about learning practical skills; often considered in terms of learning how to 'do' something

EXAMPLE

When learning to drive a car, you first of all copy the basics from watching someone else, follow instructions and start to try to remember how to steer the car while changing gears. You may need to be reminded to look in the mirror, watch out for other road users and to drive at the right speed. With practice you start to be able to drive the car with confidence. Eventually you are able to drive the car well enough to anticipate problems and make decisions, without asking anyone else. Finally, driving becomes such second nature that you may well drive a familiar route home and not be able to remember much about the journey!

Bloom's taxonomy: the cognitive domain

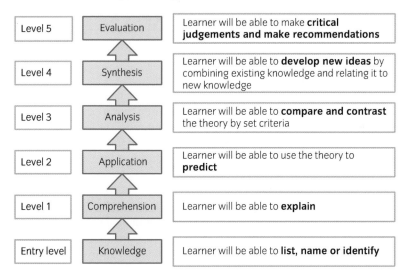

Level 5	Evaluation	Learner will be able to make **critical judgements and make recommendations**
Level 4	Synthesis	Learner will be able to **develop new ideas** by combining existing knowledge and relating it to new knowledge
Level 3	Analysis	Learner will be able to **compare and contrast** the theory by set criteria
Level 2	Application	Learner will be able to use the theory to **predict**
Level 1	Comprehension	Learner will be able to **explain**
Entry level	Knowledge	Learner will be able to **list, name or identify**

When setting tasks with a learner, a teacher must make sure that the tasks are set at the correct level and they cover what they are supposed to do. The levels within Bloom's taxonomy are useful to use to set questions and tasks. It is important to stretch and challenge the learners, but if they are only meant to be working at level 1, for instance, it would not be good practice to ask them to try to analyse or evaluate information. This could create a barrier for the learner and make them feel out of their depth.

Cognitive domain
is about learning knowledge and information; often considered in terms of theoretical subjects

Sometimes a learner may start to demonstrate a depth of knowledge and understanding that is beyond what is asked of them. In this case, it is good practice to provide support to enable them to carry on exploring theoretical concepts. However, the teacher should be aware of what they *have to* cover before looking at what they might *like to* cover during the sessions. This is part of the planning process and will be informed via initial assessments and ongoing formative assessment along the learner's journey.

Bloom's taxonomy: the affective domain

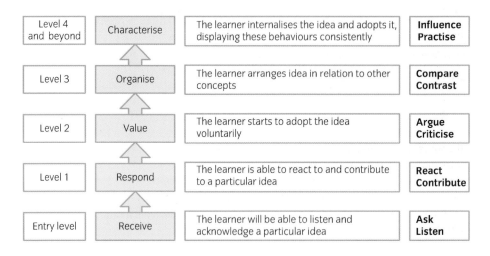

The **affective domain** is about changing people's beliefs through information and discussion. This is often an area that is covered during tutorial time, or in personal and social development (PSD) classes. It covers attitudes and approaches to what can be controversial topics, often about lifestyle choices.

Affective domain
involves learning about beliefs and attitudes; often considered in terms of trying to change a person's beliefs by providing information from a range of viewpoints

---

EXAMPLE

An individual may know some of the facts about how bad smoking is for them, but it is only through further information and discussion, and by being able to relate the idea to other information or experience they have, that they can start to take the concept on board mentally and eventually give up smoking.

Theory
is a set of principles or system of ideas designed to explain something; normally developed from research

It is important to have an awareness of the three domains and the stages of learning that take place when teaching or facilitating learning. This helps when planning sessions, writing materials and assessment tasks by ensuring that they are pitched at the right level. It also helps the teacher explain the stages of development to learners. This enables the learner to see their own progress within the subject. This helps them to apply their knowledge or skills at a level that is suitable for them.

Theory to practice: Levels within education	
Level 6	Final year of a degree programme
Level 5	Second year of a degree programme
Level 4	First year of a degree programme
Level 3	A levels or NDs
Level 2	GCSE grades A–C
Level 1	GCSE grades D–G
Entry level 3	Reading age 11–14 years
Entry level 2	Reading age 8–11 years
Entry level 1	Reading age pre-school–8 years

HANDY HINT

If your learners are looking blankly at you while you are delivering information, don't panic. This could be their thinking faces. Allow time for information to be processed and don't rush. Encourage individuals to share their own thoughts. This will also give you the chance to check understanding and go over anything that was not clear.

EMBEDDING ENGLISH, MATHS, ICT AND WIDER SKILLS

LO1.3 Explain why it is important to provide opportunities for learners to develop their English, maths, ICT and wider skills

Functional skills

Functional skills are the skills needed in order to manage life and to function in modern society. They have developed from 'basic skills' and 'key skills', but are wider and applicable to a broader group of learners. They can be 'embedded' in vocational or other mainstream subjects, or taught as a standalone subject. They are always tested as separate subjects, managed by a functional skills expert.

❝❞

Functional Skills are practical skills in English, ICT and mathematics that allow individuals to work confidently, effectively and independently in life. Functional Skills will be constituent parts of new Foundation, Higher and Advanced Diplomas. The assessment approach will be primarily task-based scenario questions ... the assessments will support problem solving, skill based approaches.

(QCA, 2007)

Functional skills provide an opportunity for learners to develop functionality in using English, maths and computer skills, in a range of different contexts. They also introduce wider skills such as thinking, applying previous knowledge and analysing different situations.

Although functional skills are tested as standalone qualifications, it is expected that an element of embedding these skills will happen within a learner's vocational subject. This is an important aspect of every teacher's role to introduce and contextualise these skills within the approaches and activities with learners. This helps to motivate learners to engage with English, maths and ICT because they see the relevance of these subjects when they are based in their own subject area that they are interested in. More importantly a main barrier can be a learner's own skills in these key areas. Many young people who enrol on a vocational subject lack the functional skills to access the vocational curriculum or make the sort of progress expected. Therefore by embedding these skills within every session the learner will be able to improve their English, maths and ICT skills, while learning their main chosen specialism.

Some suggested strategies

- Introduce the notion of a glossary that learners can use to record new and unfamiliar words in course materials or during delivery.
- Signpost when learners should be note taking during discussions.
- Provide marking criteria for learners to assess peers during tasks and activities to help embed active listening strategies.
- Model good practice when planning writing and provide a structure or scaffolded templates to support learners' written skills.
- Use ICT to record data, work out problems, research in a safe way and present information professionally.
- Provide alternative ways of working out solutions to mathematical problems ('... 20%, that is 1 in 5 ...').
- Provide supported opportunities for learners to practise maths skills in context (such as working out ratios of hair dye, mixing cement in the correct quantities).

Functional skills in English, mathematics and information and communications technology (ICT) help people to gain the most out of life, learning and work.

The skills are learning tools that enable people:

- to apply their knowledge and understanding to everyday life
- to engage competently and confidently with others
- to solve problems in both familiar and unfamiliar situations
- to develop personally and professionally as positive citizens who can actively contribute to society.

Functional skills are important also as many professions rely on a good level of functionality in the workplace; for example, working out the area of a room that needs decorating or how to write a formal business letter.

Self-assessment task

Using the information on the next pages about skills that are covered
within each subject (at level 1), identify where these could be included
within your own topic area. This represents an opportunity to embed
the skill rather than teach it explicitly.

Subject (L1) (Equivalent to GCSE grades D–G)	Skill Standards	Possible coverage in your subject area
Maths	**Representing** ■ Understand practical problems in familiar and unfamiliar contexts ■ Identify and obtain necessary information to tackle the problem ■ Select mathematics in an organised way to find solutions **Analysing** ■ Apply mathematics in an organised way to find solutions to straightforward practical problems for different purposes ■ Use appropriate checking procedures at each stage **Interpreting** ■ Interpret and communicate solutions to practical problems, drawing simple conclusions and giving explanations	
English	**Speaking and listening and communication** ■ Take part in formal and informal discussions and exchanges that include unfamiliar subjects **Reading** ■ Read and understand a range of straightforward texts **Writing** ■ Write a range of texts to communicate information, ideas and opinions, using formats and styles suitable for their purpose and audience	

ICT	**Using ICT**	
	■ Identify the ICT requirements of a straightforward task ■ Interact with and use ICT systems to meet requirements of a straightforward task in a familiar context ■ Manage information storage ■ Follow and demonstrate understanding of the need for safety and security practices	
	Finding and selecting information	
	■ Use search techniques to locate and select relevant information ■ Select information from a variety of ICT sources for a straightforward task	
	Developing, presenting and communicating information	
	■ Enter, develop and refine information using appropriate software to meet the requirements of straightforward tasks ■ Use appropriate software to meet requirements of a straightforward data-handling task ■ Use communications software to meet requirements of a straightforward task ■ Combine information within a publication for a familiar audience and purpose ■ Evaluate own use of ICT tools	

Wider skills

Alongside functional skills, wider skills are also often embedded or taught as standalone subjects. A subject that often falls into this category is personal and social development (PSD). This provides learners with the skills to work as a team, manage their own personal development, such as planning skills, communication skills and problem solving. This is often taught at a level below the one that a learner is taking for their main qualification; so if they are studying engineering at level 2, they would be taking PSD at level 1.

Other wider skills, such as recognising and understanding issues about equality and diversity, will also be covered during tutorial sessions when learners can explore some of the differences that exist within society. This is particularly important for learners who are studying a vocation that will result in them working in social settings. This is a good opportunity to challenge stereotypes and work with learners to help them develop a better awareness of acceptable codes of professional conduct.

ACTIVITY

Consider the area of vocational specialism that you will be teaching in – or are already teaching in – and identify three reasons why it is important to embed functional and wider skills.

SOME SUGGESTED WAYS TO CONSIDER INCLUSION

LO2.1 Explain why it is important to create an inclusive teaching and learning environment

Equality, diversity, and promoting inclusion

There are many barriers to inclusion in education. Some (as already discussed on page 49) relate to disability or learning difficulties, but many also concern social conditions, out-dated attitudes and stereotyping. Whatever the specialist subject, the teacher will meet with particular barriers and will be actively participating in helping to break down these barriers.

For example:

- Some occupations are traditionally associated with or dominated by one gender or the other, and it may be a daunting prospect to try to break into such a profession. Learner taster days are one way of encouraging others to try out something they would not normally consider.
- Learners who have home responsibilities, caring for children or relatives, often find it hard to access traditionally delivered learning. Offering flexible learning and support opportunities can help them to fit study around their other commitments.
- Those learners with diverse cultural backgrounds may not be available to participate at certain times on certain days. Discussing any problems and coming up with an individual schedule may be possible.
- Some learners, in particular those with disabilities or health problems, and those living in rural locations, may benefit from e-learning or online tutorial support.
- All learning materials should be representative in their examples and illustrations of a range of people from diverse backgrounds.
- The teacher will also need to guide interactions between their learners, fostering an atmosphere of mutual respect and tolerance and leading by example.

Diverse needs and diverse barriers require diverse solutions. Making a conscious effort to provide inclusive learner support requires a certain amount of flexibility.

Wherever possible the teacher will need to offer:

- a flexible attitude
- a wide range of methods of teaching and ways of learning
- a variety of materials
- flexible assessments
- outcomes that are adaptable
- at all times zero tolerance for any discriminatory practice, including bullying and harassment.

It is part of the role of the teacher always to consider whether the planned teaching methods and strategies are accessible to *all* learners. If the group is unfamiliar it is good practice to ask the programme or course manager if there are any learners with disabilities or with additional learning needs that need to be planned for specifically. However, this information should be kept confidential and only used as appropriate to inform the delivery of the sessions. A group tracking sheet may be kept and this provides a useful overview of the whole group and their specific needs.

Below is an example of a course learner information sheet based on initial assessments:

Name	Target Grade	Number of GCSE A* – C	GCSE Grades		Initial Screening Results	RETENTION: 'AMBER ALERT' CHECKLIST More than 2 ✓s = Potential Early Leaver. Learners needs extra front-loaded tutorial support								
			Maths	English	IT	Numeracy	Literacy	Late applications/late enrolments/ missed induction	Special entry criteria/or have learning difficulty	Transferring from another course/or left a course the previous year	Existing/recent medical conditions/ bereavement/looked-after children	Financial/social/ domestic pressures	Gender minority within group	Lack of motivation/ confidence/returning to classroom learning	Learners with behavioural problems or under disciplinary procedures	Poor attendance/lateness/missing work deadlines	Intended career/ambition/ progression

Always ask yourself if you have provided sufficient variety to maintain interest and to cater to the needs of individuals in the group.

The table on the next page gives some practical examples of actions to create an inclusive teaching and learning environment.

Potential issues	Inclusive actions	Achievable?
Physical barriers	■ This may include looking at holding the class in a wheelchair-friendly environment (such as a ground-floor classroom) ■ You may look at how the layout of the tables and chairs provide access to anyone with restricted physical mobility ■ Providing specialist equipment such as a hearing loop or adjustable table	
Teaching and learning resources	■ This may include providing a visually impaired learner with large font handouts ■ A learner with dyslexia may prefer coloured paper (cream is often recommended) ■ Some learners may need more visual handouts or images used to supplement the text ■ Scaffolded worksheets that identify key characteristics of a particular genre (such as the structure of a formal letter)	
Teaching and learning strategies	■ This may include differentiating activities within the classroom ■ Try to plan to use a range of activities within the session to break it up and make it engaging and active for all ■ This may be achieved by positioning a higher-level learner with someone who may need support ■ Active learning approaches that consider all learning styles ■ Different-level questions to accommodate levels in the group	
Support for learners	■ Learning support can be put in place (one-to-one) ■ Flexible tutorial times may be necessary ■ Additional time for assignment work ■ A reader or scribe for exams ■ Software that can read or write for a learner ■ A recording device so that information can be revisited ■ Provide study skills embedded within the sessions ■ Give verbal cues to learners when something is of particular note or may be in the exam/test ■ Make links to wider concepts and provide visual diagrams and/or mind maps of the topics	
Outside the classroom	■ A virtual learning environment (VLE) ■ Additional handouts or suggested websites and resources ■ Additional points of referral (outside agencies or internal networks of support) ■ Additional study skills (either individually or peer groups)	

CREATING A POSITIVE LEARNING ENVIRONMENT

Malcolm Knowles developed a theory that he termed **andragogy**. This is based on the assumption that adults can draw from a rich vault of prior experience and knowledge and tend to be self motivated and self directed as learners (Knowles, as cited in Scales, 2008). Adult learners bring with them a readiness to learn, particularly because they have chosen the course or programme that they are studying. An andragogical approach puts the learner in the driving

Andragogy is the term given to teaching adults. It is based on the idea that adults are more motivated and can draw from prior experience and knowledge. Therefore they are self directed as learners

Pedagogy is the term given to teaching children. It is based on the idea that children need to be taught directly and instructed in their learning. They are not very motivated or self directed and do not have very much experience or knowledge to draw from

seat by empowering them to take control of their learning. Although andragogy, as opposed to **pedagogy**, may be more applicable to older learners, it still remains the responsibility of the teacher, trainer or tutor to help create a learning environment that is conducive to learning. This involves giving careful consideration to both the physical and the emotional environment.

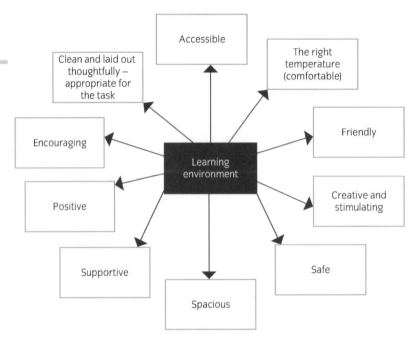

Creating a positive environment conducive to learning is linked to the teacher's own attitude to and knowledge of their learners. Learners may lack confidence at first and need encouragement to participate and contribute to activities and discussions. The teacher's ability to communicate in a non-superior, non-judgemental way and at the right level for their learners will be crucial to success in creating such an envionment.

Alongside this, consideration of the physical environment also applies when arranging rooms for teaching or selecting somewhere to meet. The teacher should consider issues of confidentiality, for example for tutorials, and of potential noise that could be distracting, for example, if running tests for initial assessments.

HANDY HINT

Hole punch all worksheets or handouts that you give to your learners, before the session. This should reduce the number that are left on the floor or tables when the learners leave the room and remove the opportunity for the learners to spend time passing around a hole punch during the session, which is an unnecessary distraction.

Classroom layout

The physical arrangement of furniture can enhance or diminish group dynamics and participation.

Traditional classroom layout

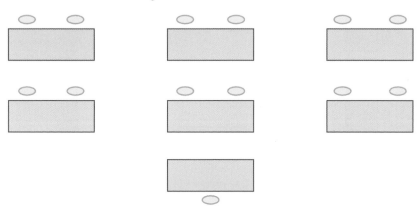

Layout 1: Traditional exam style

The traditional style of laying the room out so that all the tables are in rows is a good way to make the most of the space available in a room. However, it does not lead to effective communication or enable easy group work. One important aspect in an inclusive learning environment is that it should be possible for the teacher to have easy access to all of the learners. This is not always possible in this type of classroom layout which is only really suitable for exams or when space is short.

Group work layout

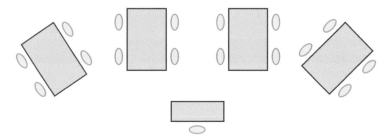

Layout 2: Group work

Laying the room out so that the tables are placed together to form small groups is a popular choice in most **lifelong learning** classrooms, where possible. This allows for learners to work together and encourages active learning activities. The tables can be arranged according to space, but the learners should be able to face the board to enable them to feedback from tasks and watch presentations comfortably. There should be enough room between tables so that the teacher can gain access to all the learners in the room, to provide support and manage behaviour.

Lifelong learning: in 2007 the lifelong learning sector was defined as comprising adult and community learning (ACL), further education (FE), higher education (HE), libraries, archives and information services (LAIS) and work-based learning (WBL)

Horseshoe layout

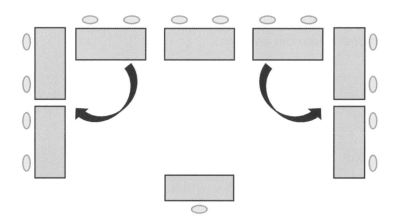

Layout 3: Horseshoe

The horseshoe layout is a good classroom layout to use when planning for a whole-group discussion to take place. All learners can see each other and the teacher can get access easily from inside the horseshoe to support and manage behaviour, if and when necessary. This layout can also be easily modified to support small-group work by moving the corner tables as shown in the diagram. However, all planned activities need to be considered carefully and, if furniture rearrangement is necessary, a note could be made as a reminder on the session plan. Any risk to personal safety has to be considered if furniture is going to be moved. If learners are to be involved in this activity then they should be alerted to any potential risk to personal safety. It is also essential to enable access for any learners who have physical needs.

HANDY HINT

Don't be worried about moving the room round to suit the needs of the lesson or the diverse needs of the group. Use the learners to help move tables. Set them the task of arranging the room to suit group work, or paired activities. This will encourage team work and create a fluid and flexible learning environment which feels creative and dynamic. If there is room, you could try sitting learners in a circle away from the desks to discuss a topic. Remember, the room is not fixed and can be rearranged at any point of the session. With practice this will not take too much time out of the session and the rewards will outweigh any disruption caused.

Note: Personal safety must be considered first at all times.

THE USE OF RESOURCES

LO2.2 Explain why it is important to select teaching and learning approaches, resources and assessment methods to meet individual learner needs

When considering how to deliver a subject, the teacher should think about the types of resources that are available for each activity within the session. Types of resources include:

- physical resources, such as rooms and practical equipment
- human resources, such as technicians, guest speakers, other colleagues, or learning support, as applicable
- practical teaching aids, such as practical tools of the trade, models, and so on
- academic teaching aids, such as handouts, DVDs and games, etc
- electronic teaching aids, such as interactive whiteboards, VLEs and internet.

Most teachers have a resource bank to draw from. This could be a learning pack that may have been commercially created, such as **SmartScreen**, previously created in-house within the department or available online. These resources should be checked first for content as, although they might not be exactly what is needed, they can make a good starting point to develop and create resources from.

SmartScreen
is the name of the resources available online from City & Guilds

A learner in a practical cooking situation

Accessibility and individual needs must be considered when making decisions about the resources to be used. Obviously it is also important to be aware of financial and programme limitations on the resources that can be used. Most organisations will have a limit on the amount that can be spent on resourcing a programme, including photocopying, so it is always worth checking.

ADAPTING ASSESSMENT FOR INDIVIDUAL NEED

When planning to assess learners the teacher has to consider any potential risks, not only health and safety risks, but also those particular to their own subject area. Following correct health and safety guidelines will help with this.

The following points should also be considered:

- Do not put undue stress and pressure on the learners.
- Try not to over-assess – only assess what is necessary or the learners will be put at a disadvantage.
- Do not expect too much, too soon. Check they are ready for the assessment and, if not, negotiate the assessment dates with them (if possible).
- Do not pass someone because there is a pressure to get high achievement.
- Be aware of subjectivity and bias and consider this when planning all assessments (for example: if teaching a family member or friend, someone else may need to assess them instead to avoid favouritism).
- The assessment decision should be based on clear criteria and this must be communicated to the learners before the assessment.
- Use the referral system as necessary to enable all learners to participate. This may mean that special adjustments have to be made, such as extra time, or a reader could be provided if someone has dyslexia.
- The assessment task could be adapted so that it is provided in an auditory format or large print as necessary.

ACTIVITY

Consider ways that you could plan your assessment to meet the following needs: a physical disability, a learning difficulty (dyslexia, a hearing impairment, a visual impairment), a learning disability (autism, dyspraxia), cultural or religious beliefs, English as a second language, mixed-ability group.

A tutor with a disabled learner

The image above is a good example of a teacher getting into a position where they can have eye contact when assessing a learner with a physical disability. This will enable the learner to be included and is a simple strategy to use when working with learners who are wheelchair users.

STRATEGIES TO ENGAGE AND MOTIVATE ALL LEARNERS

LO2.3 Explain ways to engage and motivate learners

Motivating learners

There are times when external factors can lead to demotivation in the learner and a slowing down of the learning journey. This could be owing to a variety of factors, both external and internal, as already discussed. There are different ways in which the teacher will be able to proactively increase motivation within the learners, although there will still be a responsibility with the learner as well to aid this process.

ACTIVITY

Make a record of a variety of factors – both **intrinsic** and **extrinsic** – which may demotivate learners. Make a note of which ones you can influence in the classroom and which ones you may need some external support with.

One of the main causes of inappropriate behaviour is when a learner is not motivated or engaged with their learning. Some learners will feel instantly at ease in a learning environment, while others may need varying degrees of support to be successful. A lot will depend on the nature and quality of learning experiences provided.

Learners working together

When working in lifelong learning, it is sometimes the case that not all the learners are as motivated as the teacher might want or expect them to be. It is easy to assume that learners are there because they want to be, particularly as, being adults, they have presumably chosen to do the course or study the subject being taught. However, this is not always the case. Many adult learners are sent on courses by their employer or have to 'up skill' in order to gain career progression. Some younger learners do not feel that they have many other choices and are using a college course as a way of using up time until they work out what they really want to do. Advice and guidance at the application and interview stage will help to offer clear choices for potential learners and can give the teacher a chance to set out expectations. This is not always possible as many courses are only one-day or short courses and may not have an application or interview stage. The teacher may not have any information provided prior to the course about their learners. It is important then that a large part of the teaching role is about helping the learners *want* to learn.

The table below offers some practical advice to encourage learners.

Ways to switch your learners on to learning	
Share the benefits of what they will get from the course	■ You could ask them to draw up a list of what they think they will gain, rather than lecturing them on what *you* think the benefits are
	■ Give them examples of past learners and success stories
	■ Invite ex-learners to come into the class if possible to talk to them about the course and answer any questions they might have

Think about the human side of your relationship with your learners	■ Learn their names in the first session and use these when you communicate with them so they feel important and not just an unknown face in the room ■ Engage with them on at least one topic so you can relate the learning to their own interests and experiences ■ Listen to their suggested answers and discussions and use these in future sessions to illustrate points made so they receive legitimate praise over a period of time
Develop your learners as independent and autonomous	■ Clearly tell them what they are learning in each session ■ Make links to the bigger topic and ask them to give examples of this from their own experience and knowledge ■ Provide opportunities for individual learners to demonstrate to (teach) the rest of the group
Learning by doing	■ Plan activities so that your learners can practise what they have learnt ■ Provide repetitive activities that will reinforce their learning ■ Offer a safe environment where they can make mistakes without ridicule and experiment with ideas or tasks
Encouragement and praise	■ Praise your learners as soon and as often as possible in the early stages ■ Let them know when they have given a correct or insightful answer or completed a task well ■ Offer them information that will help them to improve when they do something similar in the future. This is also known as active feedback or 'feed forward' ■ Ask direct questions to individuals and use leading questions to help them to explore what they are doing or trying to do ■ Believe in them!
Ways to switch your learners on to learning	
Be enthusiastic and positive	■ Be passionate about the subject and your learners will share your passion ■ Do not suggest that a particular topic is a bit dull but rather see it as an opportunity to explore it in a new light – often these are the topics that you have to think most about at the planning stage ■ Be enthusiastic about your learners and show them respect and interest – like them! ■ Never indicate that an area of the course is not very well planned or is not relevant. Work on making improvements out of the sight of your learners ■ Be positive about other learners, groups, other colleagues and the organisation – maintain professionalism at all times

CLASSROOM MANAGEMENT

Ask for a volunteer from the group to stand at the front and act as teacher to gather feedback from a group task. This will enable you to record the feedback, rest your voice and can work well as a classroom management strategy. It is surprising how well behaved a group can be for one of their peers. This is a short-term strategy, so it can't go on too long or happen too often!

BUILDING THE RIGHT RELATIONSHIPS

LO2.3 Explain ways to engage and motivate learners

When working in the role of the teacher it is crucial to consider the type of relationships that will be developed with the learners. This is regardless of age or previous relationships; the professional boundaries must exist while a teacher/learner relationship is taking place. Getting to know individuals and encouraging them to get to know each other will foster a supportive atmosphere. However, it is always important to be aware of potential conflict if you have a number of distinct groups of learners, or a learner who seems to work on their own. Interactive and fun icebreaker activities can help to bond the group together during induction and also sets the scene for the rest of the year. Having high expectations of your learners from the outset – and making this clear to them – will also give them all a clear message of how they need to act in your classroom.

EXAMPLE

Even if your best friend enrols on one of your courses, while you are in the classroom environment you must maintain a professional distance. How would your other learners feel or react if they thought that you were paying your friend any extra attention?

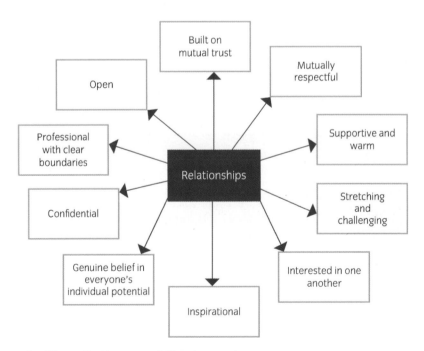

Conditions critical to a successful learning experience

Learning names

First session: ask everyone to wear a name badge displaying the name they like to be called. While learners are participating in activities throughout the session, look at them individually and repeat their name in your mind with a key piece of information; for example, Fran likes riding.

On your way home after the class has finished, try to recall as many of the learners as you can. Sometimes it helps to picture them sitting in the room. This will help their name stick in your memory. If you can't remember the odd one, look it up before the next session.

In the following session: use the learners' names as soon as they start to arrive. This will help them to relax and feel welcomed. It should prevent any minor disruptions as they will realise that you know who they are and that you will be able to act quickly if necessary! This will also help the learners learn each other's names as well.

ESTABLISHING GROUND RULES AND MANAGING BEHAVIOUR

LO2.4 Summarise ways to establish ground rules with learners

Classroom management

The idea of behaviour management is fast becoming outdated. The way in which the teacher manages the classroom and how they relate to the learners is key to promoting a positive classroom that will result in good behaviour. The idea is that if the learners are engaged, challenged and motivated they will not misbehave.

CLASSROOM MANAGEMENT

Try to learn your learners' names in the first session and use their names when addressing them, particularly when giving them praise for their contributions.

From the outset, when the teacher first starts working with new learners, they will need to establish a set of ground rules that will cover all aspects of the relationship. It is important that such rules should be 'agreed' and to a large extent 'negotiated' on an equal basis, rather than imposed on the learners. This is an important process that ensures that learners understand their responsibilities and take full ownership. This kind of open involvement will help foster rapport and a good working relationship, reinforcing the teaching role as supportive rather than judgemental. This is an important early step: the teacher should bear in mind that some learners may be returning to learning with negative memories from school days and other learning experiences.

This image shows how important ground rules are in terms of health and safety when working with groups of learners. All are wearing their personal protective equipment (PPE) and the teacher can teach safe in the knowledge that they will be behaving in an appropriate manner.

Learners behaving appropriately in a practical lesson

The precise nature of the ground rules will depend on the context of the teaching, but generally they should cover what is expected from each other and also include a framework for working together within the learning environment.

Rules should always cover issues of valuing diversity, health and safety, cooperation and restating codes for common manners and courtesy.

Some basic ground rules

- Respect each other's beliefs and unique perspectives and preferences.
- Accept each individual's rights to hold opinions.
- Share knowledge, experiences and support one another.
- Arrive on time and ready for work.
- Have fun and participate fully!

If working with a group on a short course or in a workshop, the ground rules will be simple and centre on suitable behaviour for the activities you have planned. These might include the following:

- an appropriate language standard for conversations, responses and discussions
- listening to what others are saying without interruption
- awareness of the safety of the workspace and of other learners.

If working with remote learners, ground rules will also need to cover:

- how and when you may contact each other
- time frames for submitting and returning work (and acknowledging receipt)
- what to do if a commitment needs to be broken or a deadline cannot be met.

A positive learning environment should be based on a personalised approach that is challenging, supportive and safe.

CLASSROOM MANAGEMENT

Don't interrupt the flow of learning with irrelevant information or class notices just because you have suddenly thought of something else. Make a note of it and wait until the end of the session.

Problems

In the context of working mainly with adult learners, and more mature young people, there are usually few instances of major offences of inappropriate behaviour. Most learning situations tend to be relatively problem free, with behaviour problems usually consisting of minor incidents. However, such minor offences as late arrival and inconsistency in attendance and performance continually eat away at everyone's learning time. Teachers have to waste time allowing for learners who are unprepared, repeating information the learners have missed and dealing with minor interruptions.

Major problems, when they do occur, are likely to be socially based. The organisation will have procedures and guidelines to follow if a teacher finds themselves in such situations and they should ensure they are acquainted with them.

Generally, however, confrontational situations can be diffused by calm and measured responses that do not further inflame anyone.

Ensuring that problems in the classroom are diffused quickly will lead to a happy classroom.

In a classroom, it is likely that learners will divide themselves into smaller groups or a particular learner may become an individual isolated from the internal group politics going on in the room. The groups may well bicker against each other and, no matter what the teacher tries to do, this bickering will continue either inside or outside the classroom. In these circumstances a less experienced teacher will need to seek the advice of the course manager or a more experienced colleague. However, under no circumstances should the teacher accept any prejudicial statements or attitudes.

CLASSROOM MANAGEMENT

Silence can work well when trying to get attention back to you. Ask
the group to come to an end with their activity in an assertive way
and then wait for the conversations to end. If this takes more than
three minutes then ask again. This is should be a more successful
technique than repeating yourself, or shouting for attention. This
does take practice and patience. If one particular learner is still
talking then you could refer directly to them by name, eg. 'Rachel,
finish what you are doing. Thank you.'

Putting it into practice: practical skills

An effective way of increasing learner participation is to know and
understand about different ways that learners learn and different
strategies that can be used to deliver the subject. In addition, it is
important to consider the learning environment and communication with
learners. A teacher will need to check that learning has taken place by
using a form of assessment that provides information to monitor learner
progress and support further planning. Finally, all learners should be
treated as individuals and so the session should be planned to meet the
needs of learners and personalised as much as possible.

After teaching a session, it is useful to reflect on how the session went.
This will enable the teacher to make continuous improvements to their
teaching and demonstrate a professional approach.

In summary
Within any teaching session it is important to:

- try to plan an interesting, dynamic and relevant learning experience
- tailor learning to the individuals within the group
- use a range of teaching methods and resources
- assess that learning has taken place
- evaluate how effective the session was.

The result should be that motivation will increase and any potential
barriers that may prevent or hinder the learning process for the
learners will be removed.

Planning for learning

When delivering any subject a certain amount of planning is essential
in order for the subject to be taught in the most productive way.
A number of factors will have to be considered and the process of

planning will enable the teacher to make decisions before the session takes place. There are two elements to any planning: long- and short-term planning. Long-term planning takes into account the overarching aims of the programme and maps the course over a period of time, whereas short-term planning focuses on each individual session.

Long-term planning

A scheme of work (SoW) is the name given to a document that is used to organise the entire content of a course. It sets out what will be taught over the duration of the course and is usually designed for a specific group of learners and a particular subject or qualification.

A scheme of work should include:

- a brief structure and content for each individual session
- overall aims and objectives for each session
- a range of teaching methods (strategies)
- assessment planned for the programme taking into account formative and summative assessment opportunities.

It may also show where the following topics can be embedded:

- equality and diversity
- literacy, numeracy and ICT.

A scheme of work is basically a summary of the delivery plan for each session. This planning document may be pre-written and provided for the teacher who will then use it to produce individual session

plans. Alternatively a teacher may be involved in the development
of a scheme of work. If a course results in a qualification then the
scheme should be based on the criteria as set out by the awarding
organisation.

Session number	Content and tutor activities	Learning activities	Resources (including ILT use)	Assessment
1	**Aim: To Introduce learners to unit** Handout folders. Discuss course requirements – standards. Discuss the layout of the folder Record sheets Evidence Rough work	First impressions count … activity	Folders Record sheets Activity sheets	Completed front sheet Observed group and written work
2	**Aim: To introduce learners to different types of organisation** Direct teaching	Group activity: match different scenarios to different types of customers	PowerPoint Scenario sheets	Completed work Mind map created
3	**Aim: To carry out a research activity** Differences between internal and external customers Customers and their expectations	Customer satisfaction survey	Gapped handout Presentation Survey examples	Business model identified Direct Qs Completed surveys

The table shows an example of a completed scheme of work and
illustrates the first three weeks of planned delivery for a long-term
course.

The micro-teach

The micro-teach is an opportunity for you to plan, deliver and evaluate
a 15-minute session to the other learners from your course. You will
receive feedback from your tutor and at least two of your peers. This
will be useful information to help you when you evaluate your session.
You will also be expected to observe your peers when they deliver their
micro-teach sessions and you will be expected to provide feedback to
them. This is a supportive process and a valuable experience.

Your micro-teach can be on a subject of your choice and you must
plan for the session to include a beginning, main body and summary/
end. It cannot be 15 minutes of a longer session. For practical tips see
page 260.

LO3.1 Devise an inclusive teaching and learning plan

No matter what role the teacher is in, it is essential that learning opportunities are planned for and that these use the time effectively. The session plan is the key tool in this process.

Short-term planning: session plans

There are several good reasons why a formal plan is necessary as shown below:

Before the session

A formal plan:
- acts as a checklist
- plots a sequence of activities
- identifies the resources needed
- identifies assessment methods
- gives focus and structure.

Some of the worst lessons are the un-planned ones.

During the session

A formal plan provides the teacher with a schedule to follow, showing where they (and more importantly, the learners) should be at any one time, and what comes next. This will help the teacher cope with any situation where suddenly things are going faster or slower than planned, and enable them to take action and introduce extension activities or shortcuts accordingly.

After the session

In any teaching context, good practice is reflective practice. If a teacher plans and records how the session should go, they can more easily reflect and evaluate how it went. This will give an invaluable insight into what went well and why, as well as what didn't go so well and may need to be altered for next time. This way the teacher is always adapting to their learners and improving own practice as well as revising the long-term plan (scheme of work) and further short-term planning (future session plans).

Quality assurance

In addition to all of this, the teacher may be required by their organisation to provide evidence of sound practice as part of their quality assurance procedures. A formal session plan is one of the requirements for inspection or they may be observed by someone from the organisation.

Major considerations when planning a session include:

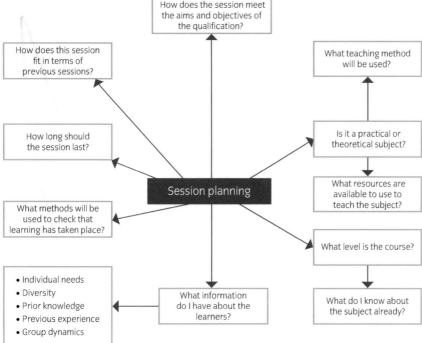

Of course, depending on the teaching role, the physical environment
in which the teaching is taking place and the type of course being
offered, the teacher may not be free to make decisions on content and
activities, as these may be predetermined. Hopefully such resources
will have been written to allow for individual styles, but practicalities
and economies of scale mean that these are, by their very nature,
somewhat generic.

EXAMPLE

Delivering a short health and safety qualification in the workplace

Even when supporting learners who are working remotely from
pre-written course materials, the teacher may need to use their
judgement to guide and support individuals through the materials in
a different order or in a different way. As individuals progress, they
may need to be provided with supplementary materials to increase
relevance and aid understanding.

Remember: everyone learns in a different way and a personalised
approach should be planned for whenever possible.

As the saying goes – fail to plan, plan to fail!

Aims and objectives

The *aim* of the session should be written in general terms and identify the overall topic that is going to be covered. *Objectives* are more specific and outline what the learners will have learnt by the end of the session. These are the statements that the teacher uses to check that learning has taken place. In order to be able to do this, objectives must be specific, measurable, achievable (within the timeframe), realistic and timebound (SMART).

A good way to make sure that they are easily measurable is by starting each objective with the sentence:

'By the end of the session the learners will be able to … .'

For example:

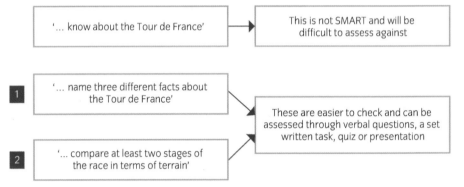

Keep away from using the verbs 'know' or 'understand' as these are not SMART which makes them hard to assess.

Example two is more challenging and uses higher-order thinking skills on Bloom's cognitive domain.

ACTIVITY

Consider how you can use Bloom's theory to write your objectives. You must try to set the objectives at the level that is right for the learners.

Using these verbs below from the different levels within Bloom's cognitive domain, write a set of new objectives for the example given above:

list   compare   discuss   recommend

If you have a session that you are planning to teach, look at the objectives and consider which level of Bloom's taxonomy they are set against. Identify which assessment method you plan to use to check that they have been achieved.

Trying to include all (differentiation)

Pitching the session at the right level will make sure that all learners are able to participate. However, some learners might find the session too easy so it is useful to think about activities that can stretch and challenge those learners in order that they do not become bored and distracted, or not learn as much as possible from the session. It is also good to consider those learners who might struggle and set some activities that are simpler or allow more time within the session for them to complete the work.

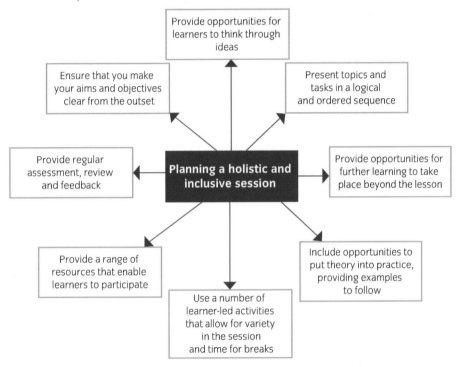

(Adapted from Fairclough, 2008)

The following example is based on the City & Guilds suggested session plan format. This is available to use to evidence your planning for the micro-teach. However, you may be required to use a session plan used by your own organisation. Make sure that you plan each part of the session by breaking it down into smaller timed slots and use a variety of assessment methods that are suitable to check against the learning objectives. Think about how you will use the resources in an interesting and relevant way.

Example of a micro-teach session plan

Teacher	B. Hopcroft	Date		Room	
Course/topic	Golf	Time		Duration	15 mins
Aim		To give learners an overview of the game of golf and the importance of using the right pressure when putting			

Objectives:

	By the end of the session all learners will be able to:	By the end of the session, some learners will be able to:
1	Accurately throw a soft ball a required distance with support	Accurately throw a soft ball a required distance and relate this activity to the amount of effort required when putting a ball using a golf club
2	Hit a golf ball to a set distance in three attempts with some support	Hit a golf ball to a set distance in two attempts without any support

Timing	Objectives	Resources	Teacher activities	Learner activities	Assessment
2 mins		Whiteboard Hand-drawn diagram of a putting green	Introduce the topic: Give an overview to the game of golf. Explain how each hole is scored and the importance of putting within the game Note: assess prior experience and knowledge	Listen and observe, asking and responding to questions where appropriate Offer information when prompted	Open questions
4 mins	1	Soft balls Pre-marked distances	Facilitate the activity: throwing a soft ball in pairs in a pre-arranged sequence Discuss how the task relates to the game of golf	Throwing and catching a soft ball a variety of different distances in pairs Participate in a discussion about the task	Observation Discussion and direct questions for advanced learners
2 mins		Putter and golf balls	Practical demonstration: using a putter. Note: relate it to the previous activity of ball throwing	Observation and listening	Open questions
5 mins	2	Putter and golf balls	Facilitate practical activity: putting a golf ball successfully	Individually practise hitting a golf ball with a putter to a marked distance	Observation
2 mins	1, 2	Whiteboard	Summary of the session: 1. Putting is half the game 2. Effort has to be proportional to distance 3. All had a go to experience putting	Listen, feedback and discuss in terms of own experience Answer questions	Direct questions

THE JUSTIFICATION

LO3.2 Justify own selection of teaching and learning approaches, resources and assessment methods in relation to meeting individual learner needs

When thinking about planning the micro-teach (mini-taught session) you need to provide evidence to support the choices you have arrived at. This is part of the planning stage and shows that you have considered theory and made links between this and the decisions made. It is a way to prove that you have considered your choices and can justify these choices.

When writing the justification, you should think about the following questions:

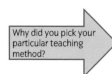

Practical subjects are better taught by:
- Demonstration
- (Supported or independent) practical task such as making something or role play

Theory subjects are better taught by:
- Presentation
- Discussion-based activity such as problem solving through a case study or debate

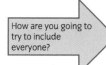

Some strategies you might consider:
- An initial assessment to establish prior knowledge and skills (simple question or ask learners to rate themselves)
- Match experienced or confident learners with less confident ones
- Give more time for learners to complete the activity
- Support less able learners
- Extended questions to stretch more able learners

Consider:
- The physical environment – can you alter the layout of the tables and if so how will you set out the room? Why will this enable learner participation?
- Do you need specialist resources for the task?
- What might you need to think about in terms of making changes to resources based on individual needs – eg large font, coloured paper, use of images
- Are your choices realistic and practical?

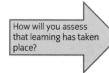

Some strategies to consider:
- Observation
- Open, directed or leading questioning
- Completed task

Don't forget to think about getting the learners to self-assess or assess each other in a peer-assessed activity

TEACHING APPROACHES

LO4.1: Use teaching and learning approaches, resources and assessment methods to meet individual learner needs

Starter activities

All sessions should start promptly and the learners should be engaged right from the beginning. This helps the learners settle into the session and establishes expectations from the outset. A simple starter activity can aid this process and a range of ideas can be used to set the scene, put the session in context and get the learners working from the moment they get into the classroom.

Practical subjects	Theory subjects
Prompt questions: ask learners to write down one thing that they completed in the last session	Prompt questions: ask learners to write down one thing that they can recall from the previous session
Tell your neighbour: ask learners to explain to their peer what they need to work on during the session	Unjumble the sayings: provide some words on slips of paper that learners have to use to create a saying related to the topic
Guess the object: put an unusual object in view of the learners and ask them to guess what it is Extension: ask them to describe it (embedding literacy)	Word search: give the learners word searches on the topic Extension: ask them to highlight any unfamiliar words to look up and write a definition for
	Pose a viewpoint: give learners a controversial statement that they have to consider and ask them to discuss with the person sitting next to them

These are some ideas of possible starter activities. Over a period of time, an experienced teacher will develop a range of starter activities that they will be able to use with their learners. These should only take a few moments at the start of the session and are useful to help learners settle down and provide something for them to do. Sometimes adult learners arrive early to the session and starter activities are particularly helpful while the teacher gets organised.

HANDY HINT

Use name cards (folded A5 card is good for this) to help you learn individual names in the first session. You could type a series of behaviour expectations on one side that your learners will be able to see throughout the session. This will promote the attitudes that you want to see and sets the scene from day one.

Resources

For each activity, whether carried out by the teacher or learners, it is necessary to plan in advance what resources will be needed, including physical resources, rooms and equipment – and even technicians, guest teachers, or colleagues if applicable. As before, accessibility and individual needs must be included in the rationale for your decisions on resources.

Remember contingencies: for example, if you are planning to use any technology, this can prove problematic – especially in unfamiliar surroundings. Unfortunately the point has not yet been reached where the reliability of technology can be taken for granted. Always plan for an alternative; hard copies of handouts and notes will all help.

You also need to be aware of financial and programme limitations on the resources you can use. Most organisations will have a limit on the amount you can spend on photocopying, so you should find this out at the beginning.

You may have a resource bank to draw from, a learning pack already, or you may have to research and create resources yourself. Whichever of these is true, you must be clear in your reasons for selection and be able to justify them in terms of effectiveness and learner needs.

Things to consider

When choosing resources that you can use in your specialist area, ask yourself the following questions:

- What would you use it for?
- How will it contribute to the objectives/ learning outcomes?
- Is it accessible to anyone with disabilities or learning difficulties?
- If it needs adapting, how might you go about this?
- Does it communicate clearly, with straightforward instructions (if applicable)?
- To which learning styles will it appeal? (Remember: visual, auditory, kinaesthetic, read/write – VARK.)

During the micro-teach you will be expected to use resources, suitable teaching and learning approaches and assessment methods. If you are preparing new resources then give yourself time to get them right. If you are using existing resources, make sure you are familiar with them and spend time practising before using them in the session.

Assessment: checking that learning has taken place

It is an important part of the teacher's role to check that the learners have learnt what was intended in the session. There are many different ways to do this. Deciding on the assessment method to use to measure learning is part of the planning stage. The assessment method will be linked back to the learning objective for the session and will provide a measure of how much the learners have learnt from the session. It should be a simple method as the micro-teach is only a very short teaching session. Try not to be over-ambitious!

When thinking about the best type of method or methods to use. You should consider:

■ the subject that is being taught
■ the resources available
■ the level of the learners
■ any additional needs that could result in barriers to assessment.

A simple way to check learning is through verbal questioning. This still needs to be planned in order to be as effective as possible. The type of questions asked can be changed to accommodate all levels of knowledge in the group.

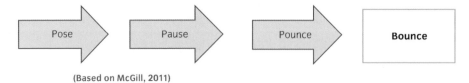

(Based on McGill, 2011)

This is a simple strategy that allows learners to consider the question once it has been posed and before the teacher pounces on a named learner. The same question can then be asked of another learner in the room. This type of assessment method needs to be managed so that learners do not shout out the answer before being asked. By setting clear guidelines before using this assessment method, learners should be able to participate in an active way that includes everyone and the teacher will be able to choose who they want to ask for the answer.

Use the table below to consider resources and ways to assess the learning when planning the micro-teach:

Type of resource	Things to consider	Alterations that can be made	Ways to make it active	Possible assessment method
Handout or information sheet	■ Is the information accurate? ■ Check for spelling, grammar and punctuation ■ Is the information clearly put across? ■ Have images and examples been included? ■ Has it photocopied clearly? ■ Are they sufficient for everyone?	■ Sans serif font such as Comic Sans ■ Size of font – minimum 12 point ■ Large font if needed ■ Coloured paper (cream if possible)	■ Include activities at the end ■ Include written questions after each paragraph ■ Offer opportunities for key words to be underlined and put into a personal learner glossary	■ Direct or open questions ■ Verbal quiz ■ Written quiz ■ Completion of gapped activity within the handout

Type of resource	Things to consider	Alterations that can be made	Ways to make it active	Possible assessment method
PowerPoint presentation	■ Is the information accurate? ■ Check for spelling ■ Is the information sufficient and at the right level? ■ Have images and examples been included? ■ Do not include too many slides or it will be death by PowerPoint!	■ Sans serif font such as Comic Sans ■ Size of font – minimum 36 point ■ Simple design and less is more! ■ Do not use too many animations or colours to complicate it ■ Make the slides available as handouts for learners	■ Ask questions during the slides ■ Break up the presentation with activities, video, images ■ Do not talk for too long	■ Direct or open questions ■ Completion of activity based on the information from the presentation such as a poster
Teaching aids such as practical equipment	■ Is the object in good working order? ■ Is it complete? ■ Does it demonstrate what it is meant to?	■ Can everyone see? ■ Can it be handed round or is there enough for everyone to participate?	■ Ask questions during the demonstration ■ Provide an opportunity for learners to use the object individually	■ Observation of finished product ■ Open or direct questions

EXAMPLE OF A JUSTIFICATION

The recipe packs to be used within a session have a basic recipe for the learners so they can produce the required dish. As it is a mixed-ability group some learners will be required to convert quantities of ingredients within the dish to ensure that they are in the same unit of measurement; for example, pounds to grams. This will help to embed numeracy skills and can also be differentiated to meet the individual needs of the group.

I will look at the resources that I use as well and try to think about ways to make these more of an active learning exercise so they are as useful as possible.

❝❞

Some teachers produce uncompleted handouts; diagrams that are not labelled, headings with missing text. Completing the hand out becomes a useful lesson activity, which personalises the handout for the student.

(Petty, 2004: 205)

Gould (2010) discusses the importance of communication when demonstrating a task. It is necessary therefore for me to make sure that I speak in a clear and unambiguous way so that the meaning is clear for everyone.

For more information on assessment methods look at Unit 305/306.

COMMUNICATION

LO4.2 Communicate with learners in ways that meet their individual needs

If the session has been well planned, and the aims and objectives are well defined, then it is easier to make sure that the message delivered by the teacher is clear. From the start of the session, a teacher should outline in simple language what learners are expected to achieve and should provide an opportunity for learners to ask questions to clarify meaning if necessary. Some teachers will write the objectives on the board and leave these in full view. This also allows the teacher to revisit these objectives at the end of the session and can form the basis for the recap and assessment of learning.

Even if a teacher thinks that they are communicating clearly, there might still be barriers to communication that could mean the message is not understood fully by the learners.

Assessing learners' work can provide an insight into how clear your communication is

Top tips

- Use simple language whenever possible.
- Give examples and anecdotes to embed meaning.
- Provide opportunities for questions throughout.
- Offer a definition for technical terms (glossary).
- Provide a dictionary to aid spelling (embedding literacy).
- Use a variety of pitch and tone to maintain interest.
- Consider positive body language (open and encouraging).

In order to uphold discipline and engage with all learners the teacher should try to make and maintain eye contact. When working with a group of learners, some teachers will start on the left side of the room and slowly move their gaze across all the learners until they finish on the other side of the room. This is a good way to make all the learners feel included and noticed and they are more likely to participate in the session.

Reading cues from your learners

Do not read too much into these; after all a person may cross their arms because they are cold! However, the teacher may get a useful assessment of how well the session or activities are being received if they are familiar with some common signs.

A group of learners working together displaying positive body language

This image shows a group of learners who all look relaxed and engaged in the conversation.

Look at the quick reference list in Unit 304 for more information on this.

During the micro-teach you will need to make sure that you communicate clearly and effectively with the learners. This could be more challenging than you might think. You will probably be delivering your micro-teach to your peers and this can make the experience stressful. One way to reduce nerves is by making sure that the session is well planned and that you have practised the session before it is delivered for real. If the experience is nerve wracking then take deep breaths, use simple language and, if necessary, plan to have prompt cards in case you go blank!

In addition you should provide opportunities for learners to ask questions throughout.

USING FEEDBACK

LO4.3 Provide constructive feedback to learners to meet their individual needs

Once the subject has been delivered in an inclusive way, the teacher has to consider how they will provide feedback – **formative** or **summative** – to their learners. The purpose of feedback is to let the learner know how they are progressing on the course. Just as the delivery needs to be tailored to make sure that everyone can participate, the way that feedback can be communicated also needs to be considered.

Formative feedback is information that is given so that learners can identify what can be further improved as they continue with their studies

Feedback can be verbal or written or a combination of the two.

Ways to make sure that feedback is constructive and inclusive

Summative feedback is information given so that a learner can see what has been achieved in the work as a final grade and end result

- Provide feedback at regular intervals, in sessions and on marked work.
- Information should be clear about how to improve as a learner.
- Always refer to the question or learning outcomes.
- Use direct, positive language to make it clear about what a learner is doing well, particularly in the early stages of their learning.
- Feedback should be timely; a learner will feel demotivated if they have to wait too long for their feedback.
- Check that the feedback is understood by the learner.
- Offer feedback in a variety of formats to cater for any special education needs.
- Always use clear, unembellished and succinct language and avoid ambiguities.
- Use a level of language and style appropriate to the learner.
- State what you want learners to do for future improvements.
- Involve the learners in completing an action plan. This could be linked to their ILP.

When teaching groups on a regular basis it is necessary to build instant feedback into the teaching and learning activities. This will be either verbal, in response to an answer or comment, or written on a piece of work.

A group of learners and their tutor looking at peer feedback

This image shows a group of learners giving peer feedback on a
completed task. This can be a good way to provide feedback for
learners but needs to be managed and structured to be effective and
not detrimental.

Whenever giving feedback, both verbally and especially when written
(as this can be re-visited time and again), make sure you are positive
and supportive and never overtly critical.

Say to the learner	Then add
'You have made a really good point here'	'Consider adding more information to this section'
'You remembered how to measure that accurately without any help'	'Next time use the list in your handbook when carrying out that task as it will help you to think about the order'
'Your sentence structure is really improving'	'Now try to use a wider range of words'
'Your written skills have really developed a lot and you are now using a wider vocabulary'	'Consider how you could take that point further and use some technical language here'

Positive, supportive feedback is not just a choice of words. Supportive
feedback uses the 'medal and mission' strategy by focusing and
congratulating on what was done well, explaining what wasn't
and why, then ending with some targets to help the learner make
improvements throughout their studies. This will ensure that the
overall feeling is positive and keeps the learner's motivation levels high
(Reece and Walker, 2003).

Giving feedback – good practice checklist

- Start with pleasantries or greetings.
- Give feedback on each point separately.
- Use clear, simple, concise language; avoid jargon and acronyms.
- Use positive openings that comment on strengths.
- Point out any mistakes with directions and suggestions for action.
- Explain grading if appropriate.
- Refer back to previous examples or materials and put the task in perspective.
- Offer further sources of information or support.
- Finish positively; acknowledge effort.
- Summarise and list further or next actions required and by when.
- Check understanding and agreement.

More information about giving feedback can be found on page 163.

REFLECTIVE PRACTICE AND EVALUATING THE SESSION

LO5.1 Review the effectiveness of own delivery of inclusive teaching and learning

Self-evaluation is an important part of being a teacher. Attending regular continuing professional development (CPD) and developing good habits of reflective practice can be considered the best ways to demonstrate and develop these skills. Using a reflective model to consider how the micro-teach went will help to provide structure.

You could use the below from City & Guilds:

SELF-EVALUATION

Micro-teaching/teaching practice delivery

Strengths:
Areas for development:
Action required to improve the same session for the future:

Alternatively you could use the below from City & Guilds:

REFLECTIVE LEARNING JOURNAL

Analysis of challenges that I faced in the task:
How I dealt with this, and why I took this approach:
What went well and why:
What I need to do to improve and how I plan to do this:

Both forms provide a simple structure to help when reflecting on the progression of a session. A set of questions will provide the teacher with some structure on which to base their reflections. After reflecting on the micro-teach it is important that some form of reflective practice is continued in the role of the teacher. This might be provided by the organisation that the teacher works for or could be developed independently. Whatever format the structure takes, the result should be the same; it is an opportunity to consider what worked and what could be altered so that delivery is improved time and time again.

Schemes of work and session plans are documents that can and should be altered and updated over a period of time based on reflective practice. It is not always necessary to consider every second of a session, but to concentrate on one key element that did not work as well as possible and arrive at solutions so that the next time improvements can be made. Whatever format the teacher uses, this should be simple and easy to refer to in the future.

Here are two examples of reflective practice after a micro-teach session:

EXAMPLE 1

I was really pleased with how I interacted with the learners. I was able to use open and closed questions and this helped me to get the individuals in the group to demonstrate they were learning. Some group members gave excellent answers to the questions and this encouraged me to ask leading questions to extend their learning further. I was able to genuinely praise the learners.

In terms of areas for improvement, I apparently talk to the whiteboard on occasion. In future, I could ask a learner to do the writing when the rest of the group are giving feedback, or just try to remain silent when writing up the answers myself. Finally, I do find that I struggle to give consistent eye contact and this is something that I have been working on and is something that should improve with practice.

EXAMPLE 2

My main teaching method involved me demonstrating what I would like the learners to do. At the same time I described the task verbally, talking through each stage and giving information about how to complete it.

❝❞

The aim of most demonstrations is to provide students with a concrete example of good practice to copy or adapt

(Petty, 2004, page 173)

Demonstration allows both audio and visual learners to gain the most that is possible from the session and have a clear idea of how to complete the set task. By using a practical task, the learners were able to have a go and this then enabled the kinaesthetic learners to participate.

I think this was successful as all of the learners were able to complete the task quickly and to a good standard. As the learners were attempting the task I walked around the room to answer any questions or to provide help.

In both examples the teacher has linked back to what they had planned to do and thought about how this worked in practice.

It is good practice to underpin all of your thoughts and reflections with some ideas from theory. This will demonstrate a depth of knowledge and understanding based on research. Example two does this successfully.

NEXT STEPS AND ACTION PLANNING

LO5.2 Identify areas for improvement in own delivery of inclusive teaching and learning

Once in the role of the teacher it is normal practice to undergo an appraisal with a line manager where the teacher is expected to continue to demonstrate a professional approach to their job.

This involves:

- making an action plan for the following year that will provide the basis for training and up-skilling
- participating in continuing professional development that will help to improve subject knowledge and teaching skills.

This is an important aspect of the role of the teacher and could have a direct influence on promotion opportunities and an increase in salary.

This could involve the use of the summative profile and action plan as shown here.

SUMMATIVE PROFILE AND ACTION PLAN

My overall development and strengths as a result of attending this programme:

Personal statement: Where I am now, the subject I wish to deliver, and what I wish to do in the future:

Action plan: What I intend to do now to help me gain a teaching/ training position or progress with my teaching/training career:

At the end of the course you will be expected to think back over the duration of the course and complete a short piece of reflective writing. This will enable you to consider what you have learnt from attending the course and how this has helped you to develop professionally. It will also provide you with an opportunity to identify some areas that you need to develop further. By writing an action plan from this reflective practice you will be able to focus on furthering your professional teaching career. The action plan should follow SMART principles so that it will be possible to measure when each action has been achieved.

UNIT SUMMARY

This unit has concentrated on some of the different inclusive teaching strategies and approaches that can be taken when delivering a subject. It has looked at some of the types of barriers that exist and identified some of the ways to try and remove these barriers to make the learning more accessible. Different teaching and learning theory, such as learning styles, teaching according to level and how to develop and use active teaching methods, have also been explored.

A key element of inclusive practice is the development of a supportive and positive learning environment. This unit has looked at ways to create ground rules that will help provide a learner with the structure and guidance they need through their journey. The individualised approach that can be developed in an inclusive environment can be an extremely successful one, but it is dependent on the relationship between teacher and learner. It is most productive when based on mutual respect and when learning needs are recognised and planned for. This is not always easy and this unit has identified some of the barriers and challenges that can arise along the way. Some possible strategies have been suggested and different teaching methods also explored.

This unit also identifies some techniques to use when planning a session. It has provided a recap about different teaching methods and approaches that can be used when delivering a subject. It has looked at some of the different documents that can be used and provided information and examples to support the practical element of the qualification. Creating resources that meet the needs of learners and communication theory have also been explored. Remember that a relevant, practical task is necessary when teaching vocational subjects. It would not be as effective to teach how to cut someone free from a car in a theory-based classroom session.

A key element of inclusive practice is the planning of sessions that meet the needs of individual learners. This unit has looked at ways to facilitate this and has provided practical examples so that taught sessions can be planned in an inclusive way. Checking that learning has taken place is critical and some possible strategies have been suggested that will make this part of the teaching cycle effective within the micro-teach.

Overall inclusive practice is a very motivational approach to learning. Tailoring sessions to individual need, and planning an engaging and interesting experience, very often results in a successful learning and teaching experience for both the teacher and the learner. Turning theory into practice is the creative part of teaching. Planning for learning to take place in an interesting and dynamic way, delivering the session in an inclusive way and reflecting back on the experience are what makes a successful teacher.

This unit has focused on understanding and using learning and teaching approaches in an inclusive way, but there is additional information in other units that will also be helpful when planning the micro-teach. There are also suggested websites and a comprehensive book list to help when researching the topic further.

ASSIGNMENT FOCUS

This unit provides you with information to enable you to understand a variety of approaches to learning and teaching that underpin inclusive practice. The learning outcomes will be assessed by a piece of written work, such as an assignment, and the practical element of the course, such as a micro-teach. You will need to cover all of the following assessment criteria in order to evidence your knowledge and understanding successfully.

Assessment criteria: Knowledge element

1.1: Describe features of inclusive teaching and learning

1.2: Compare the strengths and limitations of teaching and learning
approaches used in own area of specialism in relation to meeting
individual learners' needs

1.3: Explain why it is important to provide opportunities for learners
to develop their English, maths, ICT and wider skills

2.1: Explain why it is important to create an inclusive teaching and
learning environment

2.2: Explain why it is important to select teaching and learning
approaches, resources and assessment methods to meet
individual learner needs

2.3: Explain ways to engage and motivate learners

2.4: Summarise ways to establish ground rules with learners

Tips

You might want to consider the following when planning your
assignment:

- What types of teaching approaches do you use in your own subject
  area?
- Discuss some of the factors that have an impact on a learner's ability
  to learn.
- How will these needs be considered when planning and delivering
  learning?
- Which teaching methods are the most successful when working with
  an individual and what makes these successful?
- What sort of individual barriers might exist and what would you do to
  engage your learner and help to reduce any barriers?
- What resources would you choose to use with your learner and what
  can you do to make these more accessible?
- Give some examples of ways that you would change delivery in order
  to meet individual need more effectively.
- How would you adapt the way that you assess your learners in order
  to consider a range of learning difficulties?
- Within your own subject specialism, explain how you would try and
  embed English, maths, ICT and wider skills.
- How would you plan to create a motivating learning environment?
- Discuss ways to set ground rules with your learners that will
  encourage a respectful learning environment.
- Give some examples of how you could deliver feedback to motivate
  and encourage your learners.

Assessment criteria: practical element

3.1: Devise an inclusive teaching and learning plan

3.2: Justify own selection of teaching and learning approaches, resources and assessment methods in relation to meeting individual learner needs

4.1: Use teaching and learning approaches, resources and assessment methods to meet individual learner needs

4.2: Communicate with learners to meet their individual needs

4.3: Provide constructive feedback to learners to meet their individual needs

5.1: Review the effectiveness of own delivery of inclusive teaching and learning

5.2: Identify areas for improvement in own delivery of inclusive teaching and learning

Tips

You might want to consider the following when planning your micro-teach:

- What type of planning document will you use to help plan the session?
- Which teaching methods will suit the subject that you are planning to deliver?
- What differentiation strategies will you use when trying to meet the needs of the individual learners in the group?
- What resources will you choose to use with your learners and what can you do to make these more accessible?
- How will you plan to create a motivating learning experience?
- Give some examples of how you will assess that learning has taken place.
- How do you plan to communicate effectively with the learners?
- Is there a reflective model that you can use after the session to help you to identify future improvements to your teaching delivery?

UNIT 303

Facilitate learning and development for individuals

INTRODUCTION

There are many reasons why learners are taught on an individual basis. Some learners are supported on a one-to-one basis in the workplace or in addition to their main qualifications. This type of delivery is often more to do with assessing, coaching or mentoring rather than traditional teaching. To get the best results, a learner will be responsible for their own progression.

One-to-one delivery is often supported with online resources and often includes a personalised style of learning. This can be a successful type of experience and helps learners to develop a deep understanding of the subject. It is flexible and negotiated on a regular basis and often takes place in a real-life learning environment.

Teaching on a one-to-one basis has many benefits but can also present challenges to both teacher and learner. This unit explores ways in which learning can be facilitated on a one-to-one basis so that it is as successful as possible as a learning experience. Some of the aspects covered include:

- the different roles that the teacher may adopt, depending on the situation
- the importance of rapport and building relationships
- effective and suitable teaching methods
- overcoming barriers to learning and monitoring individual progress
- reflective models to support self-evaluation, both for learner and teacher.

This unit focuses on working with individuals, but there is additional information in Units 301 and 302 that will also be helpful.

In Unit 303 you will cover the following learning outcomes:

LO1: Understand principles and practices of one-to-one learning and development
LO2: Be able to facilitate one-to-one learning and development
LO3: Be able to assist individual learners in applying new knowledge and skills in practical contexts
LO4: Be able to assist individual learners in reflecting on their learning and/or development

WHY DO WE TEACH ON A ONE-TO-ONE BASIS?

LO1.1 Explain the purposes of one-to-one learning and development

It might seem unusual to think about teaching learners on an individual basis rather than as a group, particularly when considering the evidence in the previous unit that learners learn best in a social context, through interaction with other learners. However, there are occasions when learners do need to be taught on an individual basis as this will be the best way for those individuals to engage with their learning.

The workplace assessor

When learning is facilitated in the workplace, rather than in a traditional learning environment, the learner will often be taught on a one-to-one basis. It might not be practical, possible or necessary to teach more than one learner at a time in this type of situation. Some adults are in a role that requires them to work unsociable hours and this type of delivery can be flexible enough to enable them to participate at a time and place that are convenient for them.

EXAMPLE

A learner can study a diploma in health and social care where the evidence is gathered in the form of a portfolio. An assessor meets with the learner in their workplace about once a month for an hour. They collect completed work, observe the learner carrying out their role and have professional discussions mapped to learning outcomes. This keeps the learner on track and makes the learning relevant and a 'real-life' experience.

Private tutoring

When teaching adults, it is possible to teach one learner at a time as a private tutor. This type of teaching will be based on a bespoke delivered training programme that may take place in the tutor's home or a community venue.

A singing lesson taking place

This type of teaching is frequently offered in the form of additional classes to support the learning of an academic subject, such as GCSE preparation. Alternatively the learner could be learning a new skill, such as a musical instrument, as a leisure pursuit.

Teaching support

Another reason for one-to-one learning might be due to individual need. A one-to-one teaching and learning environment might be more suitable for learners who require specialist support. By working with these learners individually, the teacher is able to tailor a very particular, bespoke, learning experience that will effectively meet the needs of each learner. The opportunity for an individual learner to be supported on a one-to-one basis should help them to develop a deeper knowledge and understanding of the course materials and enable them to succeed on their course. This type of provision could be in addition to group learning, where the majority of the course is taught to that individual, or as a stand-alone type of programme.

EXAMPLE

A learner could be studying a level 2 qualification in animal care. If they have been diagnosed with dyslexia, then they could be entitled to some additional support. A learning support tutor will meet with the learner in the library about once a week for an hour. They will look at completed work with the learner and may act as a scribe to help the learner write essays. They may also help them to come up with coping strategies to make the course accessible for them.

Some of the benefits

This type of bespoke delivery is often one that turns the teacher's role into one of facilitating learning, often more akin to a coach, assessor or mentor. A major benefit of this type of learning experience is that it can be of a high quality, offering real ownership of the learning journey. The tasks can be tailored to meet individual need and the relationship between the teacher and learner is one built on mutual respect and understanding. The amount of **guided learning hours** (GLHs) required are fewer than traditional classroom-based, group-taught sessions, so are potentially just as cost effective. However, this will clearly not be the case if the same topic is taught on separate sessions when it could be delivered as a group, rather on an individual basis.

Guided learning hours (GLHs)
Guided learning hours are the number of hours that an awarding organisation suggests that it takes to deliver a course. This also determines how much funding will be provided per learner

In summary, one-to-one teaching:

- facilitates learning
- has a bespoke delivery style
- matches learners' needs
- offers ownership of the experience by the learner
- provides tailored personalised tasks
- means fewer GLHs.

Some of the challenges

In terms of assessment in the workplace-based qualifications, delivery often relies on the learner taking a lot of responsibility for their own progression. This active engagement with the learning means the learner has to complete tasks away from the classroom and may be supported via online resources. The result is that learning will be completed independently and shared either electronically, via email or an online assessment tool, or during each separate face-to-face meeting. Not all learners are able or willing to do this and may need constant support, particularly at the start of the programme.

This type of learning can be flexible and happen at a time and place that are suitable for both parties. However, it can mean that the teacher is travelling long distances between locations and the facilities might not always provide the right type of environment for learning to happen. I have even seen one-to-one learning taking place in a cupboard! It is important that the teacher plans the journey, allowing sufficient time to get to the location and on to further sessions if necessary. The learner might arrange to meet at the end or start of a shift, but then the learner could be tired or find it difficult to concentrate while in their workplace.

As discussed, this type of delivery can be supported with online resources; but these do need to be properly set up, managed and accessible if they are to be useful. Finally, this type of learning could result in informal conversation or an opportunity for the learner to 'off load', especially as the relationship develops. The boundaries need to remain clear so that the time can be directed and useful and so that the session stays on track.

A tutor and a learner in conversation

In summary, one-to-one teaching:

- relies on the learner taking responsibility
- means the teacher may have to travel between locations; therefore time management and access to a vehicle are necessary
- can mean an unknown teaching environment
- requires less access to 'known' teaching resources
- means the learner may need ICT skills
- may result in the learner finding it difficult to concentrate
- could become informal and more of a 'chat'.

WORKING WITH INDIVIDUALS

LO1.2 Explain factors to be considered when facilitating learning and development to meet individual needs

LO1.3 Evaluate methods for facilitating learning and development to meet the needs of individuals

A teacher's responsibilities for learners centre on the individual and their needs. The role may well include elements of:

- giving advice, guidance and conducting initial assessments
- planning and enabling specialist subject support during delivery
- providing regular assessment of coursework
- giving constructive feedback on work
- conducting regular reviews of progress
- keeping efficient and effective records of all assessment, progression and feedback
- communicating on a regular basis.

In all of this a teacher will be following set codes of practice from within the organisation, in order to ensure quality, equality and following relevant legislation.

Significant planning and organisational skills are required to provide effective learning support. When working individually, a learner can easily feel demotivated, and this can be compounded when there is a lack of peer support available. A structured individual learning plan (ILP), to be negotiated at the outset, is essential. All such plans must clearly state learning goals, target and review dates. Assessment will also be part of the plan and may take many forms, depending on the programme. Also, within the constraints of specific course delivery, the teacher will have a responsibility to ensure that assessment is focused on remaining clear and impartial. It must also take into account the specific learning needs or other requirements of the individual learner.

A tutor with a learner in a non-traditional learning setting

❝❞

Good teacher–student relationships are based on mutual respect. The student respects the teacher for his or her teaching skills, personal qualities, knowledge and professionalism and the teacher respects each student as an individual.

(Petty, 2004, page 96)

CLASSROOM MANAGEMENT

If you are asked a question that you don't know the answer to, do not bluff. Learners know when you are bluffing and this undermines your authority. Compliment them on the question asked and either say you will check and let them know the next session, or ask them to go away and find out the answer themselves. Make a note of the question and use it as a starter for the following session. This will show that you take notice and that will mean a lot to your learner.

It is worth considering the following principles. These are particular to the role of coach and mentor and will be relevant when working on a one-to-one basis with a learner.

L	Learner is capable of better results
E	Equality of conversation
A	Attention is centred on what the learner thinks and experiences
R	Relationship is built on truth, openness and trust
N	Nurture a commitment to support the individual
E	Every session will be different
R	Responsibility for the results sits with the learner

(Adapted from Starr, 2003, page 30)

Teacher, facilitator, assessor, trainer, coach or mentor

The type of role that the teacher employs when working with individual learners will depend on a variety of factors. The role will often be a fluid one, moving between the different types of support and delivery needed, determined by the situation as it happens. This flexible approach is something that can be of benefit for both the teacher and the learner.

Looking at the role of mentor, and comparing it with the coaching role, will provide information about how to best work with learners to meet their needs in a learning environment – wherever that might occur.

In lifelong learning, mentoring, according to Wallace and Gravells (2008), is '*primarily about transition*'. This involves helping someone to move from one stage of professional development to another.

Both coaching and mentoring should enable individuals to achieve their full potential and share many similarities. However, it is the type of learner, or the situation that the learning is taking place in, that will determine in many respects what type of role the teacher will adopt.

Characteristics of the coach and mentor	
Coaching (assessing/workplace training scenario)	Mentoring (learning support role)
<ul><li>Relates to performance improvement</li><li>Specific skills set/area</li><li>Goals set by the coach</li><li>Coach has ownership of the process</li><li>Direct extrinsic (external) feedback</li></ul>	<ul><li>Nurturing of whole person</li><li>Long-term relationship</li><li>Goals set by learner</li><li>Learner owns goals and process</li><li>Feedback comes intrinsically (from within)</li><li>Mentor enables the mentee to develop insight and understanding</li></ul>

(Adapted from Megginson and Clutterbuck, 2005, page 5)

ACTIVITY

Think about a one-to-one teaching session that you are responsible for. Consider which approach suits your learner the best. Do you use a coaching technique or are you acting more in the role of a mentor? What factors have you considered when arriving at your decision?

Do you think it is possible to adopt both of these approaches with the same learner? Is so, what would be the benefit of this?

As discussed by Klasen and Clutterbuck (2002, cited in Wallace and Gravells, 2008, page 14), when establishing the type of role to be adopted when working with individual learners, it is worth considering the four basic styles of helping. The majority of the time a teacher will normally operate using a **directive approach**; stretching intellectual need. This style provides clear direction, structure, guidelines and controls for the learner to work within. This is the coaching style of delivery. It can cause the learner to act in a passive manner, looking to the teacher to provide answers, solutions and set the workload for them.

Directive approach is where a teacher takes a proactive and lead role in the session, guiding and instructing the learner

THEORY TO PRACTICE

This style of one-to-one delivery could be a sensible starting approach to use when working with new learners as it can take time for a learner to take ownership of their learning, particularly if they have come straight from school or are lacking in confidence.

A **non-directive approach**, on the other hand, will put the learner in control of their own learning by forcing them to set their own targets, establish their own workload and be more self directed. This is teaching an individual via the use of questions and *active listening strategies* and is more akin to a mentor role.

Non-directive approach is where a teacher takes a back seat during the session, waiting for the learner to take control of their own learning

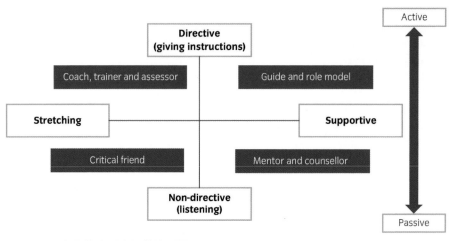

Four basic styles of helping

Neither approach is considered to be better or worse than the other, but the approach used has to be appropriate for the learner and the learning situation for it to be successful. It is the role of the teacher to consider both approaches and be flexible enough to use the one that is most suitable at the time.

THEORY TO PRACTICE

If a learner is confident in their own ability, has a lot of experience in the subject and is capable of working independently then they will become frustrated if the teacher tries to be in control of the learning. This could make the learner feel patronised and will make it difficult for them to remain engaged.

HANDY HINT

Use mind maps as visual aids to help your learners connect all of the separate parts of the lesson into one big picture.

HOW TO SET AND FACILITATE A ONE-TO-ONE ACTIVITY

LO1.2 Explain factors to be considered when facilitating learning and development to meet individual needs

LO2.1 Clarify facilitation methods with individuals to meet their learning and/or development objectives

The primary purpose of teaching a learner, whether in a group or on a one-to-one basis, is the gaining of knowledge. The top five skills, qualities and attributes that a coach and mentor should have are:

■ subject knowledge (experience, qualifications, authority, confidence)
■ organisational skills (time management, planning)

- communication skills (clarity of speech, perception, previous experiences, non-verbal)
- professionalism (boundaries, clearly defined roles, leadership; building rapport)
- analytical skills (evaluate, identify hazards, issues – including behaviour).

In order for learning to take place effectively in a one-to-one situation, the common things that need to happen, regardless of whether you have adopted a coaching, mentoring or teaching approach, include:

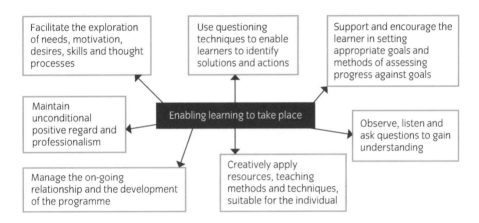

Having developed a positive rapport with the learner in the first instance, the role of the teacher is one of negotiating a learning route. This will be decided according to what best suits the learner while at the same time covering all of the criteria needed for that learner to be successful. The learner may think they know what is best for them but they will still need guidance and accurate information or they may not always choose the right options, particularly if they are in the 16–19 age bracket.

Although every one-to-one session with learners will of course be different, based on their needs, experience and the topic, a useful approach which could be adopted is based on research carried out by the DCSF, now the Department for Education (nd).

❝❞

Teaching one-to-one is not just a scaled down version of whole class teaching, and it requires a different approach from that used in group work. The basis of one-to-one pedagogy is obvious enough; if we have just one *learner* to attend to, then we can tailor the approach to their particular needs, pass quickly over the things we know they can do, and spend time improving the way they see and apply the learning, so that their weaknesses are resolved and their successes consolidated.

(page 9)

An eight-stage model could look like this:

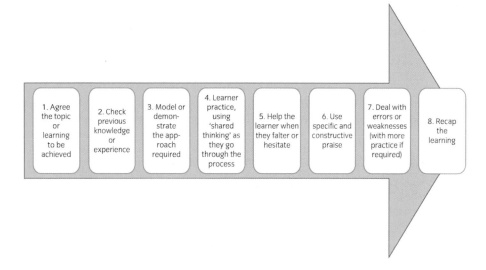

| 1. Agree the topic or learning to be achieved | 2. Check previous knowledge or experience | 3. Model or demon-strate the app-roach required | 4. Learner practice, using 'shared thinking' as they go through the process | 5. Help the learner when they falter or hesitate | 6. Use specific and constructive praise | 7. Deal with errors or weaknesses (with more practice if required) | 8. Recap the learning |

TEACHING METHODS FOR INDIVIDUALS

LO1.3 Evaluate methods for facilitating learning and development to meet the needs of individuals

LO2.2 Implement activities to meet learning and/or development objectives

Planning

Deep learning is a type of learning that will last over a period of time because the learner has understood and made sense of the information

Some teaching methods are particularly well suited when working on a one-to-one basis with a learner. Taking time to consider which will be the most effective teaching method to use with an individual learner means that the learning that takes place is more likely to be successful and end in **deep learning** taking place. This type of learning will enable the learner to make connections between what they are learning in the classroom situation and their own experience within their place of work, practical tasks or prior knowledge of the subject. This should then mean that the information will make sense to the learner and they will be able to use it in future situations.

Negotiating

Working on a one-to-one basis with a learner will provide the teacher with the opportunity to plan the learning that is best suited to each individual learner. This should be discussed and, where possible, negotiated with the learner not only at the start of the course but also during the course. This will make sure that it is the most suitable for both and should also result in 'buy-in' from the learner.

Delivery

The **teaching method** can be adapted during the session if necessary and the pace of delivery can match the needs of the learner. It is worth considering that this type of learning can be quite tiring, so offer short breaks if possible or reduce the amount of contact time for each session; short and frequent sessions can be better than a long drawn-out session.

Teaching method is the way in which you deliver a topic to your learners. Also called a teaching strategy

HANDY HINT

Take note of body language. If your learner starts to look uncomfortable, is shuffling in their chair, fiddling or leaning right back, then this could mark the end of the session. Alternatively you may be able to offer a short break and then resume teaching.

There is nowhere to hide in a one-to-one session for either the teacher or the learner. Both will need to work carefully together to let each other know when they have had enough. Younger learners might not be as mature at communicating and it will be down to the teacher to manage this environment.

Negative body language

Teaching method	Strengths	Weaknesses	Teaching tips when facilitating
Gapped handouts	■ Individual activity ■ Safe ■ Builds confidence ■ Embeds language skills ■ Simple tool to check knowledge and as a starter activity ■ Allows a learner to succeed at own pace and demonstrate knowledge ■ Easy to set up and manage ■ Tailored to individual need and ability ■ Can be adapted to include extension activities	■ May only check surface knowledge ■ Does not promote deep thinking ■ Can be easy and not challenging enough ■ Can be patronising ■ Might not naturally encourage conversation about the information ■ Can be a quick task	■ Set up the scenario carefully ■ Offer clear criteria for learners to work within ■ Be clear on expectations ■ Offer time at the end for learners to discuss the information and offer additional information as an extension task ■ Praise the learner for completing the handout and give them feedback on how they have done ■ Arrive armed with lots of handouts or use a mixed-methods approach
Practical tasks (in the workplace or workshop)	■ High in retention of information ■ The learner is practising the task ■ Good for visual and kinaesthetic learners ■ Interesting and fun ■ In context and real ■ Active learning activity	■ Can be resource heavy – time and additional resources are needed for it to be successful ■ Can make learners feel under pressure if they are being watched ■ Additional questions can be used alongside to check knowledge and understanding ■ Can be observed – but this can take time and be subjective	■ Offer criteria to signpost what the learner is expected to do ■ Might have to offer hands-on support ■ Make sure that the learner has all the resources needed ■ Provide a set of instructions for the learner to follow if necessary ■ Ask questions during the task to check learning ■ Allow time for learners to ask questions to clarify understanding ■ Make sure you cover all health and safety required for the task ■ Offer opportunity for the learner to self-assess
Verbal questioning (open and leading)	■ Easy to set up ■ Free exchange of ideas on a related topic ■ Encourages interaction between teacher and learner ■ Offers an opportunity for learner to explore new ideas and concepts ■ Can aid development of deeper understanding	■ Needs careful management as the learner could find it difficult if they are not used to thinking through ideas ■ Could lead to lots of silence as the learner might not want or know how to communicate ■ Difficult to evidence so should be used as a teaching tool	■ Decide on the topic for the discussion carefully so that it is relevant and engages the learner ■ Introduce the topic in a clear and engaging way ■ Use visual alongside written information if possible ■ Consider the questions carefully so that they allow the learner to answer honestly without being led ■ Think about how to capture the answers so that the activity can be used as assessment evidence ■ Time the activity so that it stays on task ■ Don't be afraid of silence; give the learner time to think

Teaching method	Strengths	Weaknesses	Teaching tips when facilitating
Problem solving – case studies or written tasks	■ Can help to develop deep learning ■ Can challenge the more able learners ■ Motivational as it can stimulate thought ■ Can enable conversations to emerge ■ Can embed literacy skills	■ Can be time consuming to set up ■ The learner may need a lot of input at the start if they do not have the skills or prior knowledge to tackle the task ■ Not all learners will feel that they are able to contribute and may feel out of their comfort zone	■ Decide on the case study carefully so that it is relevant and interesting ■ Present the task so that the learner can see the relevance to previous learning ■ Set it in context of the 'bigger picture' so that the intended outcome is clear ■ Offer additional resources or information to extend the discussion if the learner needs it ■ Think about how to get the learner to capture the results and thought processes ■ Ask the learner if they have a real-life case study that they would like to present and evaluate

When teaching on a one-to-one basis, it is possible to use a mixed-methods approach so that each session is varied, engaging and interesting for both learner and teacher. During the first meeting with the learner, a **learning styles** questionnaire could be completed so that the teaching methods chosen will suit the preferred style of the learner. It is best practice as a teacher to provide opportunities to help a learner to improve any weaknesses that they might have as learners. One way to do this is by using a range of teaching methods rather than only concentrating on using ones that cater to their preferred learning style. This should help them to improve any weak areas in their learning styles and become more developed in their learning styles.

For more information about learning styles see Unit 302.

Learning styles are the preferred way that a learner takes on board information. This style can be visual, auditory, read/write or kinaesthetic (practical), otherwise known as VARK

EVALUATION TECHNIQUES – GETTING THE MOST FROM A ONE-TO-ONE

LO1.3 Evaluate methods for facilitating learning and development to meet the needs of individuals

LO1.6 Explain how to monitor individual learner progress

LO4.2 Review individual responses to one-to-one learning and/or development

Reflection-in-action
Evaluating the session will happen in two stages. It will happen after the session and it will also happen during the session. This is part of being a reflective practitioner and can take time to perfect. You should arrive at the session clear about what you are going to cover with the learner and have a structured plan in place, with resources

Reflection in action is when you consider what you are doing while you are doing it and make changes along the way. It is 'thinking on your feet' or reactive reflection

that will support the learning in the most effective way. However, the session may not go to plan and this is nothing unusual in teaching. Sometimes things can happen that are out of your control and this will prompt you to make sudden changes in order to accommodate these unforeseen circumstances. This is **reflection-in-action** (Schön, as cited in Thompson and Thompson, 2008). This is more likely to happen when teaching on a one-to-one basis and it will be more profound than when teaching a group. Being flexible enables the teacher to adapt the session as it happens with little or no disruption to the learning.

Reflection-on-action

The other type of evaluation happens after the session and this is known as *reflection-on-action*. This is when the teacher can think back over the session and take a considered view about how the session went. This is a critical aspect of teaching and has to be completed in order for future delivery to be fully effective. If the teaching that takes place is not improved upon time and time again, the learning and teaching will never become excellent!

Body language

When working with individual learners an awareness of body language will help you and your learner get the most from the learning experience. When facilitating the one-to-one session try to think about the key points below:

- Their position: Offer the learner the choice of where to sit first when they enter the room. If they are feeling anxious or nervous then this will help them develop some ownership and control of the situation.
- Your position: Try to sit next to the learner as this will be less intimidating than sitting opposite them. It also means you can both look at materials together and is a partnership model, rather than 'teacher versus learner'.
- Smile and lean slightly forwards: This will help to foster positive working relationships.
- Nodding: This shows interest and engagement in the conversation.
- Eye contact: When addressing the learner try to give eye contact.
- Maintaining interest: When the session is in progress try not to shuffle papers, or spend too much time looking down at materials, but actively listen to the learner when they are talking, particularly when answering a question. It is easy to pose a question and then not listen to the answer, but get distracted with the next task.

Use the quick reference list on the next page to help you to read cues from your learner to gauge how the activity is going.

BODY LANGUAGE QUICK REFERENCE

Body hunched	Low confidence or cold
Clenched fists	Aggression
Crossed arms	Shut off, uncomfortable, defensive
Dropped shoulders	Lethargy or weariness
Fidgeting with objects, hands	Nervous, bored or had enough
Hands behind head	Arrogance, superior attitude
Hands on hips	Defiance
Hands on table	Agreement
Head down	Timidity, lack of interest, tired
Head resting on hands	Bored, lack of interest or tired
Leaning away	Discomfort with the situation
Leaning in closer	Interest, comfortable, winning
Looking at watch	Boredom, other engagement
Massaging temples	Anxiety
Nodding – interest	Agreement, understanding
No eye contact	Lack of confidence, intimidated
Shaking leg(s)	Sign of stress or anxiety
Rapid eye movement	Nervousness
Stroking chin	Thinking, in thought
Tapping foot	Impatient, nervous
Blank face	Thinking, daydreaming, misunderstanding

ACTIVITY

In no more than 100 words, write a description about a coaching or mentoring scenario that you have experienced.

What do you remember about the relationship? Consider the following and write some comments beneath each question.

- What was it about it that made it successful?
- How could it have been made more successful?
- What were the difficulties?
- How were these overcome?

RISKS AND SAFEGUARDING

LO1.4 Explain how to manage risks and safeguard individuals when facilitating one-to-one learning and development

LO2.3 Manage risks and safeguard learners participating in one-to-one learning and/or development

Risks exist in all learning environments to some degree or other. The usual measures should be taken to reduce injury and to safeguard the learner. As discussed in Unit 304, some activities pose more obvious risk to personal safety than others, but all potential risk needs to be taken into account and planned for. However, one of the factors when working with individuals is the increased possibility of risk to either the teacher or the learner.

In a one-to-one learning situation, a teacher may be in an unfamiliar environment, alone with a learner and both of these pose risk to personal safety. When working in an unfamiliar workplace, of any kind, the teacher should be presented with an up-to-date risk assessment. It is the responsibility of the teacher to be familiar with this and to let the learner know of any potential risk. If working on a one-to-one basis, a teacher should try to keep themselves safe by keeping the door ajar, letting someone know where they are and, in rare cases, they may even have to remove themselves from the situation if they feel threatened.

The teacher should take every measure to ensure the safety of their learner and their own safety. It is their responsibility to make the learner aware of potential risk from the start of the course, and put in measures to ensure that safety and well-being are considered in all one-to-one situations.

For more information on this look at Unit 304.

HANDY HINT

Don't take feedback personally! It is there to help you to improve your practice so make sure you concentrate on the information. If there is anything you do not understand, ask.

OVERCOMING INDIVIDUAL BARRIERS

LO1.5 Explain how to overcome individual barriers to learning

Many different types of barriers can be seen in a learning situation. These can be more noticeable in a one-to-one situation. The learner may not feel able to participate fully in the session. They may even stop turning up at all. It is impossible for a learner to continue on an individual programme unless they are fully engaged as there really is nowhere to hide. They can't be invisible and as their coach, mentor, or teacher you should be very aware of any barriers and look at ways to support or manage these from the outset. If these issues are not addressed, the learner is more likely to demonstrate aggressive behaviour, non-attendance or may ultimately leave the course early.

CLASSROOM MANAGEMENT

Assume nothing!

If a learner is not engaged in their learning it is less likely that any learning will be taking place at all, and the chances of it being a deep learning experience is highly unlikely. It is important for the teacher to recognise when a learner is not fully engaged, so that steps can be taken to motivate that learner. Barriers to learning can also have a damaging effect on the relationship between the teacher and the learner and this is an important aspect of working with individuals so should be resolved as quickly as possible.

The table below identifies some of the barriers that a learner may experience and some simple strategies that a teacher can adopt in order to overcome these barriers. Don't forget that the learner also has a responsibility for their learning and your role is to support and facilitate their development as learners.

Learner	Teacher
Low self-esteem Be aware that this could be due to a learning difficulty or disability	■ Asks simple questions to involve the learner from the start and give lots of genuine praise and encouragement ■ Meet the learner at a time and place that are suitable and convenient for them ■ Communicate with the learner in a non-threatening manner and be aware of your own body language so that you remain open ■ Allow time for the learner to answer for themselves. Don't be scared of silence ■ Offer structured tasks and a range of open and closed questions to help reduce any anxiety and increase the opportunity for success from the start ■ Try not to highlight any learning difficulty until the learner has raised it. Discuss any coping strategies that the learner may already have developed and encourage them to continue to do this – praise them for finding solutions ■ Offer adapted resources
Lack of motivation	■ Find out at least one thing about your learner in terms of interests, hobbies and ambitions. The topics can then be related to these on an individual basis ■ Deliver the subject with enthusiasm and use inspirational resources ■ Use active teaching methods to engage the learner and open questions ■ Link the topic to the bigger picture and put in context so the learner can see the relevance

External issues (such as housing, financial worries, relationship issues)	■ Discuss any issues that the learner might have and try to arrive at workable solutions so they can continue to attend. For example, agree to go to their workplace at the end of a shift, so they don't have to make an additional journey if finances and time are a barrier ■ Use the referral process to signpost the learner to any additional support and guidance if it is outside of your remit
Lack of understanding about the task	■ Clarify the information by providing the learner with a written record of the discussion or meeting. Include an agreed list of actions that they have to carry out before the next meeting ■ Ask open questions to check understanding ■ Provide an opportunity for the learner to contact you if they are unsure about anything at a later date, such as a work email, or work phone number ■ Ensure that any written instructions or information are written in a clear and unambiguous way (see the sections on creating inclusive resources in Units 301 and 302)

CLASSROOM MANAGEMENT

Make the session as current and relevant to your learners as possible. Make links to their interests and they will automatically be more engaged.

TEACH, REFLECT, REVISIT: ADAPTING DELIVERY TO MAKE IT WORK FOR THE LEARNER

LO1.6 Explain how to monitor individual progress

LO1.7 Explain how to adapt delivery to meet individual learner needs

LO4.2 Review individual responses to one-to-one learning and/or development

A critical stage in the delivery of learning is the constant checking and reviewing of what is happening both within a session and afterwards so that the delivery is as successful as it can be. The teacher should plan interesting and relevant sessions that are based on individual need. These will have been mapped to learning outcomes and assessment criteria and negotiated with the learner to make sure that they are engaging and delivered using a variety of methods. However, some form of evaluation is necessary to make sure that progress of the learner is monitored and that any future delivery is adapted if necessary. The most outstanding teacher will constantly reflect on what they are delivering and there are different strategies that can be put in place to make this happen effectively.

THEORY TO PRACTICE

Learners learn in different ways and they should be asked for their feedback at the end of every session. This will provide the teacher with information to use when making improvements.

Have you provided a **framework** for the learner to see the overall content in context of the bigger picture?
Are **connections** made between each session?
Is the session pitched at the **right level** – not too easy or too hard?

Is your learner **engaged** in an active way?
Have you given them positive **praise**?
Can the learner **practise** what they have learnt?
Is the **environment** suitable? Is it safe? Can anything be changed if necessary?
Is the relationship built on mutual respect?

What sort of **questions** are you using? Can these be considered in advance and pre-planned?
Do you use a **mixture of assessment** techniques? How can these be developed to make them **accessible** for the learner?

What **teaching techniques** are you using and how can these be improved?
Have you established and maintained **high expectations** and clear **ground rules**? Are these clear to the learner? Do they need to be re-negotiated?

Main questions to consider from the theory based on the teaching cycle

It is unlikely that you will need to make significant changes to delivery as it is happening when teaching learners on an individual basis. You might find that you need to spend longer on one thing than another during the session, but this is easy to accommodate without the learner being aware of any changes to the planned activities. It is more likely that the majority of evaluation will happen after the session.

It is necessary to be sure that the content that is being covered is mapped to the qualification if appropriate or at the very least mapped to an agreed set of targets. This will make sure that the learner is learning what they are meant to be and that the sessions remain focused and the learning is on track.

There are different reflective models that can be used. One such model designed by Rolfe et al. (2001) is discussed in Unit 304. An alternative, developed by Gibbs (1988), also provides a more detailed framework for the teacher to reflect on what happened in the session. The emphasis on this model is the evaluation section of the session and provides an opportunity to think about *why* things happened within the session.

Gibbs, 1988

THEORY TO PRACTICE

Example

Description What?	The session was part of a series of literacy sessions with an adult learner who has been attending for a number of weeks. It is part of a programme to help parents to improve their English skills and is taught at the primary school, during school hours. I started the session with a short recap. The main part of the hour was focused on developing written skills as this learner is struggling with sentence structure and their use of full stops and capital letters.
Feelings So what were you thinking and feeling?	I was feeling tired and a bit stressed as the IT was not working very well, so although I had planned to use a number of short activities I did not get as much done as I had hoped. The learner seemed a bit stressed as well and had not completed any of the practice tasks that I had set at the last session.

Evaluation	I had a back-up plan which was good as I could use some other resources that I had to hand. We were able to talk about how to split up sentences so that they made sense when read. The learner completed the tasks on their own and by the end of the session had managed to identify correct use of full stops and capital letters. I think that I spent too much time getting drawn into a conversation about the learners' personal problems and this got in the way of their learning.
So what was good and bad about the experience?	
Analysis	I let my own frame of mind interfere with the session and this was not very professional of me. I did not stick to my plan and so the session was not as clear in its structure as it could have been. I should have realised that this learner does not always take responsibility for learning outside of the session.
What sense can you make of the situation?	
Conclusion	I could have given the learner some words on laminated card so that they could make sentences in a practical way rather than getting them to write the sentences from scratch. This would also have helped them as they struggle with spelling. I could also have made sure that the sentences were relevant to their interests. I know this learner is also looking to apply for jobs so I could have spent time getting them to think about key words to go with personal skills to help with this.
What else could you have done?	
Action plan	In future I will focus the session on a particular topic that is relevant to the learner. I will ask them to create a bank of words that they can keep in a type of glossary.
Now what?	
	I will provide examples of sentences that are relevant to that learner – such as job adverts – and ask them to construct sentences using a bank of words. I will also start to introduce key terms in literacy such as nouns and verbs to help them to understand how a sentence is formed. The next stage is to look at the use of tenses. This can be difficult to grasp so I will make sure that I do not over-complicate it, but introduce one tense per session and not move on until I have checked that they can master this reliably.
	Don't let my frame of mind interfere with the session!

ACTIVITY

Think about a session that you have delivered recently. Using the example above, write a short reflective account about the session. Don't forget to concentrate equally on each of the headings. The idea is that you will arrive at an action plan that you can use next time you teach that learner (or are faced with a similar scenario).

Final course evaluation

The learner is a useful asset when reviewing a course and must be included somehow in the process. What might appear to the teacher as a successful session might not be experienced as such by the learner. Simple verbal questions can be asked to find out what was useful about the session while providing an opportunity for the learner to give an opinion about possible changes to future sessions. This is of particular importance when working with adult learners.

Overall changes you might want to make to the course if you are to deliver it again could be based on the following:

- application and interview stage; including access onto the course and information provided
- resources; including teaching aids, handouts and physical facilities
- course content
- assessment; both formative (ongoing, for learning) and summative (at the end of learning)
- course organisation; planning and timing of the course
- general; support given and any other information about the course as a whole.

ACTIVITY

Think about a recent one-to-one session that you have facilitated and write four questions that you could ask at the end of the session to allow feedback to be gathered from your learner.

PUTTING THE LEARNING INTO PRACTICE

LO3.1 Develop opportunities for individuals to apply their new knowledge and learning in practical contexts

LO3.2 Explain benefits to individuals of applying new knowledge and skills

When working with individual learners it is highly likely that the learner will meet with the teacher on an infrequent basis and will also be working in their chosen field of study. If this is the case the learner will be able to regularly put into practice the theory from their individual sessions. This is one of the most effective ways to develop deep knowledge and understanding of a subject. It will provide the learner with an opportunity to bring all of their knowledge and understanding of the subject together, by applying it in a real-life practical context.

Bloom's taxonomy

There are three domains altogether:

- **cognitive:** about learning knowledge
- **psychomotor:** about learning a skill
- **affective:** about beliefs and attitudes.

It is important to have an awareness of the three domains and the stages of learning that take place when teaching or facilitating learning. This helps when planning sessions, writing materials and assessment tasks by ensuring that they are pitched at the right level. It also helps the teacher to explain the stages of development to learners. This enables the learner to see their own progress within the subject. It helps them to apply their knowledge or skills at a level that is suitable for them.

The domains are covered in Unit 302 (see page 58) and should be referred to if you are teaching a practical, theory or personal development subject.

KEEPING THE LEARNER IN THE PICTURE

LO1.6 Explain how to monitor individual learner progress

Feedback

As already discussed, feedback is one of the many essential aspects of communication with learners. Good feedback should provide a learner with information about their progress. For feedback to be effective it needs to be:

- frequent – in the early stages of a learner's journey the feedback should be given verbally during each meeting and followed up with written feedback on a regular basis
- appropriate – linked to the learning outcomes, assessment criteria or topic being taught
- accessible – in both a format and language that the learner can understand and interpret for their own use
- informative – to provide information about what needs to be improved as well as what the learner has done particularly well
- positive – to aid motivation, but can have aspects of criticality
- understood – it might be worth checking with the learner that the feedback is clear and that they have taken the key points on board that you wanted them to.

Formative feedback is something that will be continually given throughout a learner's journey on the course. This will be used by the learner so that they can identify what is left to be done and to establish what they have done well. If there is an assessment at the end of the course then this type of feedback will be invaluable for the learner when preparing for this assessment.

When teaching individual learners it is necessary to build instant feedback into the session. It will be mostly verbal, as part of the learning conversation or in response to an answer or comment. This is a good way to praise your learner and let them know in a friendly and informal way when they are on track and are making positive progress. It could also be presented to the learner in a written format, either on a piece of work, or on a template that will identify their progress with the work.

HANDY HINT

Always start with a positive comment as you want the learner to relax and also to take on board all of your comments. Give some clear ideas of what they could do to improve and try to make time to talk through the feedback with them. Get your learner to record their targets on an individual learning plan (ILP) and bring this to each session. These should be negotiated and agreed mutually.

The feedback should be linked to work completed and this can be in any context, either practical or theoretical. It is good practice to support the learner by helping them formulate action points on their individual learning plan (ILP). This will also make it obvious to the teacher if they understand the feedback fully.

A teacher providing feedback

HANDY HINT

Feedback and feed *forward*. Feedback is useful for the learner so they are clear about their progress on a course. However, it should also feed forwards to help the teacher see what they still have to cover with the learner. It should be used to help inform the planning of future delivery and is part of the reflection and evaluation stage of the teaching cycle.

More information about giving feedback can be found in Unit 306.

SUPPORTING INDIVIDUAL SELF-EVALUATION

LO4.1 Explain benefits of self-evaluation to individuals

LO4.3 Assist individual learners to identify their future learning and/or development needs

Feedback

Feedback, as discussed, should help learners to make sense of what they have done so that they can take ownership of their learning, especially to motivate them to *want* to learn. This should result in the learner becoming more aware of what they can do better in future work and this will enable them in the process of self-evaluation. One way to further develop these skills of self-evaluation is through the use of self-assessment. *(More information can be found on this in Unit 305/306.)*

Self-assessment

When the learner is actively involved in the assessment process, they will be able to develop skills in making accurate judgements about their progress. This needs to be structured carefully so that the learner can make informed comments, in a supported way. One way to do this is by identifying a series of pre-set questions that can help learners to evaluate for themselves what they have learnt and what they need to do in order to continue to develop their skills and knowledge. As previously discussed, a reflective model (Rolfe et al., 2001; Gibbs, 1988) could also be introduced to learners as a way to provide structure in the process of self-evaluation.

Kolb (1984) developed an experiential learning cycle that would be a useful tool to aid self-reflection on an individual, but supported, basis. This is a cycle that can be repeated as many times as necessary. For it to be useful as a model to aid self-evaluation and as a way to make changes to practice, all the stages have to be included.

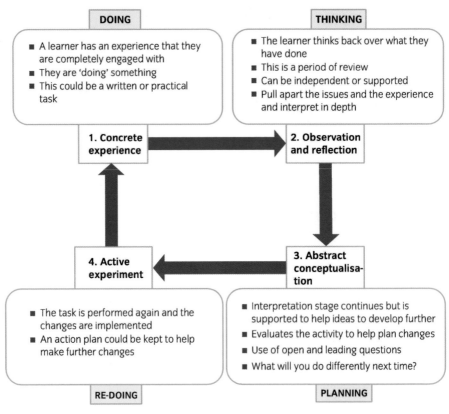

DOING

- A learner has an experience that they are completely engaged with
- They are 'doing' something
- This could be a written or practical task

THINKING

- The learner thinks back over what they have done
- This is a period of review
- Can be independent or supported
- Pull apart the issues and the experience and interpret in depth

1. Concrete experience

2. Observation and reflection

4. Active experiment

3. Abstract conceptualisation

- The task is performed again and the changes are implemented
- An action plan could be kept to help make further changes

- Interpretation stage continues but is supported to help ideas to develop further
- Evaluates the activity to help plan changes
- Use of open and leading questions
- What will you do differently next time?

RE-DOING

PLANNING

In order for a learner to identify any future development needs they need first of all to be able to self-assess. This is not an easy process and will take time, regardless of ability, age or experience. It is a skill that needs to be supported and developed with the guidance of a teacher, coach or mentor. Signposting to other courses or using a referral system can also be a positive way to support learners.

UNIT SUMMARY

This unit has concentrated on some of the different aspects that are involved when teaching on a one-to-one basis. It has looked at the reasons why some learners are taught on an individual basis and identified some of the ways to make this as successful as possible. The different roles that a teacher may embrace, such as the role of assessor, mentor or coach, have also been explored.

A key element of facilitating learning on an individual basis is the role of the learner. This unit has looked at reflective models that will help support a learner through their journey by giving them structure and guidance. The personalised approach that can be developed in this type of delivery can be an extremely successful one, but as you will have discovered, it is dependent on the relationship between teacher and learner. It is most productive when based on mutual respect and when learning goals can be negotiated. This is not always easy and this unit has identified some of the barriers and challenges that can happen along the way. Some possible strategies have been suggested and different teaching methods also explored.

Overall this is a flexible approach to learning. As it is situated in a real-life learning environment, or developed as a bespoke programme, it often results in a successful learning experience for both the teacher and the learner. This unit has focused on working with individuals, but there is additional information in other units that will also be helpful when completing the assignment. There are also suggested websites and a comprehensive book list at the end of the book to help you research the topic further.

ASSIGNMENT FOCUS

This unit provides you with information about teaching and facilitating learning and development that takes place on an individual basis. Learning outcomes 2, 3 and 4 will be assessed in a genuine workplace environment where you will have to demonstrate your understanding of the theory by putting it into practice with real learners. Learning outcome 1 will be assessed by a piece of written work, such as an assignment. You will need to cover all of the following assessment criteria in order to evidence your knowledge and understanding successfully.

Assessment criteria (LO1)

1.1: Explain the purposes of one-to-one learning and development

1.2: Explain factors to be considered when facilitating learning and development to meet individual needs

1.3: Evaluate methods for facilitating learning and development to meet the needs of individuals

1.4: Explain how to manage risks and safeguard individuals when facilitating one-to-one learning and development

1.5: Explain how to overcome individual barriers to learning

1.6: Explain how to monitor individual learner progress

1.7: Explain how to adapt delivery to meet individual learner needs

Tips

You might want to consider the following when planning your assignment:

- Why is it beneficial to teach learners on a one-to-one basis?
- Discuss some of the factors that have an impact on teaching on a one-to-one basis and why these need to be considered when planning and delivering learning to an individual.
- Which teaching methods are the most successful when working with an individual and what makes these successful? What difficulties could you and the learner experience when using these teaching methods?
- What strategies would you employ in order to minimise risk and ensure that your learners are safeguarded in the teaching session?
- What sort of individual barriers might exist and what would you do to engage your learner and help to reduce any barriers?
- Identify ways that you would monitor individual progress.
- Give some examples of ways that you would change delivery in order to meet individual need more effectively.

UNIT 304

Facilitate learning and development in groups

INTRODUCTION

There is an obvious financial incentive to teaching in groups, as it is cost effective at a time when there is increasing pressure in lifelong learning to make sure that courses are financially viable. However, there are also huge benefits for both the learner and the teacher. One of the main benefits for the learner is the chance for shared experiences and this can increase their sense of belonging and make the learning experience a rich and rewarding one. The opportunity for a group of learners to work together helps them to develop a deeper knowledge and understanding of the subject, particularly through the use of discussion and problem-solving-based tasks.

The teacher's role can become one of facilitating learning. Recognising that the learners are a rich resource of experience can help to bring the subject to life and this should be exploited to its full potential, by making the subject relevant to them. Teaching to groups is also a good way to deliver key information to many people at the same time, rather than having to repeat the same information several times.

But teaching in large or small groups can also present challenges to the teacher and the learners. This unit explores ways that group work can be facilitated so that it is as successful as possible as a learning experience. Some of the aspects covered include: effective planning; establishing clear ground rules; setting high expectations; using a range of teaching methods and different ways to evaluate sessions. This unit concentrates particularly on working with groups, but there is additional information in Units 301 and 302 that will also be helpful when working with groups of learners.

In Unit 304 you will cover the following learning outcomes:

LO1: Understand principles and practices of learning and development in groups
LO2: Be able to facilitate learning and development in groups
LO3: Be able to assist groups to apply new knowledge and skills in practical contexts
LO4: Be able to assist learners to reflect on their learning and development undertaken in groups

WHY TEACH LEARNERS IN GROUPS?

LO1.1 Explain purposes of group learning and development

Teaching in groups is a good way to facilitate learning, but it does involve careful planning, resourcing and managing if it is to be effective. In order to explore why learners are taught in groups it is necessary to think about *how* learners learn. This also provides a basis for planning the best way possible to facilitate group learning and development so that the session can run as smoothly as possible. There are several theories that set out to try to determine how learning takes place. When explaining the purpose of group learning and development it is necessary to consider some of these and look at ways that this can be applied to practice. More information on learning theory can be found in Unit 302.

Passive learning is when learning happens to the learner and they are not involved in the process

Behaviourist theory:
This theory is based on the notion that learning takes place in response to external stimuli
Note: a stimulus can be anything that causes a response
Therefore a learner is more likely to be motivated to learn when there is an external reward offered

■ Learners are given praise for work achieved
■ Learners have a clear idea of the next task that needs to be completed
■ The classroom environment is structured and controlled by the teacher
■ The learning experience is broken down into achievable steps
■ All success is rewarded with positive reinforcement
■ The learning experience tends to be one of knowledge transfer
■ Learners take a **passive role** in their learning, letting it happen *to* them, motivated by external rewards, rather than in terms of the achievement itself

Humanist theory:
This theory is based on the belief that the learner has the solutions to a problem within themselves
The role of the teacher is to create a positive, supportive learning environment
Based on developing positive self-image and a personalised approach
Note: sometimes called student-centred learning

■ Learners are provided with a safe learning environment
■ Tasks are individual to their own needs and development
■ The learning environment is fluid and creative, changing with the needs of the individual and group
■ The learning experience is holistic
■ All success is rewarded with genuine praise
■ The learning experience also covers social and personal development
■ Learners take an **active role** in their learning, motivated by personal achievement

Constructivist theory:

This theory is based on the belief that learning happens in the mind. It is about gathering and organising information. Based on the development of individual perception based on own previous knowledge and experience

The role of the teacher is to create discovery-style activities that link inform-ation together through exploring ideas

Based on learners constructing meaning often through social interaction

Note: developed from cognitivist theory that states that learning happens in the brain

Theory to practice

- Learners are provided with structure, such as concept maps, mind maps, diagrams, **scaffolded worksheets**, case studies, etc
- Tasks are tailored to help learners make connections between different parts of information
- The learning environment is often based on social interaction, such as discussions and group work
- The learning experience is challenging
- All success is rewarded with genuine praise
- The learning experience may also cover problem solving
- Learners take an **active role** in their learning, motivated by personal achievement and peer rivalry

Active learning is when a learner takes part in the learning in an involved way. They participate fully and are engaged with the process

Scaffolded worksheets are a type of worksheet that provides the learners with a template as a guide to help give structure to the content. For example, a letter template with headings to work from

Not all learners will learn in the same way so the teacher should consider how all of the three main theories of learning can be applied when teaching groups. As discussed in Unit 302, adults are able to learn in ways that are different from children as they tend to be self motivated and have prior experience and knowledge to draw from (Knowles, as cited in Scales, 2008). In addition to this, most adult learners have chosen the course or programme that they are studying. There are occasions when some programmes include additional subjects that may not be the learner's choice. However, the learner can usually see the relevance of their learning. By using an andragogical approach the learner is empowered to take an active part in the learning.

Teaching in a group is a good way to give adult learners an opportunity to share their prior experiences and knowledge. In particular it enables learners to take an active role, rather than be a passive passenger in the session.

Refer to Unit 302 for more information on this.

HANDY HINT

Greet your learners when they arrive and ask them how their week has been. Try to remember one key fact about each of them and use those as examples within the session.

An alternative type of group work. Learners are using library facilities for a self-managed research task

Learner interaction

Through the use of discussion-based activities and problem-solving tasks, which are ideally suited to group work, learners are more likely to develop a deeper knowledge and understanding of a subject. The teacher's role becomes one of facilitating learning, rather than teaching by telling. The learner can draw on past experiences and will be more likely to want to participate in the session when the subject is relevant and interesting to them. This is an aspect of teaching in lifelong learning that should be exploited fully and should result in a rich and rewarding learning experience. Working with groups is also a good way to deliver key information to a large audience, rather than having to repeat this several times on an individual basis.

When working with groups of learners:

- try to develop independent learners
- allow them to have ownership over their learning
- encourage them to arrive at key questions that will inspire and motivate them to learn more
- provide opportunities for them to start to construct meaning
- offer time for them to apply skills in a practical context
- make the purpose of the lesson clear
- support them to put into context what is being learnt.

As learners make connections to previous knowledge or skills base, their interest is sparked and the learning becomes pleasurable. They will feel in control of their learning and engaged, developing confidence as a learner within a group setting.

One of the reasons why learners are taught in groups is to provide them with an opportunity to work with other learners. Write down at least five reasons why this is seen as a good teaching approach.

WHAT IS SO IMPORTANT ABOUT GROUP DYNAMICS?

LO1.2 Explain why delivery of learning and development must reflect group dynamics

You will be aware by this point in the book that the role of the teacher is a diverse one that encompasses many aspects. One main role of the teacher is to plan to make learning happen. This involves having good subject knowledge, an understanding of the learners and using tools and techniques to enable learners to learn in an active way. Promoting deep learning will mean that your learners will retain information, rather than just being able to repeat it in a set format. This is what the teacher wants learners to do. Learning something is not just about repetition but about being able to use that information in any situation, transferring skills and knowledge from the classroom to real-life scenarios.

For example, it would not be enough for someone to be able to repeat the facts about driving a car; they need to be able to drive the car in a safe way and be able to make decisions about what to do when faced with an unexpected problem.

It is no different when teaching any topic. Learners need to have engaged with the topic and be able to relate it to different situations and deal with new circumstances, in order to demonstrate that they have processed it in a deep way that has meaning.

Considering the individuals within a group and planning to accommodate and develop their needs is only one aspect of working with groups. Another important consideration is the dynamics of the group.

Learners involved in a practical task

This image shows how learners can all actively participate in a task; they can all see and all get involved. Getting learners to stand up means they are more likely to be able to participate fully.

Choosing groups. A pack of playing cards can be used to organise your learners into groups or pairs. Simply select the number of cards in each suit that you need to make the right size group; for example five hearts, five spades, five diamonds. Identify which table is for each suit, mix up the cards and distribute them anonymously. Once all the learners have a card they can move to the correct table. This will facilitate random groupings.

Tuckman's model of group development

A model of how groups develop over a period of time was developed by Bruce Tuckman in the 1960s (NCSU, nd). This model has become widely used, particularly in the business sector, but it is also useful in terms of education when trying to understand the group dynamics that you might witness within the classroom environment.

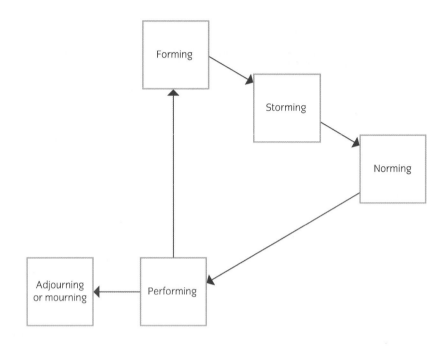

Tuckman's model identifies stages of development that occur in the lifespan of a group. The first stage *forming*, occurs when a group of people first come together, when they meet and relationships are formed between the individual members of the group. The next stage is a period of unsettled conflict, often around interpersonal issues: *storming*. Next a period emerges where conflicts are resolved and a sense of cohesion develops where the group are getting settled: *norming*. Eventually the group can be flexible and work together with all energy put into the group rather than into conflict; it is only at this stage that a group will be able to properly *perform*. The final stage, *mourning* or *adjourning*, is when the group comes to an end and the members feel a sense of loss.

Using Tuckman's model in the classroom environment

Stage	Characteristics	Considerations when teaching
Forming	■ Shyness ■ Uncertainty ■ Assertiveness from some ■ Early leaders dominate	■ Icebreaker activities can help learners to get to know each other in a supported way ■ Simple tasks that are achievable will help everyone to participate and achieve something from the start ■ Try to put learners together in groups on the basis of shared interests, experience or knowledge ■ Lots of praise and encouragement ■ Offer of one-to-one voluntary tutorial support

Stage	Characteristics	Considerations when teaching
Storming	■ Challenging behaviour towards weaker members of the group ■ 'Testing out' of the teacher ■ Disagreements ■ Initial leaders may not survive – new leaders emerge	■ Clear ground rules established and repeated with realistic sanctions and rewards ■ More challenging tasks are used to motivate and stimulate learning ■ Classroom layout is used to trial out different group environments ■ Group learners together depending on how they interact on a social level ■ Praise and encouragement where appropriate
Norming	■ A code of acceptable behaviour is developed as a group ■ Group identity is created ■ Learners appear more settled ■ Can slip back to storming!	■ Ask learners to volunteer to get themselves into groups ■ Identify positive aspects about the group to encourage the approach that you want them to adopt (see activity below)
Performing	■ Stable ■ Content ■ Settled	■ This is the stage when you can cover the important content needed for the qualification
Adjourning (mourning)	■ Sense of achievement (jubilant) ■ Sense of loss (mournful)	■ Supportive in the final stages of the course ■ Complimentary and recognising achievement and success ■ Offer information, advice and guidance

HANDY HINT

When you move your learners into new groups, ask them to introduce themselves again to one another. This isn't something that they might naturally do and will help to remove any embarrassment or uncomfortable silences.

It is important to consider the dynamics of each group so that learning can take place successfully and every learner will feel motivated and able to contribute fully to the lesson.

ACTIVITY

Think back to when you were working as a group and were given a label by the teacher/manager. How did it make you respond?

For example 'You are the best group I've ever had. You are always on time and work really hard. I am always impressed by your involvement in the lesson and by how much you seem to be learning. I think you will all get great results.'

For example: 'You are the worst group I have ever had. You never work very hard, always mess around, and I will be surprised if any of you manage to pass.'

People live up to the label they are given and groups are the same. Label them carefully as you always get the group you asked for!

PLANNING FOR GOOD BEHAVIOUR

LO1.3 Evaluate methods for facilitating learning and development to meet the needs of groups

When working mainly with adult and more mature young people, instances of challenging behaviour that can be classed as major offences are usually few and far between. Most learning situations tend to be relatively problem free, with behaviour problems usually consisting of minor incidents.

Some low-level behaviour problems may include:

- arriving late
- distracting other learners in the session by chatting
- finding opportunities to go off task
- acting as the class clown
- not participating in the activities
- using mobile devices inappropriately
- eating and drinking without approval.

Ground rules

One way to prevent some of these incidents from happening in the classroom is by agreeing a set of ground rules. This is best done during the very first session and should clearly cover all aspects of your expected working relationship. It can be tempting, when working with the 16–19-year age group, to go in with a 'heavy hand' and impose a large number of rules on your first meeting; but if the majority of the rules are negotiated, the learners are more likely to have 'buy in'. This is an important part of building a relationship with the learners and sets the scene early on, so that everyone knows and understands both their responsibilities and yours. It will help the learners to take full ownership. This kind of open involvement will help foster rapport and a good working relationship, reinforcing your role as supportive rather than judgemental.

The precise nature of the ground rules will depend on the context of the teaching or support, but generally they should cover what is expected from each person and also include a framework for working with others if applicable. This should always cover issues of valuing diversity, cooperation and restating codes for common manners and courtesy. This proactive approach is seen as a way to plan for good behaviour, rather than reacting to bad behaviour. The ground rules should be established during the first session with a group of learners. If the learners are only being taught for a relatively short period of time, it is still essential that the teacher quickly forms

some basic ground rules of what is acceptable behaviour in the
learning environment and what will not be tolerated. This will help
the learners to feel safe and more able to contribute feely. Learners
need to know that anything they say will not be open to ridicule
and reassured that anything they disclose will be dealt with in a
confidential manner.

More information about how to set ground rules can be found in
Unit 301.

Classroom layout

Learners in a traditional classroom setting

You can see in the example above that learners have been mixed
according to gender and the tables are positioned with sufficient room
and at an angle to the board. This means that all learners will be able to
see the front of the room as and when necessary.

Maslow in practice

Maslow (1970) developed a hierarchy of needs that is still recognised
and used today in many contexts. It is a valuable tool when considering
what learners require before they are able to fully engage with
learning. Basic life needs such as food, shelter and warmth are
considered in the first stage of Maslow's hierarchy of needs. The
diagram on the next page illustrates some of the issues that the
teacher needs to consider in order for effective learning to take place.

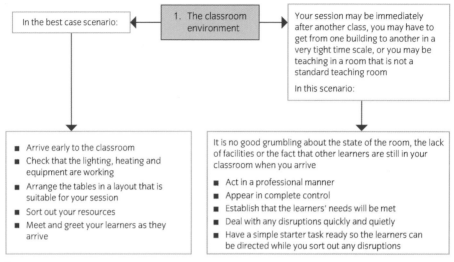

Stage one

The setting of ground rules (stage two) is important in order for learners to feel safe and secure in the group and this will encourage a more open exchange of ideas.

A sense of belonging (stage three) can be established during the induction period, when icebreakers help the learners to form friendly relationships within the group. A simple and small icebreaker is another part of establishing a positive environment, where learning will flourish. It is crucial that the teacher gets to know the learners and helps them to get to know one another. At the very least the teacher should try to learn the names of all the learners as this will help learners to feel important and recognised as individuals.

HANDY HINT

Tell your learners when they need to take notes, or when you are giving them key information. Making links to the assessment criteria will help them to make sense of the bigger picture.

When a teacher sets achievable tasks, and asks simple questions in an open forum, it quickly gives learners an opportunity to have their self-esteem boosted. Not all of the learners will want to contribute and some may have very low self-esteem or lack in confidence. However, with constant encouragement, and if they are treated with respect, eventually all learners should develop a sense of self-worth.

Remember: According to theory, it is only once a learner has had their basic needs met that they will be able to concentrate on learning.

CLASSROOM MANAGEMENT

Don't neglect the quiet learners in the group. Make time to talk to them on a one-to-one basis. Try not to ask them for contributions in front of the whole class but wait for them to volunteer instead.

In a classroom, learners may split themselves into smaller groups or an individual can get isolated from the internal group politics going on in the room. The groups may well bicker and, no matter what a teacher does, this bickering will continue either inside or outside the classroom. In these circumstances it is best to seek the advice of the course manager. A teacher should never accept any prejudicial statements or attitudes. Healthy inter-group competition is fine; derogatory statements are not.

The photo below illustrates why it is important to consider group size when asking learners to work in groups. With this seating plan the individuals will find it difficult to interact as a whole group. An ideal group size is between four and six individuals. The layout of the tables should also make sure that everyone can participate with the activity and discussion.

CLASSROOM MANAGEMENT

Approach your group with the belief that they all want to be there even if they tell you they don't. It is difficult to maintain a negative attitude when someone is convinced that you will be successful and expects you to give it your best shot.

ACTIVITY

Consider one of the teaching rooms that you use on a regular basis. How well does this meet the needs of the lesson and the learners? Is there anything that needs to be changed about the room and how can you manage this?

For more information about classroom layout see Unit 302, page 69.

BARRIERS

LO1.5 Explain how to overcome barriers to learning in groups

There are many types of barriers that can occur in a learning situation and these can be particularly noticeable in a group task or activity. Barriers to learning can result in learners not participating fully in the session, and drifting through the course, or leaving the course early. If a learner is not engaged in their learning it is less likely that any learning will be taking place at all and it is highly unlikely to be a deep learning experience.

It does not always happen that barriers will present themselves as a disruption to the session. However, it is an important role of the teacher to recognise when a barrier is stopping a learner from being fully engaged, so that steps can be taken to overcome the barrier and so engage the learner in the session. Barriers to learning can also have a detrimental effect on the dynamics of the group: it can mean that the learners may not want to work together and so any situation should be resolved as quickly as possible.

CLASSROOM MANAGEMENT

Make sure you have room to move around the classroom and make sure you *do* move around the classroom. Interact with your learners whenever possible in a friendly and approachable way.

The table below identifies some of the barriers that a learner may experience and some simple strategies that the teacher can adopt in order to overcome these barriers. Don't forget that the learner also has a responsibility for their learning and your role is to support and facilitate their development.

Barriers and possible solutions

Learner	Teacher
Low self-esteem	▪ Asks simple questions to involve all learners from the start and give praise and encouragement ▪ Put the learners in groups to enable the quiet learners to participate ▪ Offer scaffolded worksheets or questions to help aid the task
Peer rivalry or peer conflict	▪ Set up groups to avoid conflict situations ▪ Revisit the ground rules and outline acceptable behaviour ▪ Meet with the learners and act as a mediator to resolve any underlying issues (see Tuckman's model of group dynamics)
Lack of motivation	▪ Deliver the subject with enthusiasm and use inspirational resources ▪ Use active teaching methods to engage the learners ▪ Link the topic to the bigger picture and put it in context so learners see its relevance
External issues (such as housing, financial worries, relationship issues)	▪ Book in individual tutorials ▪ Use the referral process to signpost the learners to appropriate support and guidance
Lack of understanding about the task	▪ Clarify the information ▪ Ask questions to check understanding ▪ Give out task instructions that are written in a clear and unambiguous way (see creating inclusive resources in Unit 301)
Low levels of literacy (learning difficulties)	▪ Arrange learners in mixed-ability groups or separate learners according to level ▪ Give clear instructions and scaffolded task sheets ▪ Use learning support if possible to work with individuals within the group tasks ▪ Offer adapted resources ▪ Set differentiated tasks to accommodate different levels of learners

For more information about barriers to learning see Units 301 and 302.

Although the learners in the group below are positioned in close proximity so are able to communicate with one another easily, there is limited space on the table for everyone to work comfortably.

Learners in a traditional classroom setting, but the table is too small for purposeful engagement

 CLASSROOM MANAGEMENT

Get down to eye level when talking to a learner on a one-to-one basis. This will make the situation less intimidating and enable you to have an adult conversation quietly.

RISKS AND SAFEGUARDING

LO1.4 Explain how to manage risks and safeguard individuals when facilitating learning and development in groups

LO2.3 Manage risks to group and individual learning and development

Recognising that risks exist when working in a group environment is part of the role of the teacher. It is important that any potential risk to the safety of any learner is assessed and that measures are taken to either remove or manage the risk. All workplaces will have a health and safety policy and risk assessments in place for many of the group activities that are used when teaching in different locations and different subject areas. Some group activities pose more obvious risk to personal safety than others, but all potential risk needs to be taken into account and planned for. Not all risks to the safety of the learner are obvious and, depending on the age or vulnerability of the learners, the teacher will need to raise awareness about some of these less obvious risks. The following points should help when identifying risk and safeguarding learners:

- All learning facilities and activities should be risk assessed. This means that the potential hazards have been identified and measures taken to greatly reduce or remove the risk.
- Brief the learners on all activities at the beginning of a session. Use a risk assessment, often a written document, to prepare the briefing. Encourage learners to see the risk assessment at any point or have it displayed.
- Insist that all learners must follow any safety points that have been outlined. This might include wearing any personal protective equipment (PPE).
- On some programmes it might be necessary for learners to gain experience of preparing their own risk assessments; this is often a requirement when working in a vocational setting.
- Learners need to demonstrate respect to peers and staff, regardless of differences, and look out for the welfare of others. Any suspicious behaviour should be reported, as well as any physical threat to health and safety such as faulty equipment.
- Guidance should be provided on how to use internal and external internet systems in a safe and secure way.

Bags can be a trip hazard if not stored correctly

Safety

It is the individual's perception of whether they feel safe that is important. Personal jokes – either within the group setting or put on a social networking site – may be seen as harmless by some, but could be hurtful to the person concerned. The teacher should make learners aware of this from the start of the course, to try to prevent these instances occurring.

An obvious but still a potential risk that can occur in the classroom is trip hazards. These can be caused by bags and coats left by the side of chairs. If learners are using laptops then trailing leads can also be a potential risk. However, this risk can be reduced by simply reminding learners to put their personal belongings in a safe place, beneath the desks, or hung up out of the way.

ACTIVITY

Think about some of the potential risks when working with your own groups. List five things that you are going to do to ensure that your learners are safeguarded.

Risk	Impact on learner	What will you do to minimise or remove risk?
The Electricity at Work Regulations	All electrical equipment must be portable appliance tested (PAT) annually. All equipment must be used correctly by the teacher and learners	

GETTING THE MESSAGE ACROSS

LO2.1 Clarify facilitation methods with group members to meet group and individual learning objectives

Communication skills

When working with learners in a group situation it is important that communication skills are considered, of both the teacher and learners. This will make sure that the learning that takes place is as productive as possible. Expectations of the learners will already have been established by the setting and use of ground rules. A positive rapport should also have developed, not only between the teacher and the learners, but also between the individuals in the group. It is important that this is based on mutual respect and is underpinned with **equality** and **diversity**.

Language

Teachers need to consider the implications of ambiguous and over-complicated language, particularly when setting tasks using written instructions or when giving verbal instructions to a group. This will include thinking about possible language differences, not only of learners who have English as a second language, but also thinking about the age group being taught. Encouraging learners to look up any words they do not understand in a dictionary (this can be an online application) will further promote independence. This activity can also be an opportunity for learners to create a group glossary of key terms via a **wiki**, or to make their own glossary of terms using another tool with which they are comfortable (such as a small pocket book or tablet).

Communication will always be more successful if you ask the right kind of question and listen carefully to the answers. This sounds obvious; but it is really surprising how easy it is to ask complicated or confusing questions. Take some time to set questions before the session, rather than trying to conjure them up on the spot. You might want to write down the instructions for the task and hand these out so that the learners have something for referral during the group task. This will also mean that you will be able to move about the groups, facilitating rather than constantly answering questions about 'what' learners are meant to be doing.

Equality is about giving every learner an equal opportunity to succeed. This may include making reasonable adjustments

Diversity is about recognising and celebrating differences between individuals and groups

Wiki is a website developed collaboratively by a group of users. It is built by allowing any user to add and edit content. For example, wikipedia

---

CLASSROOM MANAGEMENT

If you try to always stand in a certain place whenever you want your learner's attention, they will quickly recognise this as a cue and respond appropriately.

Body language

When working with groups of learners an awareness of body language will help both the teacher and learners get the most from the learning experience. When facilitating group activities try to consider the three key points below:

- Smile and laugh: this will help to foster positive working relationships.
- Nodding: this shows interest and engagement in the conversation.
- Eye contact: when addressing a group try not to leave anyone out but move your gaze from one to another to involve everyone in the group.

Introduce these techniques to the learners if they are inexperienced with their own communication skills and encourage them to use them when involved in a group activity. For more information about body language see page 120.

HANDY HINT

Nod, smile and be encouraging when a learner asks a question. There is no such thing as a stupid question!

GETTING GROUPS TO WORK TOGETHER

LO1.3 Evaluate methods for facilitating learning and development to meet the needs of groups

LO2.2 Implement learning and development activities to meet learning objectives

There is no one 'model-answer' way to set up and facilitate a group activity, as all learning environments, groups of learners and teachers are unique. It means being able to adopt flexible approaches that suit each particular group, topic and teaching style. However, there are good practice examples that can aid with the planning stage and management of a group activity. Peer observation (of experienced colleagues) can be very beneficial when looking at how to implement learning and development activities, as can adjusting to the learning environment and feedback from the learners as the activities are taking place.

Some suggested strategies:

- Negotiate clear ground rules at the start of the course and remind learners of these at the start of a group activity.
- Plan who will be grouped with whom; this can be in terms of ability, experience, behaviour management, previous performance or motivation.

- Have sufficient resources available and make sure these are clearly presented, interesting, contextualised, relevant and pitched at the right level.
- Give clear instructions at the start of the activity, including how much time is available and expectations of what will be achieved.
- Move around the groups to assist and gauge how the activity is progressing.
- Provide additional support, extension activities, leading questions or additional time, as necessary.
- Make explicit links to the overall course, so that learners can see how it will be useful for their assignment, practical task, or exam.
- Give lots of positive praise and feedback throughout the activity to encourage full participation and keep motivation high.
- Make it fun!
- Think about how you will gather and record feedback at the end of the activity and plan sufficient time for this to happen.

TEACHING METHODS FOR GROUPS

LO1.3 Evaluate methods for facilitating learning and development to meet the needs of groups

LO2.2 Implement learning and development activities to meet learning objectives

Group teaching methods

There are a number of different strategies, or teaching methods, that are particularly well suited to groups. It is important to plan to use the most effective methods that will foster and encourage deep learning rather than surface learning to take place. **Surface learning** can be explained as the process involved when something is learnt by rote; the learner will be able to recall information but will not necessarily be able to apply the information in an unfamiliar situation or in a different context. Deep learning is seen as taking place when a learner can connect the information to previous knowledge and make sense of it. This means the learner has a deep understanding of the topic and its underlying principles. Deep learning is normally facilitated by tasks that involve problem solving, evaluation and interpretation, rather than simply absorbing information.

Surface learning
is when something is learnt by rote resulting in information recall

The following teaching methods foster a deep learning approach so that the learners are involved in learner-centred activities which encourage them to get actively involved in the learning process.

Teaching method	Strengths	Weaknesses	Teaching tips when facilitating
Role play	■ Active learning activity ■ Whole-group participation ■ Safe ■ Builds confidence ■ Embeds language skills ■ Tool to teach affective domain and social aspects ■ Team building ■ Practise and make mistakes ■ Explore scenarios and practise by doing	■ Needs to be carefully planned ■ Needs careful consideration and monitoring/ facilitating ■ Does not suit everyone – out of comfort zone ■ Can be resource heavy – time and additional resources for it to be successful – clear boundaries and guidelines of acceptable practice	■ Set up the scenario carefully ■ Offer clear criteria for learners to work within ■ Guidelines can be negotiated at the start ■ Be clear on what is acceptable behaviour ■ Offer time at the end for learners to debrief and come 'out' of the role ■ Think about the groups that you choose and always offer an option for learners to observe rather than participate
Demonstration	■ High in retention of information ■ Involves everyone in activity ■ Good for visual learners ■ Interesting and fun ■ In context and real	■ Can be resource heavy – time and additional resources for it to be successful ■ Can make learners feel inadequate if the demonstration is given by an experienced person ■ Can be quite a passive activity unless additional questions are used alongside to help focus the learners	■ Offer criteria to signpost what the learners are looking at ■ Might have to give the demonstration more than once ■ Make sure that everyone can see and that the demonstration is delivered in stages ■ Provide images at each stage that the learners can use to make notes against ■ Ask questions during the presentation to check learning ■ Allow time for learners to ask questions to clarify understanding
Case study	■ Active learning strategy ■ Whole-group participation ■ Easy to set up and manage ■ Can be tailored to individual experiences and needs ■ Can be in context and current ■ High-level thinking skills are required ■ Level of understanding about the subject is required ■ Offers an opportunity to explore all of the aspects of the case study and arrive at solutions	■ Needs to be explained and managed or facilitated ■ Can be emotive and needs to take into account all needs ■ Some learners could take over the discussion ■ Might not capture all of the discussion	■ Decide on the case study carefully so that it is relevant and interesting ■ Present the study in a clear and engaging way, use visual alongside written information ■ Offer additional resources or information to extend the discussion if learners need it ■ Think about how to get the learners to capture the discussion and thought processes ■ Time the activity so that it stays on task

Discussion	■ Easy to set up ■ Free exchange of ideas on a related topic ■ Encourages social interaction between group members ■ Offers an opportunity to explore new ideas and concepts	■ Needs careful management as learners can be easily distracted or put forward controversial ideas ■ Can lead to confusion if the task is not clear from the start	■ Decide on the topic for the discussion carefully so that it is relevant and engages the learners ■ Introduce the topic in a clear and engaging way – a video clip can spark imagination ■ Use visual alongside written information if possible ■ Pose a set of questions to help the discussion develop
	■ Can aid development of deeper understanding ■ Balanced teacher and learner input	■ Not all learners will want to participate or some learners will monopolise the discussion ■ Difficult to evidence	■ Think about how to get the learners to capture the discussion and thought processes ■ Time the activity so that it stays on task
Problem solving and small-group tasks	■ Can help to develop deep learning ■ Can challenge the more able learners ■ Motivational as it can stimulate thought ■ Fosters a sense of competition	■ Can be time consuming to set up ■ Learners may need a lot of input at the start if they do not have the skills or prior knowledge to tackle the task ■ Not all learners will feel that they are able to contribute and may feel out of their comfort zone	■ Decide on the problem or small-group task carefully so that it is relevant and interesting ■ Present the task so that learners can see the relevance to previous learning ■ Set it in context of the 'bigger picture' so that the intended outcome is clear ■ Offer additional resources or information to extend the discussion if learners need it ■ Think about how to get the learners to capture the results and thought processes ■ Time the activity so that it stays on task

It is good to maintain variety in the teaching methods that you use as this will ensure that everyone will be able to participate at some point. Not every learner will be motivated by the same style of teaching method, but it is the role of the teacher to encourage the learners to develop as learners; introducing a range of methods ensures that all learning styles will be catered for.

This image illustrates the use of demonstration and practical task as an effective teaching method for this type of subject.

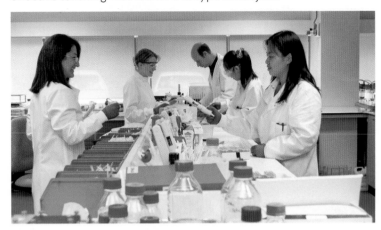

Learners in a workshop on a practical task in a laboratory

ACTIVITY

Write a list of the teaching methods that you use the most often. Consider how active the learners are and how well the methods used promote deep learning. Is there anything else that you could do to make your sessions more interactive and engaging?

ADAPTING DELIVERY AS IT HAPPENS AND AFTER THE EVENT

LO1.7 Explain how to adapt delivery based on feedback from learners in groups

LO4.2 Review individual responses to learning and development in groups

See, do, revisit
An area that is sometimes overlooked in the teaching cycle is the evaluation stage of teaching, particularly if it is a short course that is being delivered. However, an essential part of teaching is checking and reviewing what is happening – both within a session and afterwards – so that the delivery is as successful as it can be. It is not enough

simply to plan interesting, stimulating sessions that take into account individual need, which are relevant and delivered using a variety of methods; it is also necessary to put in place some form of check that will help evaluate the success of the session. A successful teacher is one who is constantly reflecting on what has occurred in order to make changes to future delivery. By breaking down the parts of the session, and then analysing them, the teacher is able to improve their practice.

Success indicators

Not all learners learn in the same way and key elements of the three main theories of learning should be applied when teaching adult learners in a group setting. The main points to consider from the theory are as follows.

- Active learning is considered more successful than passive.
- Learners should be given positive praise.
- All learning should be connected to prior knowledge and given within a framework of the overall concepts.
- Learners should be able to practise by 'doing'.
- Opportunities should be provided for social interaction with others.
- Learning should be relevant and challenging.
- The learning environment should be safe and supportive.
- Learners should feel valued and be encouraged to develop a positive self-image.
- A range of teaching methods should be used.
- Learners need time to discuss and reflect on new information.
- High expectations and clear ground rules should be established from the start.

Session evaluation

Evaluating the session as it is happening is a skill that develops with experience. The important thing is not to panic but always to try to have a plan B ready just in case the session is not going as you thought it would.

There are many ways to evaluate the teaching methods that are being used, and a simple reflective model developed by Rolfe et al. (2001) is based on three questions: what, so what, now what? This provides a framework for the teacher to reflect on what happened in the session in order to think about what changes could be made in the future.

Example	
What?	Small-group activity:
	I started the session by getting the learners into pre-arranged groups as they entered the classroom. The groups were arranged to mix up abilities and according to group dynamics (there is tension between some of the learners, so I made sure they were not sitting together). Each table of four learners was given a large piece of A3 paper and a range of coloured felt-tip pens.
	The learners were asked to produce a poster about first impressions.
So what?	Although this was a recap activity and the topic had been covered the previous session, the learners seemed to lack ideas, seemed confused and did not grasp what they could include on their poster. They also wanted to create individual posters as they are not used to working in groups, although I thought that they would be able to talk through their ideas with one another. They needed a lot of support throughout the task and although I thought they would be able to share ideas, this did not happen. Also they could have been given more resources to help them.
Now what?	In future I will need to introduce the activity to the whole group first and check understanding before setting up the task. I will ask them individually to come up with one aspect of 'first impressions' that can be included on the poster before they start and record these on the whiteboard for reference during the task.
	I will also go back over ground rules when working in a group and remind the learners of the importance of working together, treating one another with respect and valuing individual contributions. I will provide more resources, such as magazines to help with images, and may even bring in an example of a finished piece of work to show them.
	I need to work on my communication skills when setting tasks or writing a set of simple instructions. Also I need to make sure that I link the task to their assignment so they can see the relevance of it.

Course evaluation

The learners are a valuable asset when evaluating a session and, by involving the learners in this part of the teaching cycle, the teacher can get a more rounded view. On a short course a couple of simple questions can be asked to establish what was particularly good about the session and provide an opportunity for learners to offer advice on possible changes that could be made.

On a longer course, a questionnaire could be created and distributed midway through the course as well as at the end of the course. Make sure that expectations are clearly communicated before handing out the questionnaire and, if possible, leave the learners to complete it independently.

Evaluation could take into account the following aspects:

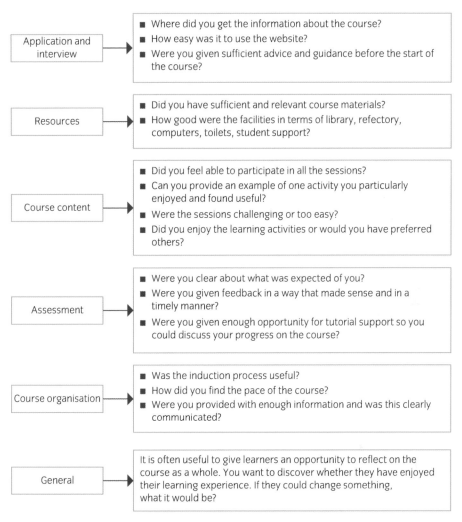

Application and interview	■ Where did you get the information about the course? ■ How easy was it to use the website? ■ Were you given sufficient advice and guidance before the start of the course?
Resources	■ Did you have sufficient and relevant course materials? ■ How good were the facilities in terms of library, refectory, computers, toilets, student support?
Course content	■ Did you feel able to participate in all the sessions? ■ Can you provide an example of one activity you particularly enjoyed and found useful? ■ Were the sessions challenging or too easy? ■ Did you enjoy the learning activities or would you have preferred others?
Assessment	■ Were you clear about what was expected of you? ■ Were you given feedback in a way that made sense and in a timely manner? ■ Were you given enough opportunity for tutorial support so you could discuss your progress on the course?
Course organisation	■ Was the induction process useful? ■ How did you find the pace of the course? ■ Were you provided with enough information and was this clearly communicated?
General	It is often useful to give learners an opportunity to reflect on the course as a whole. You want to discover whether they have enjoyed their learning experience. If they could change something, what it would be?

In addition to assessment methods that check that learners have learnt what was planned, and formal evaluation techniques, there are several indicators the teacher can use to help determine if the learners are engaged and successfully learning. Use the list on the next page to check your own learners and evaluate how well you are teaching.

Evaluation techniques enable teachers to assess successful learning

Are your learners?	Yes/no	Reasons why this is not happening
Arriving early and participating fully in all sessions		
Willing to explain how they are progressing with their own learning		
Taking responsibility to catch up with any missed work in their own time		
Voluntarily trying to ask and answer questions		
Asking for extra guidance and advice in order to complete work to the best of their abilities		
Exhibiting a supportive and caring attitude towards fellow learners		
Completing all pre-session work in a thorough manner		
Independently completing research before a topic, unprompted		
Bringing additional resources to the sessions that they can use to support class activities		
Achieving an excellent standard of coursework that exceeds the standards required		
Offering useful feedback and evaluation of the course and their own experience		
Going the extra mile in all aspects of the course		

(Adapted from Race and Pickford, 2008, page 17)

FROM THE CLASSROOM TO REAL LIFE

LO3.1 Develop opportunities for individuals to apply new knowledge and skills in practical contexts

Once a learner has knowledge of a subject, an important aspect of their development will be how they can apply the knowledge in a practical context. Being able to repeat the information is not enough; they will need to demonstrate that they have understood the information and one way to check this is by asking them to apply the knowledge, with an example, or in practice. Some subjects lend themselves to this more than others. However, if it is not possible to create a real-life scenario where practical application can be easily demonstrated, then it will be necessary to set up simulated, or role-play, situations.

Learners working outdoors to develop
skills in agriculture

EXAMPLE

Working outdoors on a practical task is suitable for a variety of
practical subjects. There are often opportunities for learners to
complete voluntary tasks in the local community as a good way to
demonstrate skills in a real-life setting.

FEEDING BACK TO YOUR LEARNERS

LO3.2 Provide feedback to improve the application of learning

The importance of feedback

One of the many forms of communication with learners will be giving
feedback on their progress. Learners need frequent and appropriate
feedback at regular intervals in order to feel confident about their
progress, gain information about how to improve as learners and
remain motivated to continue. Never underestimate feedback: how
the teacher handles it is all-important, and can be the make or break
factor that results ultimately in continuance or withdrawal from a
course. Learners need to know they are doing well, possibly more
than being told about what is not going so well, particularly in the early
stages of their learning.

Feedback during the course should be *formative*, so that learners
can identify what can be further improved as they continue on their
studies, as well as *summative*, so that they can also see what has been
achieved in the work. For feedback to be successful it needs to be
timely, constructive, positive and *understood*.

When teaching groups on a regular basis it is necessary to build instant feedback into the teaching and learning activities. It will be either verbal, in response to an answer or comment, or written on a piece of work. In primary schools the use of smiley faces or stars is common practice and, although this might not seem appropriate in lifelong learning, you may be surprised how much learners like positive praise and encouragement (Warren, nd).

Feedback is an essential part of the teaching cycle and although some adult learners can be reticent about calling attention to themselves, it is important to constantly monitor progress and ensure that feedback is given at the right time.

Positive feedback

Whenever giving feedback, both verbally and especially when written (as this can be re-visited time and again), it must always be positive and supportive and never overtly critical. Never use a red pen to mark a learner's work. Blue or black ink is recommended by the External Quality Assurer (EQA). Pencil may be required by some awarding bodies so it is best to check first with the organisation.

Use phrases such as, 'You seem to have misunderstood ...' and never statements like, 'You have got this completely wrong!'

Another one to avoid is, 'You haven't read the question' or, 'Read the question again'. (I have even seen 'Now try answering the question'.) Unless it has been established that a learner has a learning difficulty that could affect their reading skills, it is safe to assume that of course they have read the question. Even if they have such a learning difficulty, it does no good to remind them time after time; it is demotivating. However, if a learner missed something out or their efforts do not satisfy the criteria, then they did not fully understand the question or what they were required to do. Sometimes people misunderstand or misinterpret what to others seems obvious. Allow for this; re-phrasing of the question may be all that is needed.

As already discussed, positive, supportive feedback is not just a choice of words. Feedback that is supportive uses the 'praise sandwich' strategy by concentrating and congratulating on what was done well, explaining what did not go so well and why, then ending on a further positive note and motivating remark. This will ensure that the overall feeling is positive and keeps the learners' motivation levels high (Reece and Walker, 2003).

It is important always to use clear, unembellished and succinct language when giving feedback, employing a level and style appropriate to the learner. Avoid ambiguities; use direct language to make it quite clear how they are doing and, more importantly, what you want them to do. Always refer to the question or learning outcomes.

Link the feedback to work done – either written or performance – and complete an action plan, making clear what is to be achieved and then ask the learner to initial that they agree and understand. This is obviously not always a possibility with formative feedback to a group in a session.

This image is an example of the use of positive body language when giving feedback on an individual basis. Both participants appear relaxed and engaged.

A teacher providing positive feedback

Giving feedback – good practice checklist

- Start with pleasantries or greetings.
- Give feedback on each point separately.
- Use clear, simple, concise language; avoid jargon and acronyms.
- Use positive openings that comment on strengths.
- Point out any mistakes with directions and suggestions for action.
- Explain grading if appropriate.
- Refer back to previous examples or materials and put the task in perspective.
- Offer further sources of information or support.
- Close positively; acknowledge effort.
- Summarise and list further or next actions required and by when.
- Check understanding and agreement.

SUPPORTING INDIVIDUAL SELF-EVALUATION

LO4.1 Support self-evaluation by learners

Feedback should help learners to make sense of what they have done so that they can take ownership of their learning, especially to motivate them to *want* to learn. This should result in the learner becoming more aware of what they can do better in future work and this will enable them in the process of self-evaluation. One way to further develop these skills of self-evaluation is through the use of self-assessment.

Actively involving learners in the assessment process will enable them to develop skills in making accurate judgements about their progress. This needs to be structured carefully so that the learner can make informed comments, in a supported way. One way to do this is by identifying a series of pre-set questions that can help learners to evaluate for themselves what they have learnt and what they need to do in order to continue to develop their skills and knowledge. The reflective model – What? So what? Now what? (Rolfe et al., 2001) – could also be introduced to learners as a way to provide structure in the process of self-evaluation.

ACTIVITY

Supporting self-evaluation. Look at the statements below and discuss these with a colleague in terms of how suitable they would be to use with your learners. Identify at least five new statements that you can use in your teaching role.

1. I prepared for the task by allowing plenty of time.
2. I completed a plan of action before I started to read up on the topic.
3. I talked about the work with my friends outside the classroom.
4. I asked the teacher when I wasn't clear about the task.
5. I checked my work over before handing it in.

In addition, all learners should be encouraged to keep a reflective journal or diary alongside their studies to help them make sense of their learning journey, as well as keeping an individual learning plan (ILP). This will have areas for development identified and an action plan to support each learner as they make progress on the course.

An example of an ILP can be found on page 169.

CLASSROOM MANAGEMENT

If possible put up a display of your learners' work. This will promote a sense of ownership and respect for the learning environment.

THE INDIVIDUAL WITHIN THE GROUP

LO1.6 Explain how to monitor individual learner progress within group learning and development activities

LO4.2 Review individual responses to learning and development in groups

LO4.3 Assist learners to identify their future learning and development needs

Review and evaluation

As a reflective practitioner, it is important that you review and evaluate every teaching session in terms of how well it met the planned session objectives so that any changes can be made for future delivery. The best source of information to help the teacher evaluate their own practice is the group of learners.

The dynamics of a group will often determine how successfully a task is completed, but as discussed this can be managed within the classroom environment through a variety of strategies. It is important that the teacher also considers the individual learners within the whole group so that any necessary adjustments to the teaching and learning activities can be considered. This is something that can be carried out within the session or planned for to take place in the next session.

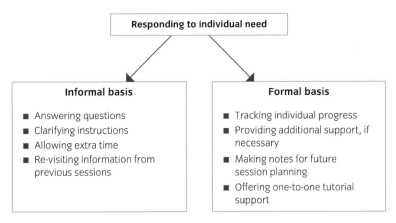

As previously discussed, evaluation forms can be used to record formally the learner evaluation of the session. These do not need to be complicated but can provide a rich source of information.

Communication

Communication plays a big part in enabling the learners to identify future learning and development needs. As discussed there are many ways to provide a learner with feedback, whether it is verbally or written. The language should be appropriate to the level of learner and easy to understand. It should not be over-complicated, too brief or alternatively in too much depth. It may be better to identify no more than two development areas, even if there are more that could be pointed out. A learner could become demotivated if the feedback is overly critical or appears too much of a hurdle. Additional development points can be introduced to the learner as they progress on the course. Identifying key areas on which to focus means the process will be more manageable and the learner is more likely to feel able to address these independently.

Some points to consider

- Provide assessment tools to help the learner to identify own areas of strength and development at the start of the course.
- Offer examples of targets that are SMART (specific, measurable, achievable, realistic, time bound – see Unit 302 for more information).
- Encourage learners to review their own targets throughout stages of the course.
- Plan all feedback so that it is timely (as soon after the task has been completed as possible – normally within three weeks).
- Give feedback in a way that the learner will understand. Link to the specific outcomes throughout as well as commenting on the overall task.
- Try to provide a combination of written and verbal feedback. This will help you and the learner to discuss the feedback and clarify any uncertainties and provide the learner with the opportunity to revisit the information.
- Point out at least one strength to encourage the learner and help them to see what they are already doing well so that it can be repeated in future work.
- Point out at least one development point.
- Involve the learner by asking for their own opinion on their performance.
- Provide some examples of previously completed work to help the learner to gauge their own performance. Even if the work being assessed is a pass, fail or refer, many adult learners like to know if their work is a *threshold* pass, good or excellent piece of work. This will motivate them to continue to make improvements and strive for excellence. Add developmental points to help them attain a higher standard next time.
- Make note on future work where a learner has taken on board previous feedback and demonstrated improvement. This will keep them engaged and motivated in reviewing targets and setting new ones.

ACTIVITY

Look at the ILP on the next page and consider how this could be adapted to be used with your own learners.

Individual learning plan	
What am I good at? (strengths and past achievements):	
What do I need to learn? (areas for development):	
Language skills	
Numeracy skills	
ICT skills	
Academic skills	
Practical subject skills	
What are my personal development objectives for the period of this ILP? (Use SMART objectives: 2–3 objectives could be an appropriate number.)	
1	
2	

Progress against each objective – complete this section regularly during the period of the ILP. Use any feedback given during the course to help with this.			
Date		Progress	Date achieved
1			
2			

UNIT SUMMARY

This unit has identified some of the benefits and challenges of teaching learners in groups. The chance for shared experiences and participating in group work can make the learning experience a dynamic and rewarding one which helps to develop a deeper knowledge and understanding of the subject. The role of the teacher becomes that of facilitating learning. Drawing on the experience and knowledge of the learners can make the sessions enriched and relevant and is an effective way to bring information to a number of learners at the same time.

This unit has explored and discussed some of the ways that group work can be facilitated so that it is a successful learning experience and draws on the theory that helps to increase motivation and participation. Some of the aspects covered include: effective planning; establishing clear ground rules; setting high expectations; using a range of teaching methods and different ways to evaluate sessions. This unit focuses on working with groups, but there is additional information in Units 301 and 302 that will also be helpful when working with groups of learners.

ASSIGNMENT FOCUS

This unit provides you with information about teaching and facilitating learning and development that takes place in a group setting. Learning outcomes 2, 3 and 4 will be assessed in a genuine workplace environment where you will have to demonstrate your understanding of the theory by putting it into practice with real learners. Learning outcome 1 will be assessed by a piece of written work, such as an assignment. You will need to cover all of the following assessment criteria in order to evidence your knowledge and understanding successfully.

Assessment criteria (LO1)

1.1: Explain purposes of group learning and development

1.2: Explain why delivery of learning and development must reflect group dynamics

1.3: Evaluate methods for facilitating learning and development to meet the needs of groups

1.4: Explain how to manage risks and safeguard individuals when facilitating learning and development in groups

1.5: Explain how to overcome barriers to learning in groups

1.6: Explain how to monitor individual learner progress within group learning and development activities

1.7: Explain how to adapt delivery based on feedback from learners in groups

Tips
You might want to consider the following when planning your assignment:

- Why is it beneficial to teach learners in a group?
- Discuss elements of group dynamics and why this needs to be considered when planning and delivering learning in a group.
- Which teaching methods are the most successful when working with groups and what makes these successful? What difficulties could you and the learner experience when using these teaching methods?
- What strategies would you employ in order to minimise risk and ensure that your learners are safeguarded within the session?
- What would you do to engage your learners and help to reduce barriers to learning?
- Identify ways that you would monitor individual progress.
- Give some examples of ways that you would change delivery based on feedback from learners.

UNIT 305/306

Understanding assessment in education
and training and understanding the principles
and practices of assessment

INTRODUCTION

These units will introduce the main principles and purpose of assessment and the many assessment methods that are available for a teacher to use with their learners. It is increasingly important that assessment is used effectively to support learners and help raise achievement. The differences between initial, formative and summative assessments are discussed, together with how to plan for assessment and yet still meet the diverse needs of learners. Clear guidelines are given on how to make assessment decisions fairly and how to minimise any of the risks involved. Examples of how assessment fits in with current legislation are given in addition to some helpful practical tips. Some of the aspects covered include:

- why teachers need to assess
- how teachers assess
- the responsibilities of the assessor
- initial, formative and summative assessment
- the strengths and limitations of a range of assessment methods
- how to meet the needs of learners
- the key factors to consider when planning assessment
- the benefits of a holistic approach to assessment
- the types of risks involved with assessment
- how to minimise those risks
- the importance of involving the learner and others in the assessment process
- how peer and self-assessment can be used effectively
- how to judge if evidence is sufficient, authentic and current
- how to ensure that assessment decisions are valid, reliable and fair
- the importance of quality assurance and standardisation
- the procedures that need to be followed when there are disputes concerning assessment
- how feedback and questioning contribute to the assessment procedure

In Unit 305 you will cover the following learning outcomes:

LO1: Understand types and methods of assessment used in education and training
LO2: Understand how to involve learners and others in the assessment process
LO3: Understand the role and use of constructive feedback in the assessment process

LO4: Understand requirements for keeping records of assessment in education and training

In Unit 306 you will cover the following learning outcomes:

LO1: Understand the principles and requirements of assessment in learning and development
LO2: Understand different types of assessment method
LO3: Understand how to plan assessment
LO4: Understand how to involve learners and others in assessment
LO5: Understand how to make assessment decisions
LO6: Understand quality assurance of the assessment process
LO7: Understand how to manage information relating to assessment
LO8: Understand the legal and good practice requirements in relation to assessment

WHAT IS THE FUNCTION OF ASSESSMENT?

LO306.1.1 Explain the function of assessment in learning and development

Assessment is one of the many tools at a teacher's disposal to help learners learn. It is a method of finding out what learners know and what they have learnt. It is part of a teacher's role to check that learners really understand what they are being taught and that learning is taking place. Steward (2006, page 5) states that, 'Assessment is about making a judgement about the progress of a particular student's learning or their achievement.' This should take place at all key points during the session. A good teacher will assess whether learning is taking place from the start of the session (if not before).

Starting with a quick recap on the previous session will serve to remind and focus learners. It also offers the teacher a chance to assess who has remembered what.

CLASSROOM MANAGEMENT

Learners quite often arrive in an unsettled state. They might have been rushing to get to the class from work or from taking the children to school. Using a quick recap at the start of the session will help them focus and prepare themselves for the session.

A teacher checks that learning is taking place

Teachers use assessment to measure knowledge, skill and understanding. This helps them to know a learner's strengths and weaknesses, so they are able to plan sessions that are pitched at the correct level and therefore move at the correct pace. A session that moves too fast will leave learners confused and frustrated while a session that moves too slowly will leave them feeling bored. By including regular assessment within a session a teacher will be continually checking what the learner knows and how much learning is taking place. Assessment should not just take place at the end of a session as this is too late.

HANDY HINT

Don't leave assessment to the end of the session. If you are not sure that the learners understand, then use a few oral questions to check their understanding before continuing. Oral questions are instant, free and they could make all the difference to the outcome of your session. (See page 231 for some examples.)

Why assess?
A teacher needs to include a variety of assessment methods, including oral questions, within their teaching. Learners don't want to be continually tested and grilled but they do expect to learn something or gain a new skill. It is up to the teacher to get this balance right and choose appropriate assessment methods to use with their learners. It is always a good idea to assess what learners already know before highlighting what they don't.

The following table shows some of the many reasons why a teacher has to assess learners.

Why?	How?	Function/purpose
To establish entry requirements	Check previous qualifications	To make sure that the learner is on the correct course
To identify any learning needs	Literacy, numeracy assessments Include the teaching of study skills	To enable the teacher to get support in place for the learner as soon as possible To assist learners with their learning
To measure knowledge, skill and understanding	By using a range of assessment methods	To give each learner the chance of a fair assessment of their ability
To motivate learners	Constructive feedback	To provide learners with a precise picture of exactly where they are at and where they need to be
To help the teacher plan future sessions	The teacher can make changes and amend planning documents, eg schemes of work and lesson plans	To make sure that all teaching is delivered at the correct level and pace to enable *all* learners to learn
To help the teacher know that the learner is making progress	Through tracking documents and progress reports	Teacher is able to monitor the progress that the learner is making
To help the learners know that they are making progress	Through feedback from the teacher	Learner is able to monitor the progress that they are making
To check that learning is taking place	By using a range of assessment methods	To monitor that all learners are making progress with their learning. To check the teaching
To meet the requirements from OFSTED, awarding organisations and, examination boards	By using official paperwork as supplied by awarding organisations, examination boards and other external agencies	To provide evidence that the criteria from external sources have been satisfied
For selection or grading purposes	By looking at previous qualifications and grades achieved to date	To help the teacher make an informed decision on whom to select

❝❞

Assessment is not only a mandatory requirement of awarding and validation bodies for whose qualifications you are preparing students, but you will need to assess in order to maintain a record of students' progress and to assist them in planning their own learning.

(Huddlestone and Unwin 2008, page 162)

CLASSROOM MANAGEMENT

Always have a well designed, engaging lesson planned. Bored learners equal trouble!

CONCEPTS AND PRINCIPLES OF ASSESSMENT

LO306.1.2 Define the key concepts and principles of assessment

LO305.1.1 Explain the purposes of types of assessment used in education and training

A teacher will make sure that learners are making progress

Assessment should not be seen as something to worry about as it can benefit both the teacher and the learners. When used effectively it will help to complete the learner's learning experience. It is a vital part of teaching as it helps a teacher ensure that their teaching is working and that their learners are achieving. It is also a requirement for external agencies, such as awarding organisations and those who provide any funding.

❝❞

If you are to teach effectively it is important that you understand the part that assessment can play in making teaching and learning effective

(Haydn, 2008, page 301)

There are many assessment methods available for a teacher to choose from, including oral questions and assignments. Assessment methods require careful consideration, planning and preparation before the start of the lesson. A teacher who plans to use a range of assessment methods regularly throughout their teaching will be taking a large step towards letting their learners know how much progress they are making.

> **" "**
> In the right hands, assessment can inspire, motivate and provide the feedback which is essential for targeting prompt corrective help.
>
> (Petty 2009, page 479)

A teacher will assist learners as required

CLASSROOM MANAGEMENT

Work to engage all learners while teaching. Do not base the pace of the entire group on one or two learners.

Types of assessment

For each stage of the course a teacher will have to decide which type of assessment will best meet the requirements of the awarding organisation, the subject they are teaching and the ability of their learners. The table below shows the different types of assessment.

Type of assessment	Description
Formal	Planned, structured assessment
Informal	Relaxed, possibly not planned assessment
Initial	Assessment that takes place at the start or beginning of something; for example, a course, unit or topic
Formative	On-going assessment that takes place throughout the course
Summative	Assessment that takes place at the end of something; for example, a course, unit or topic

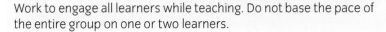

Formal and informal assessment

Assessment can take place both formally and informally. A teacher should consider the use of both of these within their teaching.

- Formal assessment is organised, planned and might be conducted under exam conditions, such as tests, assignments and exams. Learners are fully aware that they are being assessed.
- Informal assessment takes place in a continual way and at any time; it is probably not even planned. This informal assessment is very useful to a teacher. An informal discussion is actually a teacher's way of assessing in
an on-going, effective way.

Both formal and informal assessment could be used at the beginning, during or at the end of a course. This allows for initial, formative and summative assessment to be used in either way. An example of a *formal* initial assessment might be an interview whereas a telephone conversation might be considered as an *informal* initial assessment. All these types of assessment are used to help both the teaching and the learning process. These will be examined in more detail throughout this unit.

Methods of assessment

Whatever type of assessment a teacher plans to use, there are several different methods and ways that they are able to assess their learners.

❝❞

A cardinal rule of assessment practice is that methods are selected for their fitness for purpose and their validity.

(Armitage and Renwick 2008, page 38)

When any assessment is set, a teacher must also make sure that the instructions are *clear*. People can often interpret instructions in different ways. A teacher might have a wonderful assessment method planned but it will be useless if the learners do not understand what it is they have to do. Instructions that are not clear might lead to learners feeling confused, frustrated and, if it continues, they may lose confidence in the teacher. (See Communication skills, page 153.)

A teacher agrees the assessment method with
a learner

Assessment methods should be planned and agreed with the learner
before the assessment. The assessment methods chosen should
be relevant for the assessment criteria and allow the learners to
demonstrate competency in a natural, occurring way. Awarding
organisations might set some assessment methods that have to
be used. Teachers might also be able to choose some assessment
methods that they think are appropriate for both the subject they are
teaching and their learners.

HANDY HINT

Make sure that you consider both the advantages and
disadvantages for each assessment method. A teacher needs to
make sure that, whatever assessment method is chosen, the details
are well presented and link to the assessment criteria.

INITIAL ASSESSMENT

As the name suggests, initial assessment is undertaken at the start of
a course or a unit. It can also take place prior to a course, for example
application forms, auditions, interviews, initial course questionnaires
and diagnostic assessments (self-assessment tests).

❝❞

one of the first things you are going to do is assess what your student already knows or can do!

(Corder, 2008, page 76)

Obtaining information about learners before the course starts is extremely beneficial to a teacher. This would help the teacher to know about, for example, prior learning, reasons for the course being chosen, any qualifications gained and any specific requirements that the learner may have.

The information gleaned from initial assessment will help the teacher to get to know their learners and check that they are on the right course. It will also check that they have met all of the entry requirements and that they have the minimum necessary level of literacy and numeracy skills. It also allows the teacher to identify any specific individual learning needs. The teacher needs to obtain this information as early as possible in order to make suitable changes to their planning documents. Petty (2009, page 532) writes that 'however you diagnose needs, they must also be addressed'. This is also one of the first steps towards making an inclusive learning environment. (See page 49.)

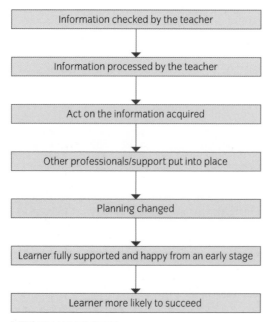

Initial assessment stages

There are several **initial assessment** methods that a teacher can use before a course starts that will help to provide valuable information about their new learners. The following table shows the advantages and the limitations of each method and it also considers the needs of the learner. Some of these methods might also be used during the first few sessions of a new course.

Initial assessment
involves checking what has gone on in the past to help improve future learning

LO306.2.1 Compare the strengths and limitations of a range of assessment methods (initial) with reference to the needs of individual learners

LO305.1.2 Describe characteristics of different methods of assessment in education and training

LO305.1.3 Compare the strengths and limitations of different assessment methods (initial) in relation to meeting individual learner needs

HANDY HINT

For your assignment, include examples of the main initial assessment that would take place within your own subject area. Think about the initial assessment that you have undertaken.

Initial assessments can provide valuable information about new learners

The strengths and limitations of initial assessment methods are outlined in the following table along with how the individual needs of learners can be met.

Advantages and limitations of initial assessment methods

Method	Initial, formative or summative, formal or informal	Strengths	Limitations	Needs of the learners
Interview	Initial Formal	Allows key questions to be asked directly of the learner Learner can ask any questions re concerns/worries that they may have Allows the teacher and learner to meet on a one-to-one basis Teacher is able to find out about the personal circumstances of the learner The teacher can check that the learner has all the prerequisites to join the course and that they are enrolling on the correct course	Time consuming It is not always the teacher who does the interview so not all information gets passed on to the teacher	Is the learner sure that they are enrolling on the right course? Check to see if learner has any learning difficulties including health problems, ESOL, etc Have all of the learner's questions been fully answered?
Application form	Initial Formative Formal	This should contain information about details of the learner's prior qualifications, grades, personal details, medical conditions, etc. Initial assessment of literacy level can be determined if the application form has been completed by hand Most application forms now have sections that a learner can tick to request more information on various areas, eg learning support, childcare, finance etc.	Not always seen by the teacher Admin staff tend to use application forms to process the details onto various systems, eg enrolment Some application forms need to be completed online so there could be a lack of IT skills	Learners might be worried about enrolling on a course. It is important that the application form is clear and easy for the learner to complete The learner may have some initial questions about the application process so it is helpful if there is someone that they could talk with

Basic skills assessment	Initial Formative Formal	Allows the teacher to assess the level of literacy, numeracy and IT skills of the learner	Some learners will be scared of such assessments due to previous experiences	Learners might need extra support with a basic skill. This help might come from the teacher or from another professional
Induction	Initial Informal and formal	Learners are given all the information needed about the course and learning provider Learners are able to ask any queries that they may have Learners will be able to meet their peers	Can take up a lot of time in the first session Learners who have already completed an induction with that learning provider may become bored	Learners might feel apprehensive about the new course A teacher needs to make a good first impression and make sure that a learner feels welcome and safe, eg all health and safety issues are discussed – Fire drill
References/reports	Initial Formal	Provide the teacher with an account of the previous work ethic and character of the learner. They allow for action points to be set	It depends on who has written the report Plagiarism	Learners might be concerned if they do not have any references
Learning style questionnaire	Initial Formal	Informs the teacher and learner of the learner's preferred learning styles The teacher is able to adjust planning documents as necessary	Sometimes the results depend on when and where the questionnaire was completed and also the state of mind of the learner at the time	Learner can reflect on the results and build these into their CPD action plan Learning needs must be taken into account to make sure that the assessment is fair, eg some learners might need more time

Advantages and limitations of initial assessment methods

Method	Type			
Practical skills assessment	Initial Formative Informal and formal	Enables the learner to demonstrate their practical skills Helps the teacher to plan the level and pace of the course	Some learners will have more practical skills than others Some learners may not have worked in a practical setting before	Some learners might be worried that they will not be able to perform at the required level They might also be worried that their peers will have better skills than they do Learners with disabilities might need the task adjusted in some way
Online diagnostic testing	Initial Formative Formal	Online testing means that the assessment is marked straight away Can be completed at home	Lack of IT skills Learners might not have access to the test Plagiarism	Learners might have free use of computers from the assessment provider Extra time might be needed by some learners with learning needs Learners might need help with IT skills
Psychometric tests	Initial Formal	Provides a standardised and objective way of assessing learners. Normally quick and easy to mark Can be administered to groups of learners at the same time This method might help a learner who might not be as confident at interview as others	Learners might feel nervous and uneasy about this method. Training might be required to mark some tests (can be quite complex) Can be costly to set up initially Should only be used in conjunction with other assessment methods – not standalone	Clear instructions will need to be given to the learner Learners will need constructive feedback and action points from the teacher

Getting to know learners

Initial assessment also allows the teacher to get to know their learners.
Any such information can then influence decisions they make about
the planning of future sessions.

A new group of learners

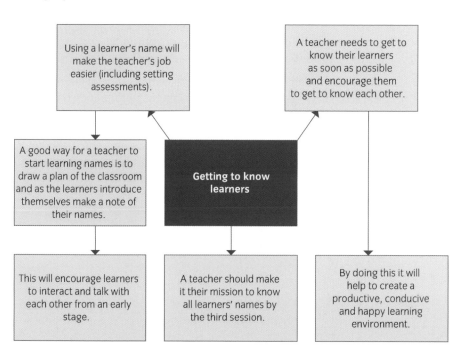

HANDY HINT

Learning names: at the start of the third session ask all the learners individually to write down everyone's names – and you should do this also. Then ask everyone to say their own name and each person should correct their own list. Who had them all right? Aim for it to be you. This is a bit of fun and it really works.

Imagine a teacher has a group of learners for one hour a week for 30 weeks. They are all girls aged 17 to 18 years. If time is not taken to learn their names then it is not hard to see the problems that might occur. (See the tips for this on page 77.)

By undertaking initial assessment a teacher will get to know their learners as individuals with different needs. Learners bring with them a range of prior knowledge and experiences which, when known, enable the teacher to help motivate and support their learners. Changes can be made to planning documents such as lesson plans. This will increase the learner's chances of passing each assessment and completing the course. Information can also be used to set targets in an independent learning plan (ILP) or action plan (see page 169).

From the start of the course a teacher should lead by example and show a keen interest in, and support for, *all* of their learners. The learners will then show an interest in and support each other. Initial assessment is not just about assessing each learner's needs or learning their names; it also checks a learner's prior knowledge and experience. This can have an even greater effect on lesson planning.

Sometimes the first contact a teacher has with a group of learners is at the start of the first session. It is possible that information has been passed to the teacher from a line manager but this does not always happen so it is up to the teacher initially to assess their learners. An icebreaker activity is a good way of assessing learners and it also helps the learners to relax at the start of the course and get to know each other (see section on icebreakers in Unit 301, page 29).

CLASSROOM MANAGEMENT

It is important to strike a balance between being your learner's teacher and being their friend.

ACTIVITY

1. Make a list of the initial assessments that your learners undertake before the start of a course; it might not be with you so you will need to find this out from your line manager.
2. Add to the list any initial assessment that you do with your learners during the first few sessions.
3. Are you missing any information that will help you to support your learners?
4. Plan how you will find this out.

FORMATIVE ASSESSMENT

❝❞

The key role of formative assessment is the giving of feedback to students for a variety of reasons: the assessment itself can be a means of learning; students are able to monitor and improve their learning; feedback if effectively given can motivate students and reinforce learning.

(Armitage and Renwick, 2008, page 5)

Formative assessment can be defined as ongoing and is part of the learning process. Black and William (1998) suggest that this is 'assessment *for* learning'. It takes place during the course and it is probably the most widely used type of assessment in teaching. It means the learner can:

Formative assessment is continued checking of learners' progress to help move them towards achieving their individual learning goals

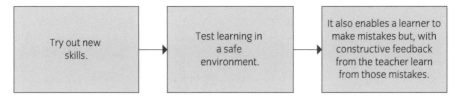

Most teachers will use this type of assessment throughout a session; it provides the opportunity for a teacher to:

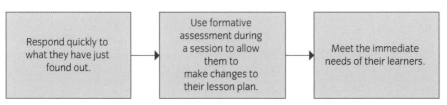

Formative assessment gives the teacher information on how a learner is progressing. Both the strengths and weaknesses can be discussed and an action plan with clear targets can be created.

There are several formative assessment methods that a teacher is able to use during a course that can provide valuable information about the progress their learners are making. The table on the next page shows the advantages and the limitations of each method and it also considers the needs of the learner. Some of these methods might also be used at the initial or summative stage.

ACTIVITY

1. Make a list of what it is you need to assess in your session and then state at least four possible ways of doing this (the following chart will help you).
2. Consider which methods you would use and discuss why you have chosen these methods with a colleague.

LO306.2.1 Compare the strengths and limitations of a range of assessment methods (formative) with reference to the needs of individual learners

LO305.1.2 Describe characteristics of different methods of assessment in education and training

LO305.1.3 Compare the strengths and limitations of different assessment methods (formative) in relation to meeting individual learner needs

Advantages and limitations of formative assessment methods

Method	Initial, formative or summative, formal or informal	Strengths	Limitations	Needs of the learners
Written work	Initial	Allows the teacher to assess the level of literacy and grammar	It could favour the more academic learner	Learners might need support with their written work
	Formative	Learning support could be put into place at an early stage of the course	Learners might be worried about their level of literacy, spelling or grammar	Reassurance from the teacher would help to put learners' mind at ease
	Summative			
	Formal			
Assignments	Formative	Learners can show a range of skills such as research, application of theory, evaluation, etc	Some learners are better at writing about theory than putting it into practice	Learners might need extra support with literacy skills
	Summative	It makes learners focus on a particular area of study	Plagiarism – the use of the internet makes this far too easy	Showing learners previous learners' work might be reassuring
	Formal	Assignments can help focus a learner	Assignments are marked on the learners' ability to write assignments not the content	Learners need to be given enough time to complete the assignment
		Demonstrate the learner's level of literacy	Some input or research needs to have been undertaken before the assignment can be written	Learners need to be clear on hand-in dates – so they can manage their time
		Easy to set	Time consuming to mark	
		Assess the use of language and grammar	Learner may have poor literacy skills	
Written assessment within a set time	Formative	Encourages learners to streamline their answers and include the key points	Key points might be missed	Extra time might be needed by some learners with learning needs
	Summative	Makes learners work quickly and efficiently	Benefits learners who work well under pressure	Some learners might need help planning their study
	Formal	Prepares learners for time-bound exams	Benefits learners who can work quickly	Teacher needs to teach some study skills within the sessions
		Limits the time spent on the assessment	Some learning styles really don't like this method	
		Some awarding organisations provide set assignments with marking criteria		

Advantages and limitations of formative assessment methods

Presentation	Formative Summative Informal and formal	Develops a learner's confidence Allows learners to perfect presentation skills – which they might also need in other areas, eg work Good for developing key skills	Learners can dread presentations Time consuming Information can be repeated	Some learners will be very nervous so they will need a lot of support from both teacher and peers
Learning journals	Formative Summative Formal	Encourage learners to reflect on their own learning Help learners to identify areas that they might want to improve on Feed into ILPs and tutorials Develop self-assessment skills Relate theory to practice Help assess literacy skills	Sometimes learners don't really understand the importance of these and if not shown how then they might be conceived as a waste of time They might be seen as something to do to meet the criteria Time consuming to read and mark	Learners need feedback on how to write a learning journal. They need to be reflective not descriptive
Case studies	Formative Summative Informal and formal	Learners can gain experience in a real working environment with 'real people' Learners could receive feedback from their case studies Case studies provide valuable real-life evidence from which learners can learn	Time consuming People/resources need to be found Might not be relevant to the subject	Learners might need help with communication and social skills

Unit 305/306: Understanding assessment in education and training and understanding the principles and practices of assessment

191

Method	Type	Advantages	Disadvantages	Considerations
Projects	Formative Summative Formal	Can include a range of assessment methods but all linked to the same learning outcome Learners can work in groups or individually Project could be put on display for different people to assess	Time consuming Difficult to get all members of the group to work together effectively Could be expensive	Learners need to know that they have enough time to complete their project Learners might need access to resources
Observations	Initial Formative Summative Formal	Allow learner to demonstrate their skills while the teacher is assessing from a safe distance Natural skills that learners have can be seen The same thing can be seen at the same time by different assessors Other people can be involved in this process Allow learners time to realise their own mistakes Can assess several aspects of criteria at the same time	Lack of resources may hinder the learner's progress Timing A permanent record needs to be made A teacher might misinterpret what they are seeing A teacher can't watch everything	Clear observation guidelines will need to be given to the learner Learners will need constructive feedback and action points from the teacher
Professional discussions	Initial Formative Summative	Teacher can prompt learners (appropriately) to expand their answers as needed Teacher can lead the discussion if needed Allow for a more complete assessment	A teacher could lead the discussion too much Lack of professionalism with other people involved Different standards A record of the conversation needs to be kept, eg recording or paper copy	Learners might be worried about the questions the teacher will ask Time needed to prepare for this by the learner

Advantages and limitations of formative assessment methods

		Advantages	Limitations
	Informal and formal	Develop skills that will be needed in the workplace Instant feedback can be given Fill the evidence gaps if the criteria have not been fully met Group participation Freedom to voice opinions (if relevant)	Teacher might 'lead' the learner Personality clash between learners
Workbooks/ short-answer question/ gapped handouts	Formative Summative Formal	Can be fun Sections can be set at different times (bite-size chunks) They can include a variety of assessment methods Several teachers could mark the same workbook Learners can work at their own speed	Easy to mark Questions must be written carefully Plagiarism – learners could share answers Questions need to be phrased carefully
Portfolio of evidence	Initial Formative Summative Formal	Shows the progression of a learner over a period of time Can contain a wide range of assessment evidence Can be produced electronically or on paper	Plagiarism Large and bulky If lost, a lot of evidence gone at once Learners might need some assistance to organise their portfolio A clear index for each section given at the start of the course will help Learners might need extra support with literacy skills

Product evidence	Formative Formal	To support observation and questioning. It must be the product of an actual work environment Can assess several areas of learning over a period of time	Needs to be planned to a time scale on scheme of work	Some learners might have access to more resources than others (unfair)
Multi-choice questions	Formative Summative Formal	Ease of marking Totally objective marking Easy to make, amend and use again	Hard to write Learner does have the opportunity to expand answer They could guess Teacher must be careful not to reuse the same test too often	Learners must have had time to prepare for the test Expose learners to mock tests to build confidence and technique Extra time might be needed by some learners with learning needs
Quizzes	Formative Informal	Fun Lots of resources readily available, eg puzzles on line Prepare learners for future tests Good informal assessment of learning to date	Time consuming Some learners might find them childish	Put learners into groups carefully so that everyone is comfortable

Advantages and limitations of formative assessment methods

Mock exams	Formative Formal	Allow learners to practise their exam technique Highlight areas that learners need to work on Highlight areas that teachers need to recap	Time consuming Learners might do so well in a mock exam that they don't revise for the actual exam Time consuming to mark	Some learners need to be reassured as they might be very nervous and stressed Embed study skills into course and make sure that the learner is aware of exam technique Extra time might be needed by some learners with learning needs
Open book tests	Formative Summative Formal	Allow learners to refer to a text book with the answers in it Some subjects need learners to be able to access a lot of technical information and use charts and formulae which would be impossible to remember	If learners are not familiar with the text book then they will not find the information in the time allowed Learners need to be able to read and digest information quickly Learners could be too dependent on the book instead of their own knowledge	Extra time would be given to learners with learning needs, eg dyslexia

SUMMATIVE ASSESSMENT

LO306.2.1 Compare the strengths and limitations of a range of assessment methods (summative) with reference to the needs of individual learners

LO305.1.2 Describe characteristics of different methods of assessment in education and training

LO305.1.3 Compare the strengths and limitations of different assessment methods (summative) in relation to meeting individual learner needs

Learners check the results of their online assessment

Summative assessment happens at the end of a course or unit. Black and William (1998) say that this is 'assessment *of* learning'. It is the final assessment that determines what a learner has learnt. A final judgement or decision is made and there is normally a grade attached. Some awarding organisations use pass, refer or fail for their theory and practical assessments while other awarding organisations might award an actual grade. It is often this final judgment that indicates how well a student has learnt something.

Theory assessments are normally undertaken at a formative level which allows the teacher to mark it in a draft form and give clear feedback on how the assessment could be improved. A learner is then able to make those changes and resubmit at a summative level. Practical assessments, where it is necessary to acquire a skill, might require several formative assessments until the skill has been learnt and the learner can prove that they are working confidently at the required standard. Once a teacher feels that a learner has achieved this then they will let the learner demonstrate that skill at a summative level.

Summative assessment
is the proof that learners have learnt

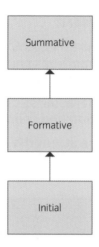

Assessment results

When a learner fails at a summative level, a teacher will have to adhere to the procedures of the awarding organisation. A learner failing to meet all of the requirements to pass a practical task will receive feedback from the assessor and then try again after a stated period of time.

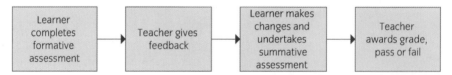

This method is quite commonplace for NVQs. However, some practical and theory-based assessments, such as exams, might require an external assessor and failure here might require the learner to resubmit for another assessment at a later date.

The teacher needs to ensure that a learner has prepared for a summative assessment, especially in the case of exams, as it is quite often the results of such assessments that interest employers.

The following table shows the advantages and the limitations of different summative methods and it also considers the needs of the learner.

Advantages and limitations of summative assessment methods

Method	Initial formative or summative. Formal or informal	Strengths	Limitations	Needs of the learners
Test/exams	Formative Summative Formal	Help to focus learners to work towards a set goal Can be marked externally and a grade is awarded Provide evidence for statistics Can assess lots of learners at one time Test of knowledge There are a range of tests to choose from	Learners can be very intimidated by exams Learners have to perform well on a particular day Some learners are able to cram – which does not require deep understanding of the subject Teachers might teach learners to pass the exam rather than for understanding of the subject Memory-based assessment Marking criteria will be needed	Embed study skills into course and make sure that the learner is aware of exam technique Expose learners to mock exams to build confidence and exam technique Extra time might be needed by some learners with learning needs
Witness statements and communication with other professionals	Initial Formative Summative Formal	To provide evidence that the learner is working consistently over a period of time All professionals involved can contribute to the assessment process A teacher can liaise with other professionals regarding the progress of the learner	A record of the conversation needs to be kept, eg recording or paper copy Lack of professionalism with other people involved Different standards	Learners need to be made aware of any communication between professionals Learners might be worried about the questions the teacher will ask Time needed to prepare for this by the learner

Advantages and limitations of summative assessment methods

Show/performance/exhibition/display	Summative Formal	Can include a range of assessment methods but all linked to the same learning outcome	Time consuming	Teacher needs to make sure that all learners have a role within the group and that learners know exactly what their role is
		Learners can work in groups or individually	Can be expensive – lots of resources may be needed	
		Encourages team-working	Some learners might have a larger role than others	Learners will need time to prepare and be fully aware of all deadlines
		It can be seen/assessed by a range of people	Some learners 'might take over'	
		Offers an enjoyable way of presenting information and knowledge gained	Learners might be very nervous and not perform well on the day	Learners will need to feel confident before the final assessment
		Good opportunity to share success		
		Teaches learners to work to a deadline		
		Presentation of work will improve		

RESPONSIBILITIES OF THE ASSESSOR

LO306.1.3 Explain the responsibilities of the assessor

The main responsibilities of an assessor are towards the awarding organisation, their own organisation and their learners. An assessor will also need to consider why and how learners need to be assessed. The responsibility of the assessor will be continually examined within each section of this unit.

The assessor has a responsibility towards the awarding organisation to:	The assessor has a responsibility towards their own organisation to:
■ Complete all assessments in accordance with the awarding organisation's specifications	■ Be a qualified assessor
■ Use all the awarding organisation's paperwork and templates	■ Remain up to date within their own subject area
■ Give feedback to learners in accordance with the awarding organisation's guidelines	■ Complete regular continuing professional development (CPD) both within their subject area and to meet organisational requirements
■ Make sure that all the evidence submitted by learners is at the correct standard and meets the criteria	■ Attend regular team meetings
■ Mark and return any assessments within the agreed time scale.	■ Attend regular standardisation meetings
■ Liaise with the internal quality assurer (IQA) and submit evidence of marked assessments regularly throughout the course	■ Keep accurate and up-to-date records
■ Attend events held by the awarding organisation to enable them to stay up to date with any developments within their subject area	

The assessor has a responsibility towards the learner to:

- agree an independent learning plan (ILP) with the learner
- explain all assessment procedures and requirements
- provide clear and objective feedback following every assessment
- support and guide learners throughout the assessment process
- complete all required paperwork linked to the assessment

- involve the learner in the assessment process
- check that any prior qualifications and experience are considered before the start of the course (see below).

EXPERIENCED LEARNERS

There are two categories to consider here.

Recognised Prior Learning (RPL)

RPL, formerly known as Accreditation of Prior Learning (APL), is a system that allows a learner to carry forward any qualification that they already hold. For example, a plumbing student might already have completed the generic health and safety unit as part of a previous qualification. Evidence will need to be seen by the teacher and a copy of the certificate kept as proof. This system prevents the learner from having to repeat areas in which they already hold a recognised qualification.

Accreditation of Prior Learning and Experiential Learning (APEL)

This recognises that a learner might already have experience and/or developed skills in a chosen area but they do not hold a recognised qualification. They would have to complete an application form for APEL and provide evidence in the form of references, letters and log books. Some awarding organisations do not accept APEL/RPL and this should always be checked first with the internal quality assurer (IQA) (see page 223).

ACTIVITY

Find out if learners are able to use RPL and APEL on your course? State as many examples of this as possible.

LO306.1.4 Identify the regulations and requirements relevant to assessment in own area of practice

Education and training sectors

There are several sectors within education and training in which a teacher could work. These include:

- further education (FE)
- higher education (HE)
- adult-based learning (ABL)
- work-based learning (WBL)
- private training provider
- the voluntary sector.

Each of these sectors will have their own way of providing learning and there will be procedures and regulations in place for teachers and assessors to follow. It is important that a teacher is aware of how the organisation for which they work operates. Teachers should attend events held by their own organisation to stay up to date with any mandatory training, such as data protection, equal opportunities and safeguarding. They will also need to be made aware of any recent changes that have been made to any of the organisation's procedures or policies.

It is important that teachers are fully aware of the assessment criteria as set by their awarding organisation. The process of writing a scheme of work will familiarise a teacher with the contents and learning outcomes that they will be required to assess against. Objectives vary from one awarding organisation to another and the assessment criteria could be quite different. There is a huge difference between teaching and assessing an NVQ compared with teaching and assessing an exam-based subject.

Within a teacher's own organisation and subject area there could be specific assessment criteria that will need to be planned for. Each subject will bring its own assessment challenges.

Further education	NVQs normally require both practical ability and theoretical knowledge to be assessed. Workshops provide a real working environment (RWE) for learners to perfect their practical skills. A learner enrolled on a plumbing course will need to be assessed on their welding skills, which brings with it the challenges of health and safety as well as the required skills to complete the assessment. The assessor/teacher will need to ensure that all the required resources and safety requirements are in place before the assessment is able to take place. This type of practical assessment is commonplace within FE colleges.
Higher education	Within HE, an assessor/teacher might need to prepare their learners for end-of-course, summative exams. They will need to include mock tests and exam techniques into their scheme of work to equip their learners with the skills to pass these assessments.
Work-based learning	Work-based assessment (WBA) takes place in the workplace and it is often completed in a continuous way. The assessor will be assessing that the learner has the ability to perform work-related tasks in a competent manner.
Adult-based learning	Adult-based learning also brings its own assessment challenges. In the absence of any criteria from an awarding organisation the teacher/assessor might have to create their own. Learners will still want conformation from the teacher that they are achieving their goals and making progress throughout the course.
Private training provider and the voluntary sector	The voluntary sector and private training providers are able to set their own assessment criteria, although this will depend on the type of course and training that they offer. An assessor/teacher should make sure that they are fully aware of the assessment criteria when writing the scheme of work.

ACTIVITY

What are the regulations that you need to be aware of within your subject area? Are there any special requirements that you need to take into consideration when preparing assessments for your learners?

PLANNING ASSESSMENT

LO306.3.1 Summarise key factors to consider when planning assessment

When planning any sort of assessment, there are some key questions that a teacher should ask themselves.

When?	Where?	What?	Which?	Who?

HANDY HINT

Don't be predictable. Plan to use a variety of assessment methods on a week-to-week basis. Try to engage your learners by using different approaches to your teaching and the way in which they will be assessed.

When to assess

At the planning stage a teacher should space all assessments as evenly throughout the course as possible (see the assessment plan below). Communication with other teaching staff might be needed to avoid learners having to complete too many assessments at once. This information should be shared with learners at the start of a course to enable them to organise their time. The actual time of the assessment should also be taken into consideration when the session plan is written.

Assessment method	Sep	Oct	Nov	Dec	Jan	Feb	Mar	Apr	May	Jun	Jul
Assignment 1	X										
Assignment 2		X									
Observations		X			X			X			X
Test unit 1/2			X								
Presentation for unit 2				X							
Assignment 3					X						
Test unit 3/4						X					
Assignment 4							X				
Assignment 5									X		
Test unit 5											X

Where will the assessment take place?

The correct environment should be provided to enable learners to complete their assessment successfully. The teacher should ensure that the layout of the room will be appropriate for the chosen assessment method and that all assessment resources should be prepared and ready ahead of time. Some assessments might require a different room or location to be used; for example, an IT room might be required if an assessment involves the use of computers or a workshop might be needed if a practical task is being assessed.

Assessment taking place in a real working environment (RWE)

What is being assessed?

The teacher needs to be very clear on what it is they are going to assess and they must ensure that the learner fully understands what they have to do to pass the assessment. The learner must be allowed suitable time to prepare for the assessment and ask any questions prior to being assessed. It is also the responsibility of the teacher to ensure that the planned assessment meets the requirements from the awarding organisation and that all the correct assessment paperwork is completed.

How are the learners going to be assessed?

A teacher will need to choose the most suitable assessment method to assess their learners. They will need to consider both the ability of their learners and the level of the course. A teacher should also take into account how their learners are normally assessed and what assessment methods they have recently used.

Who is being assessed?

A teacher should always remember that it is the individual learner who is being assessed. They should allow for some interaction between the teacher and the learner so that the pace can be adjusted to match the learner's progress. There should not be any comparison made between learners as each learner should be assessed on their own ability and skill by the teacher.

A teacher needs to decide what is really important and what they want to get out of the assessment. There will be elements of the assessment that the learner *must know*, elements that they *should know* and some elements that they *might know*.

The assessment needs to inform the teacher that learners are on track to achieve the learning outcomes for that session or unit. The learners must be fully aware of the assessment criteria and what is expected of them. Other professionals (see Unit 301, page 43) might need to be informed of the assessment decision.

❝❞

Assessment planning must integrate closely with the curriculum philosophy and design. The assessment strategy chosen must be consistent with the course aims and philosophy, and therefore with the model of achievement being used.

(Avis et al., 2010, page 165)

HANDY HINT

Select assessment methods that are suited to the learning objectives and make the objectives SMART (see page 86) – this will help make it much easier for you to check that they have been met.

There is also a range of teaching methods and techniques available for a teacher to consider when planning any assessment. The teacher is able to embed several different assessment methods when using these techniques, which will help to create more varied opportunities to assess their learners.

The table on the next page shows the advantages and the limitations of some of these methods/techniques and it also considers the needs of the learner.

Field trip
(Initial, formative, informal and formal)

Strengths
Provides a change of learning environment for the learner. New experience for learners. Chance to see a real-life example within their own subject area. Encourages group bonding.

Limitations
Travel time and cost. Lots of paperwork for teacher to complete. Risk of injury to learners.

Needs of the learners
Make provision for any learners with physical disabilities or medical conditions and reassure them that considerations have been put into place.

Tutorial
(Informal and formal)

Strengths
Allows the teacher and learner to talk confidentially. Enables teacher and learner to agree and set goals. It lets both the teacher and learner assess how much progress the learner has made since the last tutorial.

Limitations
The teacher can speak with only one learner at a time so cover has to be arranged for the rest of the group or work set. Time consuming.

Needs of the learners
The learner is able to talk freely with teacher about any of their needs.

Questionnaire
(Initial, formative, summative and formal)

Strengths
Used by the teacher to assess information on the progress and views of their learners. Teacher able to make changes from the feedback gathered.

Limitations
Learners don't always take questionnaires seriously. If given to learners at the wrong time it could affect the results.

Needs of the learners
Learners need to know that their views are asked for, valued and acted upon.

Body language
(Initial, formative and informal)

Strengths
It lets the teacher know how the learner is feeling. Teacher might be able to change what they had planned to do in response to a learner's need.

Limitations
Could be interpreted wrongly.

Needs of the learners
The learner needs to see open and relaxed body language displayed by the teacher.

Simulations **(Formative, summative and formal)**
Strengths Teacher can observe from a different location which helps to relax the learner. Offers a safe environment for the learner to practise a potentially difficult process.
Limitations Cost. Could require lots of resources.
Needs of the learners Clear instructions will need to be given to the learner. Learners will need constructive feedback and action points from the teacher.

Role play **(Informal)**
Strengths Encourages group work, interaction, use of imagination and demonstrates that learners have put what they have learnt (theory) into practice.
Limitations Lack of confidence. Embarrassment – need clear defined roles. Quite a lot of people dislike this method. Learners don't always see the value of this method until it is over.
Needs of the learners Quieter learners will need a lot of encouragement.

Group work **(Initial, formative and informal)**
Strengths Learners are supported and can interact with their peers. It enables teachers to group learners in several ways. Learners can share and exchange ideas. Teacher able to observe and assess each group.
Limitations Learners might not get on. Different learning styles might clash. Learners might lose focus and go off on a tangent. Time consuming. Some learners might dominate.
Needs of the learners Some quieter learners feel less confident working in groups. Teacher needs to make sure that all learners have a role within the group.

HOLISTIC APPROACH TO ASSESSMENT

LO306.3.2 Evaluate the benefits of using a holistic approach to assessment

LO306.3.3 Explain how to plan a holistic approach to assessment

Holistic assessment

Holistic assessment is achieved when the learning objectives are interrelated and measured against a set of standards.

Holistic assessment is progressive and it could take place over a period of time, with a variety of assessors, or it could also take place on the same day where the assessor observes a learner in a workplace setting completing a variety of tasks. All assessments – from initial to summative –
must be well thought out and planned before the start. All assessment must be consistent and include sufficient depth of evidence so that learners will be clear on the requirements of the assessment.

Individual learning plans or tutorials should be planned into the course and these will link to the objectives for each unit. This will help to identify any areas of concern or gaps in knowledge for the learner and allow individual targets to be set by the teacher and agreed by the learner. A holistic approach can also be made at the time of actually marking as learning outcomes may have been met elsewhere and can be cross-referenced.

The three main parts of assessment are:

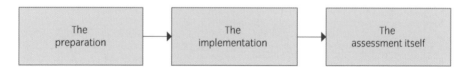

| The preparation | → | The implementation | → | The assessment itself |

When all these parts are achieved by the teacher, they will come together to help form a holistic assessment of the learner. Holistic assessment aims to link all the aspects of assessment together and work interdependently, not separately, to enable the teacher both to gauge how a learner learns and to help them make as much progress as possible. It encourages a teacher to look at all aspects of a learner's ability to learn, including their attitude, social and emotional development.

HANDY HINT

The learner should always be at the heart of holistic assessment.

A teacher observing a learner

CLASSROOM MANAGEMENT

An experienced teacher will choose to use a range of assessments methods during a session/course as this will help to involve and motivate all learners and help to keep each session interesting.

By varying the assessment methods a teacher can take into consideration the different learning needs, different learning styles (see diagram below and page 52), preferred learning methods (see page 56) and possible barriers to learning (see page 27) of their learners.

When planning which assessment methods to use, a teacher must try to meet the individual learning style of each learner within the group. Each learner will usually have a preferred style of learning and therefore they will also have a preferred way of being assessed (see Unit 302, page 72).

VARK	
Visual	Like to make charts, use pictures = **seeing**
Auditory	Like to have input but then write assignments and undertake research = **listening**
Read/write	Like to read through text either silently or aloud
Kinaesthetic	Like to produce and make things = **doing**

It is important that the assessment method chosen should be at the correct level for the course. It should also be well structured and planned ahead of time as this will encourage *all* learners to remain engaged, motivated and on track to pass.

As well as looking at the individual learner, it is also important to have a holistic approach to the whole course. Learning and course objectives should be interlinked. Assessments should be carefully planned into a programme of study. Too many assessments at one time might cause learners to become stressed and fail. Assessments should be planned into the programme at suitable times to give the whole course some structure and balance. This will also support learners as it makes assessments more achievable. A teacher needs to make sure that the correct amount of time is allocated to each assessment and that it has been set at the correct level; for example, a simple oral question or a higher-order question (see page 59).

RISKS

LO306.3.4 Summarise the types of risks that may be involved in assessment in own area of responsibility

LO306.3.5 Explain how to minimise risks through the planning process

Whatever the assessment method that a teacher chooses there is always a potential risk that the assessment might not go as planned. It is therefore essential to consider any factor that might hinder or disrupt the assessment and, with careful planning, try to eliminate any risk. It is important to have resources ready, to prepare all equipment and learners and allow enough time for the assessment to take place.

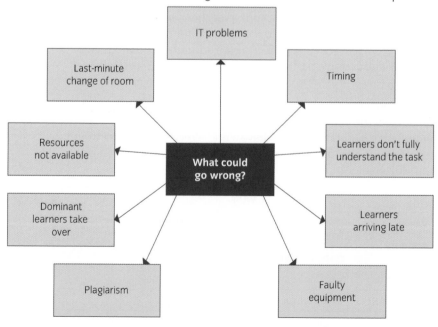

CLASSROOM MANAGEMENT

An assessment that might take 20 minutes with one group of
learners might only take 15 minutes with a similar group. A teacher
should plan for such eventualities and always have a plan B.

ACTIVITY

Make a list of the potential risks for the assessment methods used
within your own subject area.

HANDY HINT

Remember that lesson plans are not written in stone but they are a
guide (see page 84) which can be altered as needed. The planning
process allows a teacher time to ponder the risks and plan around
them.

Subject-related risks

Within a teacher's own area of teaching there will be subject-related
risks. For example a learner studying on a beauty course might take far
too long when performing a treatment for a case study which means
that the working area will not be available for the next learner to use
with their client. Their client might also arrive late.

CLASSROOM MANAGEMENT

To minimise the risk it is always a good idea to have a plan B. A
beauty teacher might plan to have one working area that is used in a
more flexible way by any learner who needs it, due to a client being
early or if a treatment is running late.

How to minimise these risks

The main responsibility for assessing learners will lie with the teacher
(assessor) but both the awarding organisation and the assessment
centre also have a responsibility to the learner.

A teacher is advised to use all the templates and paperwork as provided by the awarding organisation. Sometimes this paperwork might confuse a learner if the assessment centre is not offering all of the options. A centre might prefer to standardise its own documents to meet the awarding organisation's requirements.

A teacher also needs to keep up to date with all changes within their own subject area, to ensure that the spec from the awarding organisation has been met.

The wording in assessments needs to be clear, understandable and written at the correct level for the subject being taught. It is vital that suitable language is used when wording assessments and a teacher should include some input on study skills to help the learner prepare for the assessment.

Once a teacher has created any form of assessment they should make sure that it is *clear*, so that learners fully understand what is expected from them. A good way of doing this is for a teacher to get a colleague to check the instructions before using the assessment with their learners.

Other considerations are to make sure that the advantages of the chosen method outweigh the disadvantages and that there is enough time for the assessment to take place (including the feedback).

A variety of assessment methods should be used as this will help to motivate and keep all learners engaged despite their style of learning (see page 52).

A teacher needs to make sure that the learners are assessed across the whole syllabus. This responsibility might not solely lie with one teacher as different assessors may assess different parts of a course. Meetings with other teachers are vital to enable a teacher to plan key areas of assessment into their scheme of work.

It is good practice to space assessments evenly throughout the course and to make sure that they are progressive. Formative assessments should be used to prepare learners for summative assessments.

Standardisation meetings

Another risk is that assessors could be marking at different standards. Regular team/standardisation meetings should be attended by the whole teaching team so that everyone is assessing at the same level. At these meetings teachers should undertake some blind marking or mark another group's work and compare the feedback that they have given to learners.

The whole teaching team should also agree the consequences of plagiarism and make sure that all learners are aware of the sanctions (see page 39.) Inexperienced teachers should shadow or be mentored by more experienced members of the teaching team and all assessors should be fully qualified or, if working towards their TAQA, have their assessment decisions countersigned by a qualified assessor.

Learners need to be informed in plenty of time when, where and how they will be assessed and when they will get the results – as this will help them to feel more prepared. Support should be made available to any learner with special or learning needs and a teacher must ensure that everyone has an equal opportunity to pass the assessment (see page 238).

A teacher should plan that all assessment methods must be at the correct level, time and stage of the course, with constructive feedback given as soon as possible after the assessment has taken place. Informal assessments can be 'instant' while learners should always be informed about any formal assessments.

A teacher informs learners of how they will be assessed

HANDY HINT

You need to ensure that assessment methods are planned at each stage so that you can assess that learning has taken place.

INVOLVING LEARNERS IN THE ASSESSMENT PROCESS

LO306.4.1 Explain the importance of involving the learner and others in the assessment process

LO306.4.2 Summarise types of information that should be made available to learners and others involved in the assessment process

LO305.2.1 Explain why it is important to involve learners and others in the assessment process

LO305.2.3 Identify sources of information that should be made available to learners and others involved in the assessment process

Teachers should try to involve the learner in the assessment process from the earliest possible stage. Involving them in the planning of any assessment is a requirement of most awarding organisations and allows the learner the opportunity to ask questions about the assessment process. It will also help learners to understand:

- exactly what is expected from them
- what they have to do and
- how they will prepare themselves for the assessment.

Learners are more likely to perform to the best of their ability when they are fully informed about the assessment. They should also be made aware of:

- the assessment itself
- the grading criteria and
- the appeals procedures.

Time should be made available if there are special requirements to be put into place for any particular needs that a learner may have. Teachers should check that learners understand the assessment process before the assessment starts. Involving the learner will also encourage them to feel included, valued and motivated.

When learners are actively involved they can participate in selecting evidence (for example, samples of their work) that best demonstrate the intended learning outcomes. They also develop a greater confidence in the assessment method and the teacher/assessor's judgment. The main person to assess learners will be the teacher or assessor who has set the assessment. At a summative level it is possible that a colleague or an external assessor will complete this stage.

Learners also need to be informed when and where they will receive feedback on the assessment. Constructive feedback is vital to the whole process as it will enable learners to move forward with their learning (see page 96).

Other professionals involved in assessing

On some courses a teacher/assessor might be the only person assessing learners at a formative level. On other courses there might be several different people assessing learners. Sometimes the employer, work-based assessor or mentor might also be involved with the assessment of learners. Some awarding organisations state there has to be a different assessor at summative level from the person who taught the course. It is part of a teacher's role to ensure that there is good communication with any other professionals involved and also with the learner. A teacher will need to make sure that any other professionals and the learner are fully aware of the assessment criteria, legislation and all deadlines.

SELF-ASSESSMENT

LO306.4.3 Explain how peer and self-assessment can be used effectively to promote learner involvement and personal responsibility in the assessment of learning

LO305.2.2 Explain the role and use of peer and self-assessment in the assessment process

Self-assessment takes place when the learner is asked to assess themselves. This works really well as it encourages learners to self-evaluate, although learners can be over-critical of themselves.

A learner will need to be taught the skills needed for successful self-assessment. A detailed checklist should be given to the learner so that they have something to follow and guide them. This can be used by an individual learner for self-assessment or in small groups for peer assessment. Some learners can be very self-critical and others will not be critical enough.

CLASSROOM MANAGEMENT

Getting learners to mark their own test is a valuable experience as it will create discussions within the group which can lead to a learner understanding why they got it wrong. Care will need to be taken not to humiliate those who get low scores. Although this method takes up quite a lot of class time, it does save the teacher marking time and the learners get their score and feedback straight away.

Self-assessment

- Self-assessment is a valuable method as it can highlight that some learners know a lot more than a teacher realised.
- A learner is able to work towards their own goals.
- It encourages reflection on learners' own performance.
- It helps to make learners more selfaware.
- It promotes independence.
- A learner will also have to evaluate how much progress they are making.
- It can encourage learners to take responsibility for their own learning.
- Learners have to work out what they have to do differently next time in order to improve.

Peer assessment

> **❝❞**
>
> Making judgments about their own or a peer's work clarifies their understanding of the subject matter.
>
> (Petty, 2009, page 491)

Peer assessment is when a teacher encourages learners to assess and give feedback to each other. It helps if the teacher gives the learner clear guidelines to use when assessing their peer.

Asking a learner to observe and feedback to their peer on how improvements should be made to their work, or what they would have done differently, will help that learner to become more objective with the feedback that they give. Both their feedback skills and understanding of the criteria will improve along with their confidence in making assessment decisions.

EXAMPLE 1

A task could be set to learners who are working in small groups. Two
learners complete the task while the third learner observes. At the
end of the task all learners
give feedback to each other and discuss the key points. This
exercise is then repeated with learners taking a different role.

EXAMPLE 2

A micro-teach is another good example; one student will present
something to the rest of the group and receive feedback from
their peers at the end. This should be done orally but with written
comments completed to enable the learner to read through these
at a later time. Inviting peers to assess each other's work should
encourage interaction and everyone should learn.

A teacher needs to be aware of the risk that, if a task is not completed
successfully, the learner might feel very 'exposed'. Also, learners need
to learn to give constructive feedback first – a simple format to start
them off could be 'what went well?

Another example is to give each learner a copy of a piece of work from
a previous student (who has given their permission for their work to
be used). Ask each learner to mark it. This will lead to a discussion and
in turn it will help your learners to understand what they have to do to
pass the criteria. This is called a spoof assessment.

Which to use?
For some learners it will be easier to see the areas of development
required in others first before seeing it in themselves. A micro-teach is
a great example of this: when learners are giving oral feedback to each
other they quite often say, 'You are difficult to hear as you keep looking
at the floor; I know because I think that I do this too …'

Some learners will be more comfortable than others with peer
assessment so it might be a good idea to start with self-and spoof
assessment.

HANDY HINT

Sometimes quite a few learners will get the same question wrong,
making the same common mistake. Introduce some group
discussion as this will help them to understand what they did wrong
and research shows that they won't make it again. It may also mean
that the question was badly phrased!

The benefits of involving the learner in the assessment process

The benefits of involving the learner in the assessment process

- Planning to include some self- and peer assessment within your lesson will also free up the teacher so that they are able to move around the classroom and observe, listen and intervene where they feel it is most appropriate
- It makes the learner take responsibility for their learning
- Learners will learn from each other, eg different methods and approaches
- Encourages a learner-led environment
- Encourages a more open and honest learning environment
- Makes learners interact with each other
- Takes a bit of pressure off the teacher
- Gives the learner the opportunity to practise feedback skills
- Encourages the learner to be a reflective learner
- Learners often work harder to impress their peers
- Learners are more motivated when they have control over their own learning

CLASSROOM MANAGEMENT

Use peer assessment to create the opportunity to pair learners who don't know each other very well, have similar/opposing views or to split up more challenging learners. This will all help with managing behaviour within a group.

ADAPTING ASSESSMENT METHODS

LO306.4.4 Explain how assessment arrangements can be adapted to meet the needs of individual learners

LO305.1.4 Explain how different assessment methods can be adapted to meet individual learner needs

Teachers should ensure that learners are included in the planning process and that any special requirements to meet the needs of individual learners have been considered. Unit 301 explored how to meet the needs of learners with disabilities and/or learning difficulties. In the table on the next page there is further information on how assessment arrangements and methods can be adapted to meet the needs of individual learners.

Learner need	How assessment arrangements and methods can be adapted to meet individual learner's needs
Dyslexia and dysgraphia	Learners will be allowed extra time to complete written work
	The use of computers will be encouraged (spell check)
	Coloured overlays for reading
	Instructions printed on coloured paper
	The opportunity to answer questions orally. This will be recorded as evidence for the External Quality Advisor (EQA)
	A reader could be provided
Physical disability	The environment will be altered to suit a learner with a physical disability
	Higher tables might be needed if a learner is in a wheelchair
	Learners can be allowed extra time to complete assessments
Hearing impairment	A signer might be provided
	A portable loop system could be installed
	Teacher might provide written instructions
	Visual resources might be included
	Learners might have to sit nearer the front
	Headphones could be provided
	Computer software packages might be used
	A carpeted room will minimise the noise level
Partially sighted	Instructions could be produced in a larger font size
	Instructions could be produced in Braille
	Lighting and seating could be adjusted
	Computer software packages might be used
	The opportunity to answer questions orally (this will be recorded as evidence for the EQA)
	A voice recorder could be used
English as a second language	Instructions could be given in the learner's own language (awarding organisations often provide these)
	An interpreter could be provided
	Computer software packages might be used

HOW TO MAKE AN ASSESSMENT DECISION

LO306.5.1 Explain how to judge whether evidence is: sufficient, authentic and current

LO306.5.2 Explain how to ensure that assessment decisions are made against specified criteria, valid, reliable and fair

❝❞

Everyone is a genius. But if you judge a fish by its ability to climb a tree, it will live its whole life believing that it is stupid.

(Albert Einstein)

Practical assessments are needed for practical subjects

This is quite often one of the most daunting prospects for new teachers as it is so important that the correct assessment decision is made. Teachers should ask themselves the following questions in order to make the correct choice of assessment method.

Is it fair? For an assessment to be fair it should reflect what has been taught to date, it should be made against the specified criteria from the awarding organisation and it should offer every learner the equal opportunity to pass it. The assessment method chosen by a teacher should give all learners the same opportunity to pass it. For a teacher to use assessment methods that are fair, then they should consider if it is valid, current, authentic, sufficient and reliable. Consider the following:

Is it valid?	Is it current?
■ Does this method assess what it is meant to assess? It should assess no more, no less	■ Is the learner demonstrating an up-to-date knowledge of their subject?
■ Is this assessment method designed to measure the required skill or knowledge as required by the awarding organisation?	■ Has the work been produced recently? Are they aware of any recent changes in legislation regarding their own subject area?
■ Is the assessment set at the correct level?	■ Are they aware of any recent changes in legislation regarding their own subject area?
■ Does the learner understand what they have to do, eg do they understand the question?	■ Is the teacher up to date with current knowledge, methods of assessment and the awarding organisation's guidelines?

Is it authentic? Has all work that has been submitted been produced by the learner?	**Is it sufficient?** Has the learner produced enough evidence to meet the requirements/ standard of the assessment criteria?

Is it reliable?	
■ Reliability increases if more than one method is used. ■ Are learners assessed in a consistent way, at the same standard regardless of who is assessing them or when the assessment takes place?	■ Is the work produced by learners consistent? Would the assessment results be similar if the assessment had been sat by a different set of learners at a different time? ■ Have clear marking criteria been set in advance to enable all assessors to arrive at the same result?

HANDY HINT

If you are assessing the baking ability of a cook then a valid assessment of their cooking ability would be to get them to bake a cake, not write an essay about it!

O⊓ **HANDY HINT**

Get learners to sign a statement on any work that they are submitting to prove that it is their own work. This should have been agreed with learners at the start of the course.

❛❛❜❜

Reliability of a test refers to the extent to which it consistently measures what it is supposed to measure

(Reece and Walker, 2007)

O⊓ **HANDY HINT**

Try marking learners' work without looking to see who has written it (blind marking). You might get some surprising results.

ASSESSOR QUALIFICATIONS

LO306.6.1 Evaluate the importance of quality assurance in the assessment process

LO305.4.1 Explain the need to keep records of assessment of learning

LO305.4.2 Summarise the requirements for keeping records of assessment in an organisation

Teachers are required to hold a recognised qualification or be working towards one before they can start assessing as part of the quality assurance team. These qualifications are listed in the table on the next page. Some of the assessment terminology changed when new assessment qualifications started and a new teacher might still experience colleagues using the old titles. Both titles have been included for reference.

Before assessing quality assurance, teachers must have or work towards a recognised qualification

Old job title	New job title	Description	Qualification (old)	Qualification (current)
Assessor	Assessor	Assesses learners using a range of methods	D32	A1
Assessor	Assessor	Assesses candidate's performance through observation	D32	A2
Internal verifier (IV)	Internal quality assurer (IQA)	Conducts internal quality assurance process	D34	V1
External verifier (EV)	External quality assurer (EQA)	Conducts external quality assurance process	D36	V2
A (assessor) and V (verifier) Awards	TAQA	Qualification titles	Assessor awards	Assessor awards
Internal verification	Internal quality assurance	Internal quality assurance (verification)	Internal verification	Internal verification
External verification	External quality assurance	External quality assurance (verification)	External verification	External verification

Each centre needs to ensure that all assessors and internal quality
assurers (IQA) hold a TAQA qualification. It is possible that a teacher
can also be the assessor; however an assessor cannot also be the IQA
on the same course.

Internal quality assurance

❝❞

Internal quality assurance is meant to ensure that a range of functions
are carried out.

(Pontin, 2012, page 26)

Quality assurance is a way of making sure that learners are achieving
the outcomes as set by the awarding organisation.

The quality assurance process is something that a teacher needs
to be fully aware of and in which they play an active role. It is
essential that a teacher keeps all paperwork up to date and tracks
the progress of their learners. A simple tracking document will
inform the teacher of which learner has passed each assessment
and at what grade. This will help to keep the teacher fully up to
date with the progress that individual learners are making. This
information can be used when feedback is given to learners and
during individual tutorials. Other colleagues, inspectors, mentors
and observers might also find this information useful.

❝❞

Assessment is not only a mandatory requirement of awarding and validating bodies for whose qualification you are preparing students. But you will need to assess in order to maintain a record of a student's progress and assist them in planning their own learning.

(Huddlestone and Unwin, 2007, page 162)

Tracking records also highlight possible patterns; for example, if a group of learners all get quite a low score for a set piece of work then maybe the teacher needs to look at how *they* are delivering that unit. Questionnaires also form a valuable source of feedback from learners regarding all aspects of a course. This provides a teacher with the opportunity to give feedback to learners and make changes to any planning documents or delivery.

As part of the awarding organisation's quality criteria, each assessment centre needs to make sure that all work has been quality assured. This means that an assessor will have their work checked to make sure that they are consistent, fair and meeting the standards as set by the awarding organisation. Tracking documents will also be checked by the IQA.

Pontin (2012, page 28) groups the functions of an IQA into four main areas.

Sampling	Ensuring
■ Planning	■ Consistency
■ Sampling strategies	■ Reliability
■ Rationales for sampling	■ Fairness
■ Feedback to assessors	■ Accuracy
Supporting	**Monitoring**
■ Co-ordinating assessor team	■ Quality
■ Supporting assessor team	■ Compliance
■ Developing assessors	■ Issues and trends

The IQA normally works for the same organisation as the assessor but their responsibility is to check the assessor's judgements and the consistency of any assessment undertaken. An IQA will sample work that an assessor has marked, including written and oral feedback.

Horizontal sampling
This should not take place just at the end of a course but it should be an ongoing process from the start. There should be at least one piece of work internally verified for each assessor, each learner, each assessment and each location. This sampling ratio might be higher for new assessors, a new course or on request from an EQA.

ACTIVITY

What are the names of your IQA and your EQA?

Internal Quality Assurance Tracking Document

Full Title of the Qualification and Qualification number

Group Name: IQA name:

Assessor(s) name:

Name	Task 1	Task 2	Task 3	Task 4	Task 5	Task 6
Learner A	X 11/11/13 JW					
Learner B		X 11/11/13 JW				
Learner C			X 16/12/13 JW			
Learner D				X 06/01/14 JW		
Learner E					X 06/01/14 JW	
Learner F						X 13/01/14 JW
Learner G	X 11/11/13 JW					
Learner H		X 11/11/13 JW				
Learner I			X 16/12/13 JW			
Learner J				X 06/01/14 JW		

STANDARDISATION

LO306.6.2 Summarise quality assurance and standardisation procedures in own area of practice

An assessor, using the awarding organisation's assessment template, ensures that standards are being met

Within a teaching team it is good practice for each teacher to look at and check each other's feedback to learners. Standardisation meetings should take place regularly to give teachers the opportunity to check that they are all marking at the same level. An assignment could be copied and marked independently by each teacher. The group should then hold a discussion to see whether they have all awarded the same grade or spotted the same mistakes. They should also discuss whether the same amount of feedback is being given or if one teacher is stricter than another.

When assessment marking/feedback has been standardised within a team it will help to avoid friction between learners and teachers and also between teachers. It demonstrates to the learners that there is strong communication between all teaching staff and that teachers are working together. This process is also supportive for a less experienced teacher as it reassures them that they are assessing correctly.

HANDY HINT

Keep all paperwork up to date. Plan to do all paperwork straight after the assessment, as you will feel less stressed and appear more professional! All paperwork should then be passed onto the IQA.

External verification

The awarding organisation will regularly visit the assessment centre and check that the internal verification process has been implemented and is working. The EQA will want to be able to follow the trail of evidence for any chosen learner. All internal quality assurance records will have to be made available in addition to learners' work. EQAs also like to talk with learners about their learning experience and the teaching that they have received. They also check that the assessment criteria from the awarding organisation has been closely followed and delivered at the correct level.

This is normally done on a percentage basis, with new assessors having 75% to 100% of their marking verified (checked) and more experienced teachers having between 10% and 20% checked. A new course requires a 100% check, regardless of the teacher's experience.

The EQA has the ability to prevent learners from passing the course if they are not happy with the standard of internal verification or the work of a teacher. In a worst case scenario an EQA can remove accreditation from the assessment centre, which means that the assessment centre will not be able to continue to run that course in the future.

HANDY HINT

Make sure that you allow time to keep all records and paperwork as up to date as possible so that you are able to access information quickly and efficiently.

The EQA will also check that there are procedures in place for possible disputes concerning assessments. It is vital that learners know whom they can approach if they are not happy with an assessment decision. The teacher should obviously be the first person they approach; however, if a learner is not happy with this then they should be made aware of who is the line manager or section leader. These contact details should be given to all learners at the start of the course.

Other external interested parties might also want to be informed of a learner's progress, for example parents and employers. It is important to have reliable, up-to-date and accurate records as this demonstrates that a teacher is professional and able to provide valuable evidence when required.

Quality assurance can have an impact on retention and achievement which in turn will have an impact on funding. It is important that a teacher is meticulous about keeping *all* records as up to date as possible.

ACTIVITY

Make a list of everyone within your teaching area who is involved with quality assurance.

LO306.6.3 Summarise the procedure to follow when there are disputes concerning assessment in own area of practice

As previously mentioned it is vital that a teacher thinks carefully about any assessment that they undertake with their learners. All instructions should be clear and the learner should fully understand what is expected from them. The assessment decision should be fed back to the learner in a professional and constructive way.

If a learner does not agree with the assessment decision then they should be able to discuss this with the teacher/ assessor. The assessor should be able to state how they have reached their decision and provide written documentation to explain to the learner how the decision was reached. If the learner is still not happy with the decision then an arrangement would be made for them to talk with the IQA.

Depending on the type and method of assessment it might be possible for a learner to retake the assessment with the IQA present. Learners should be made aware of this procedure at the induction stage of their course.

Tips for dealing with complaints

- Remain professional at all times.
- Avoid having ongoing informal chats with the learner.
- Make sure that someone else is present when you are talking with the learner.
- Keep meetings formal.
- Keep dated, written records of what has been said.
- Follow all procedures carefully.
- Make sure all relevant documents are stored securely.

ASSESSMENT RECORDS

LO306.7.1 Explain the importance of following procedures for the management of information relating to assessment

Assessment records must be kept up to date

A teacher will have to complete and manage a lot of documentation relating to assessment and legislation. It is important that they are familiar with all of the procedures that are in place, along with any paperwork that will need to be completed. All records must be kept as up to date and accurate as possible to provide evidence of the learner's progress. These records will have been agreed with the learner and might be needed as evidence for funding purposes. A line manager might also ask for certain data at any time.

Some assessment records that a teacher might be required to keep →

- Independent learning plans (see page 169)
- Group profiles
- Witness statements
- Tracking documents (see page 225)
- Observation reports
- Learning style results
- Correspondence with employers/parents
- Tutorial records
- Reflective journals (see page 247)
- Action plans
- Results from literacy and numeracy assessments
- Assessment plans
- Feedback sheets
- Recordings from personal discussions

EFFECTIVE QUESTIONS

LO306.7.2 Explain how feedback and questioning contribute to the assessment process

Q: Can you teach without asking questions?
A: Yes, but it won't be very effective.

Asking effective questions is a skill that teachers need to learn as soon as possible.

Scales (2012, page 149) talks about questioning:

> **❝❞**
>
> Like many other skills can be taken for granted, assuming they are such everyday skills that people can just do them naturally.

Questions are used by everyone on a daily basis but a teacher should think carefully about the purpose and reason for the question.

Why ask questions?

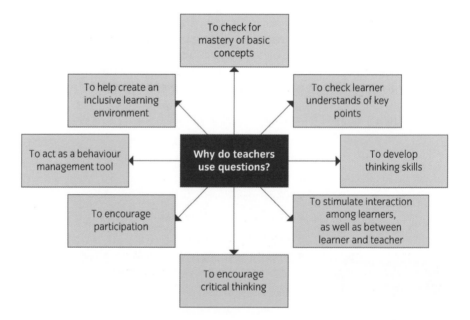

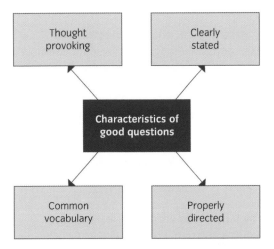

Teachers should think carefully about the type of question that
they ask. A good question is one that has been clearly stated by the
teacher and understood by the learner. An experienced teacher will
use a range of questions to engage all their learners and encourage
participation from learners with a range of abilities.

Types of question

Open questions

These are questions that require an answer using more than one word
or small sentence. They require a learner to think about their answer
and to demonstrate some level of knowledge. Open questions will
challenge a learner and help to keep them engaged and motivated
during a session.

HANDY HINT

Use the following words at the start of your question to help create
an open question: Why? Where? What? When? Who? Which? How?

Closed questions

These are questions that normally only require a 'yes' or 'no' answer
or the one correct answer, for example 'Are lemons a good source of
vitamin C?' Closed questions are good for checking knowledge and
understanding.

Extended questions

These are questions that normally follow another question and require learners to expand or add to the original answer, for example 'What effect does vitamin C have on the body?' The extended question could be directed towards the learner who answered the original question, which is a way of encouraging less confident learners to speak in the session, or it could be directed to a learner who has not answered any questions yet. It normally involves a longer answer. When a teacher continues with a line of questioning on one theme and directs questions at different learners this is called linked questioning.

Hypothetical questions

These questions are used by teachers to encourage learners to consider possible consequences and direct their thinking in a new direction. Hypothetical questions encourage learners to think beyond the obvious and also to stimulate conversations. These are normally thought-provoking questions that will make a learner reflect and consider different aspects of an issue; for example, 'What would you rather be – rich or good looking?' A teacher might start a hypothetical question with phrases such as, 'Imagine that …' 'What would you do if …?', 'Imagine that you are …', 'If you could …' These questions are also useful when there is a lack of resources, facilities or time.

Allow learners time to think

Directed questions

These questions are used by teachers when they want a question to be answered by a particular learner or small group of learners; the teacher is able to name a learner or direct the question to anyone in a particular area of the room. An experienced teacher will use this method to include all learners during the session. Easier questions can be posed to less confident learners while more challenging questions can be directed towards more able learners. This method needs to be used carefully as learners must not feel that they are being 'picked on'.

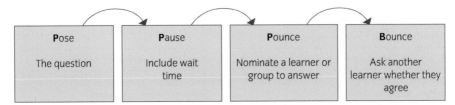

Pose	Pause	Pounce	Bounce
The question	Include wait time	Nominate a learner or group to answer	Ask another learner whether they agree

HANDY HINT

Plan to include the following directed questions in your next session.

'I would like someone who hasn't answered a question yet to answer this next one.'

'I would like someone from this side of the room to answer.' Use your hands to indicate which side.

Your learners will soon get used to you teaching in this way and they will start to answer questions more willingly and earlier in the session.

Consensus
This technique is a good method of getting the attention of all learners. The teacher will ask a question and when they get an answer they will not confirm if it is correct or not. Instead they will ask another learner what they think, then they will ask the whole group; for example, 'Who agrees that the answer is A?' All learners will have to state whether they think it is A or B. The teacher will then reveal the correct answer. This method works well because learners will want to know if they have the correct answer.

CLASSROOM MANAGEMENT

A teacher should plan to use a range of questioning techniques throughout the session and scatter them evenly around the classroom to include all learners. This will help to keep the learners engaged and on task and therefore minimise the risk that they will misbehave.

Things to consider when asking questions

Ask one question at a time	Ask questions of the inattentive
Use the consensus method	Require learners to give complete answers
Avoid 'leading' questions	Encourage learners to speak loudly enough so that everyone can hear
Use questions that require learners to demonstrate their understanding	Keep questions on the subject
Encourage learners to ask questions at any time	Use the correct grammar and terminology
Give adequate consideration to all questions – never evade a question	Write 'key' questions in your lesson plan but also use spontaneous questions
Scatter questions around the entire class	Pose questions that lack a single right answer
Pose questions within the ability of the learner to whom the question is addressed	Ask focused questions

O┐ ▶   HANDY HINT

Remember, if you didn't like the answer then maybe you didn't ask the right question!

See page 96 for details of how to give constructive feedback to learners.

LEGISLATION

LO306.8.1 Explain legal issues, policies and procedures relevant to assessment, including those for confidentiality, health, safety and welfare

Teachers must be aware of the legislation that affects their subject area

As mentioned in Unit 301, a teacher must be aware of all current legislation and codes of practice that apply to the subject area in which they teach. Within the area of assessment it is vital that a teacher particularly takes heed of the following.

The Health and Safety at Work Act (1974)

Whatever assessment method a teacher decides to use it is essential first to assess whether there are any risks to their learners. Some methods will have a higher risk factor than others. Taking a group of learners on a field trip will be a higher physical risk than giving them a multi-choice test. Wherever there is a risk it must be explained clearly to the learners. Some subjects are safer to teach than others; for example, catering, motor vehicle technology or chemistry will pose a higher risk than maths, English or business management.

The Equality Act (2010) and equal opportunity legislation

A teacher should make sure that the assessment methods chosen
do not discriminate against learners in any way. Some learners speak
more than one language so, before the assessment, they should be
asked in which language they would like to be assessed. Teachers
should think carefully about which learners to put together for group
work: a mix of male, female, experienced, less experienced, young,
old, British, Asian etc should be considered beforehand, also taking
cultural differences into account. A teacher needs to be fair and treat
all learners with respect – it could be seen to be rather insulting to put
all the males in one group and all the females in another. The Equality
Act states that educational establishments must modify any physical
barrier and a teacher must make sure that any learner with a disability
is able to access and complete the chosen assessment.

Data Protection Act (1998)

A teacher should keep all information that they have about their
learners in a safe place. Any information with a learner's name on, such
as assessment tracking records, should be locked away and not left
on display when the teacher is away from their desk. The assessment
data that a teacher might collect about a learner should only ever be
shared with other professionals who are involved with that learner; for
example, other members of the teaching team.

Code of Professional Practice (2008)

A teacher should encourage their learners to continually reflect on
the assessment they have completed and build this into their ILP and
action plans.

The Copyright Design and Patents Act (1988)

A teacher must make sure that all resources used for assessment
purposes compile with this legislation.

Every Child Matters (ECM)

A teacher should consider the five outcomes of ECM and try to embed
these within all of the assessment methods that they use.

ACTIVITY

A teacher will need to look at their own subject area and make sure that they are complying with specific legislation for that area. Complete the table below by adding the subject areas that might have to comply with each piece of legislation.

Legislation	Specific subject area
Manual Handling Operations Regulations	
RIDDOR (Reporting of Injuries, Diseases and Dangerous Occurrences)	
COSHH (Control of Substances Hazardous to Health)	
SENDA (Special Educational Needs and Disability Act (2001))	
Electricity at Work Regulations (EAWR)	
The Fire Precautions Act	

USE OF TECHNOLOGY

A teacher gathers learners around a computer

LO306.8.2 Explain the contribution that technology can make to the assessment process

A teacher will need to keep as up to date as possible with any improvements within their own subject area and with any new developments in ICT. Technology is constantly changing and this will provide new possibilities to assess learners. The use of virtual learning environments (VLE) is now common in most organisations to store course information and to provide links to other websites, along with forums and wikis. These allow communication between the teacher and learners and between learners themselves. Assessment resources can be stored on the VLE and tasks set for learners to complete.

Learners will have varying degrees of computer proficiency. Most courses now require work to be computer generated, using a variety of IT resources. Learners are also able to include pictures, diagrams and photos within their work which all help to improve the presentation and raise the standard of work submitted for assessment. However these need to be appropriate to and within the guidelines of the awarding organisation and the qualification level. Some learners prefer to submit their assignments via email or compile an e-learning portfolio as this saves on paper.

The internet has made it very easy for learners to research and access information. Most learners are happy to use electronic resources to complete assessments.

ICT resources that can support learning

■ Flip cameras	■ Email
■ Photoshop	■ Virtual learning environment (VLE)
■ PowerPoint	■ Wikis
■ Interactive boards	■ Spreadsheets used for tracking documents
■ Internet	■ Teachers can use online tests to assess learners with instant results
■ Mobile phones and tablet devices	

HANDY HINT

There is a lot of inaccurate information on the internet. Learners should use 'Google scholar' when undertaking any research, as this only contains approved, academic work.

The use of technology within assessment in teaching has:

- improved the presentation of assignments
- reduced the amount of marking a teachers has to do
- improved communication between teachers and learners
- provided some assessment resources for teachers
- reduced the amount of paper being used.

EQUALITY AND DIVERSITY

LO306.8.3 Evaluate requirements for equality and diversity and, where appropriate, bilingualism in relation to assessment

All learners deserve to be treated fairly

Equality means treating all learners fairly regardless of race, religion, gender, disability, age and sexual orientation. Diversity is about valuing the differences between learners. This has been covered in detail in Unit 301. Once the teacher has decided what assessment will be use, they will then need to consider if it is suitable for all of their learners.

In today's culture a teacher might be faced with learners from a range of different backgrounds and with a variety of different needs. Whatever assessment method is chosen it is important that it will give *all* learners an *equal* chance of passing it. A teacher should take time to get to know their learners and complete an assessment plan with them.

It might be necessary for the teacher to adapt the assessment method. This can be achieved by:

- using a larger font for learners who are partially sighted
- printing instructions on coloured paper for learners with dyslexia
- providing a signer for any learner who is deaf or partially hearing
- providing a translator if English is their second language
- providing a scribe if writing quickly is difficult
- speaking clearly
- using plain English
- using correct English (avoiding jargon and difficult words)
- ensuring that there is enough space for wheelchair access.

Learners should be able to demonstrate their knowledge and understanding more easily if the teacher chooses an assessment method that will help and not hinder them. A professional discussion might be a fairer choice for a learner who finds it difficult to write things down, due to their dyslexia, or because English is their second language.

Bilingual learners

Many bilingual learners will be able to demonstrate a good understanding of learning in a practical skill; however, they may find it difficult to record everything in a written format.

Teachers need to ensure that bilingual learners receive enough learning support to help them succeed in their learning. This will involve:

- using clear communication
- providing one-to-one support for learners before the session
- providing learning support assistants to work with the learner and teacher during the session
- providing support for a group of learners
- adapting or developing specific resources to support the learning
- using plain English
- encouraging bilingual learners to work alongside learners who are of a similar ability
- implementing a buddy system so that some peer support is also in place
- using good models of written and spoken English.

REFLECTIVE PRACTICE AND CONTINUING PROFESSIONAL DEVELOPMENT

LO306.8.4 Explain the value of reflective practice and continuing professional development in the assessment process

Learners should be encouraged to reflect on the assessment process that they are undertaking. Trying to be reflective is a skill that a learner must learn to master if they are going to be effective within their own subject area. Once the learner has completed the assessment they need to look at themselves objectively and ask some of the following questions:

- Have I learnt anything?
- What would I do differently next time?
- What skills do I lack?
- What knowledge do I lack?
- What did I enjoy the most?
- What did I enjoy the least?
- Do I need help to improve?
- Where can I get that help from?
- Who can help me?

The answers to these questions can be built into an action plan or ILP and, with the help of their teacher, peers or line manager, learners should be able to set goals that will lead them to develop and improve their knowledge, skill and confidence. This will form part of a learner's CPD evidence.

HANDY HINT

A reflective learning journal is an ideal way of helping learners to think in a reflective way. This is a skill that takes time to develop so make sure that it is completed during and after each assessment. A standard form with tick boxes may be a more appropriate starting point at Entry level – space for free comments can be introduced gradually as learners become more confident.

A learner needs to take responsibility for their own development and must be able to plan and record their own progress throughout the assessment process. Being more self-aware will help a learner to develop the skills that they need to become a professional teacher.

UNIT SUMMARY

This unit has identified some of the benefits and challenges of assessing learners. The way in which assessment is used to support individual learners has been discussed, as well as the importance of the teacher choosing the correct method of assessment to use with their learners. The differences between initial, formative and summative types of assessment have been explored, along with how important it is for the teacher to make assessment decisions fairly. Within any form of assessment there will always be risks. These risks have been identified and ways to minimise these risks have been examined.

This unit has explored and discussed the importance of including peer and self-assessment to help increase a learner's motivation and participation. Using a holistic approach to assessment lends itself to a successful learning experience and draws on theory that enables learners to develop a deeper understanding of the subject.

Ensuring that any assessment is carried out in an appropriate way, and that all assessments are valid, reliable and fair, has also been a focus of this unit along with the importance of both quality control and standardisation. Some helpful tips and suggestions of good practice have been included to relate this theory to practice.

The way in which assessment fits in with current legislation has also been discussed and examples of how assessment methods can be adapted to include legislation have been stated. The unit has also looked at the correct procedures that need to be followed when there are disputes concerning assessment. Other aspects covered in this unit include how feedback and questioning contribute to the assessment procedure.

ASSIGNMENT FOCUS

This unit provides you with information about assessing learners using a variety of methods. The advantages and limitations of each method have been explored as well as how a teacher ensures the quality of any assessment used. You will have to demonstrate your understanding of the theory by putting it into practice with real learners. Some of the learning outcomes will be assessed by a piece of written work, such as an assignment. You will need to cover all of the following assessment criteria in order to evidence your knowledge and understanding successfully.

Assessment criteria

Unit 305

1.1 Explain the purposes of types of assessment used in education and training

1.2 Describe characteristics of different methods of assessment in education and training

1.3 Compare the strengths and limitations of different assessment methods in relation to meeting individual learner needs

1.4 Explain how different assessment methods can be adapted to meet individual learner needs

2.1 Explain why it is important to involve learners and others in the assessment process

2.2 Explain the role and use of peer and self-assessment in the assessment process

2.3 Identify sources of information that should be made available to learners and others involved in the assessment process

3.1 Describe key features of constructive feedback

3.2 Explain how constructive feedback contributes to the assessment process

3.3 Explain ways to give constructive feedback to learners

4.1 Explain the need to keep records of assessment of learning

4.2 Summarise the requirements for keeping records of assessment in an organisation

Unit 306

1.1 Explain the function of assessment in learning and development

1.2 Define the key concepts and principles of assessment

1.3 Explain the responsibilities of the assessor

1.4 Identify the regulations and requirements relevant to assessment in own area of practice

2.1 Compare the strengths and limitations of a range of assessment methods with reference to the needs of individual learners

3.1 Summarise key factors to consider when planning assessment

3.2 Evaluate the benefits of using a holistic approach to assessment

3.3 Explain how to plan a holistic approach to assessment

3.4 Summarise the types of risks that may be involved in assessment in own area of responsibility

3.5 Explain how to minimise risks through the planning process

4.1 Explain the importance of involving the learner and others in the assessment process

4.2 Summarise types of information that should be made available to learners and others involved in the assessment process

4.3 Explain how peer and self-assessment can be used effectively to promote learner involvement and personal responsibility in the assessment of learning

4.4 Explain how assessment arrangements can be adapted to meet the needs of individual learners

5.1 Explain how to judge whether evidence is:

- sufficient
- authentic
- current

5.2 Explain how to ensure that assessment decisions are:

- made against specified criteria
- valid
- reliable
- fair

6.1 Evaluate the importance of quality assurance in the assessment process

6.2 Summarise quality assurance and standardisation procedures in own area of practice

6.3 Summarise the procedures to follow when there are disputes concerning assessment in own area of practice

7.1 Explain the importance of following procedures for the management of information relating to assessment

7.2 Explain how feedback and questioning contribute to the assessment process

8.1 Explain the legal issues, policies and procedures relevant to assessment, including those for confidentiality, health, safety and welfare

8.2 Explain the contribution that technology can make to the assessment process

8.3 Evaluate requirements for equality and diversity and, where appropriate, bilingualism in relation to assessment

8.4 Explain the value of reflective practice and continuing professional development in the assessment process

Tips

You might want to consider the following when planning your assignment:

- What are the key principles of assessment?
- State reasons why assessment is needed within your subject area.
- What are your main responsibilities as an assessor?
- Explain how your learners are assessed initially and at a formative and summative level.
- Give some examples of the assessment methods that you use with your learners.
- State some of the advantages and limitations of each method and why you use them.
- Consider how you are able to meet the needs of your learners and include some examples.
- Include why it is important to build a rapport with your learners and state how you get to know them.
- State the difference between formal and informal assessment and include some examples from your own subject area.
- What are the key factors you have to consider when planning assessment?
- How do you plan a holistic approach to assessment with your own learners?
- Give examples of how you adapt your assessment methods to consider the learning styles of your learners.
- Consider the risks involved with assessment and give examples of how to minimise these risks.
- What type of information might you have to make available to others who are involved in the assessment of your learners?
- Include examples of how and why you include self- and peer assessment.
- How do you make sure that all assessment is valid, reliable, current, sufficient and fair?
- Explain your role within quality assurance. Include reference to standardisation, internal and external verification.
- Discuss the procedures you have in place for keeping assessment records.
- Explain any legislation that you need to be aware of within your subject area.
- How do you include the use of technology within your assessment of learners?
- State examples of reflective practice and CPD in your assessment process.

Helpful information, suggestions and tips

INTRODUCTION

This unit has been included to assist learners with the writing of the reflective learning journal; it also covers how to reference work, how to prepare for a micro-teach session and how to study for, structure and present work. It includes lots of practical tips and suggestions that will help learners pass the Level 3 Award in Education and Training.

BACKGROUND

It is worth remembering that the requirements from each awarding organisation will be different, as will the requirements from the organisation that a teacher/trainer works for. It is the responsibility of the teacher to ensure that they are clear on exactly what they are expected to do. All teachers/trainers are also different and learners should always check with their teacher exactly how and what they have to do. These differences between organisations might include the way in which work needs to be presented or how feedback is given for a micro-teach. The core aspects remain the same and link to the learning outcomes for each unit.

It is important for learners to record and reflect on their own progress throughout their course. By keeping a reflective learning journal learners are encouraged to examine their own experiences and learning and plan to use the new skills they have learnt within their future teaching.

At level 3 there is not a requirement that written work needs to be referenced, but a section on referencing is included as this will help learners to start appreciating how and why it is important. While researching for this qualification, learners should try to expand their reading and written skills. Some learners might choose to include quotes and a bibliography within their work, especially if they are thinking of progressing onto a level 4 course in the future. Some learners might already hold a higher qualification and want to reference their work. This is considered to be good practice and will encourage learners to 'have a go' at referencing during the Award in Education and Training.

The micro-teach section offers some practical advice on how to prepare and present a micro-teach. Checklists have been included to help learners make sure that they have considered all aspects of this assessment and that they are fully prepared before the start. It gives examples of how the micro-teach might be structured and how feedback is given.

Another key aspect of this unit is to consider how work should be presented. The study skills section will provide guidance on how to present work along with tips on how to manage time and meet deadlines. It also offers help with note-taking and reading skills. Key aspects are as follows.

- How to write a reflective learning journal
- The benefits of a reflective learning journal
- How to use quotes and references
- How to write a bibliography
- How to prepare for your micro-teach
- How to manage your time
- Where to study
- How to read
- How to take notes
- How to write assignments
- Tips on grammar

REFLECTIVE LEARNING JOURNAL

❝❞

A sign of a true professional is to undergo an experience, reflect on it and learn so there is an improvement in professional practice.

(Reece and Walker, 2007, page 422)

Reflection

It is a requirement of the course for all learners to keep a reflective learning journal. The teacher should encourage learners to reflect and write down how they are feeling at the start of the course, at key points throughout the course and at the end of the course. After each session learners should think about what they have learnt and how they are able to develop their skills as a result of the session. They should set themselves some action points on how they are going to manage this. Kolb's learning cycle is often referred to as providing the foundation for learning from experience; he describes the cycle of stages that a learner will go through.

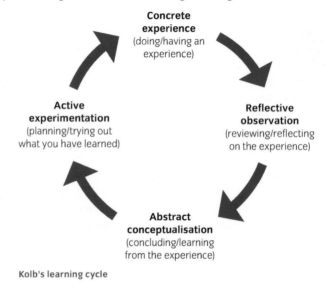

Concrete experience
(doing/having an experience)

Reflective observation
(reviewing/reflecting on the experience)

Abstract conceptualisation
(concluding/learning from the experience)

Active experimentation
(planning/trying out what you have learned)

Kolb's learning cycle

What is a reflective learning journal?

A reflective learning journal is a document that a learner keeps from the start of a course. It should grow and develop with the learner as it is used by them to record their progress. A learner should regularly make contributions to it in much the same way as someone might keep a personal diary. Learners should be encouraged to think about what they have learnt and how this knowledge might change the way that they do things in the future. It should be a helpful and beneficial piece of work that eventually can be used to look back on learning and so track progress. A journal is a record of both thoughts and reflections and, by writing it down, a learner will start to think about their own learning in a different way. This should also encourage them to focus on the way that they react to situations and to what they have read.

A learner keeps a hand written journal which can be completed at any time

The benefits of keeping a reflective journal

A learner themselves will be the person who benefits the most from keeping a reflective learning journal. The fact that a journal is being kept is an incentive for a learner to keep improving their knowledge, understanding, performance and ability.

It has been said, 'You don't know what you know till you've written it down.' When learners keep a reflective learning journal they are also tracking the progress that they are making. Patterns might emerge which can make the learner question certain aspects of their own learning or knowledge and targets can then be set and monitored by the learner.

How to write a reflective journal

The key for learners when writing a reflective journal is for them to think about how they felt. The most common mistake is that learners write in a descriptive way, not a reflective way (see Example 1).

EXAMPLE 1

Tonight was the first night of my new course. It was a teacher training course which started at 6pm. There were about twelve other people in the class.

This is a very descriptive entry and it will not encourage the learner to think about or challenge what they were feeling on the first night of their new course. Therefore they are unlikely to analyse it further or set themselves any targets.

A more reflective account will mean that the learner will have to ask themselves some questions (see Example 2).

EXAMPLE 2

It was the first night of my new course, although I don't normally get nervous, I did feel a little anxious about this as I haven't attended an educational establishment for over fifteen years. I felt much better as soon as I met the teacher who appeared to be really nice and seemed genuinely pleased to see me. There was a nice atmosphere in the room and I felt a lot happier as it didn't feel like school at all. I must remember to make sure I am as welcoming to my learners if I ever get a class to teach. It was a teacher training course which started at 6pm so this meant that I had to go straight from work and I didn't have time for anything to eat before I got there. The teacher gave us a quick tour of the college and pointed out where there was a coffee shop that sold snacks. I had missed this on the way in so next week I should have time to grab a sandwich and a coffee before class. There was another guy called Mannan who said the same thing and we have arranged to meet before the class starts next week. The teacher said that she appreciated that some learners will be coming straight from work and that it is important to make sure we have something to eat first otherwise we won't concentrate so well. Although she made a little joke of this it did make me think about the times at school when I found it difficult to concentrate when I was thirsty or hungry. I felt that she had our best interests at heart but I also wondered if she was making sure that we were all mentally prepared for her class.

There were about twelve other people in the class. They all looked so clever and I was really conscious of the fact that I haven't undertaken any study for such a long time. I did begin to question why I had enrolled onto this course. However we all had to introduce someone else to the rest of the group and I found myself beginning to relax as my partner Jayne seemed really nice and I think she was even more nervous than me! I wonder if the teacher chooses this activity on purpose as it really helped me and the rest of the class, to relax or if she was just trying to find out a bit more about us. Both I guess …I have made a note of this icebreaker to use at the start of any teaching I get in the future. I hope that I will be able to make my learners relax as well on the first session of my course. I think that I might go back next week …

The same three points have been covered but Example 2 clearly demonstrates that the learner has started to reflect in a positive way. Wilson (2009, page 246) talks about constructive, honest help of the teacher.

A learner recording her own reflections in her journal

Teachers often ask for the reflective learning journal to be handed in at the start of the second session so that they are able to check that learners are writing in a reflective way. An example template is shown on the next page.

This form should be used to record your reflections as you progress through your qualification. You should link your reflections to reading, principles, theories and professional values as relevant.

REFLECTIVE LEARNING JOURNAL

This form should be used to record your reflections as you progress through your qualification. You should link your reflections to reading, principles, theories and professional values as relevant.

Analysis of challenges that I faced in unit/task:

How I dealt with this, and why I took this approch:

What went well and why:

What I need to do to improve and how I plan to do this:

Reflective learning journal template

Things that can be mentioned in a reflective learning journal

- Interesting points that a learner has discovered within their reading. This might require further research.
- After a class a learner could reflect on the main learning points from that session.
- From which activity did they learn most? Which did they learn least? Why was that?
- What are they doing well and what can they develop further?
- The learner could comment on how well the course is meeting their needs.
- They could also consider their skill levels in literacy, numeracy and ICT.

Learners are able to type or write their reflective learning journal. A notebook that is kept by the learner can be written in at any point and it might take the form of notes, bullet points or written prose. It is also possible for a learner to record their journal orally.

Each learner will have their own preference and should choose a method that best suits their learning style and ability. More reflection might be needed for some sessions than for others so it is impossible to prescribe how much should be written at a given time. However if a reflective learning journal is to be really effective it should be updated and reviewed regularly. It is also a good opportunity for learners to raise any issues, show the extent of their reading and set themselves targets that emerge from their reading.

A journal should be something that a learner can read through at a later date to remind them of what they have learnt on the course.

HANDY HINT

Write clearly and in a logical way as you might not remember *all* the details when you read it back in the future.

Keeping a reflective learning journal
Keeping a reflective learning journal is quite often a new experience for learners and they might find it difficult to get started. It can be hard for learners to determine whether reflecting upon their learning is a natural process that they go through on a daily basis or if it is a forced process that they were adhering to as a requirement of the course.

Learners might need to be encouraged to look at their learning in a different way. Quite often what they need to write down are their thoughts. Then as they get more used to this process learners should start to feel that they can extend their thinking by writing.

The advantages of this are that:

- reflection helps the learner to step back and put experiences and developments into perspective
- it should help the learner to realise their own capacity to learn
- they should realise that reflection is a part of the learning experience
- it will give the learner a greater understanding of their learning process
- encouraging a learner to be fully in charge of their own learning experiences will help them to feel more able to guide the learning experiences of others.

Being a reflective learner will help to make you a reflective teacher
A reflective learner will continually strive to improve themselves. They are more likely to learn from their mistakes by evaluating what went wrong and working out how to stop the same thing from happening again. They will be more prepared to try out new ideas and take calculated risks. As they become more aware of the gaps in their knowledge they will realise the need to keep up to date with their subject knowledge and skills and set possible targets on a regular basis. Schön (1983) talks about the need for reflection-in-action, which could be described as 'thinking on your feet', and reflection-on-action, which is thinking about something after the event has taken place. It encourages learners to look at their experiences, connect with their feelings, and put theory into practice.

> **❝❞**
>
> The practitioner allows himself to experience surprise, puzzlement, or confusion in a situation which he finds uncertain or unique. He reflects on the phenomenon before him, and on the prior understandings which have been implicit in his behaviour. He carries out an experiment which serves to generate both a new understanding of the phenomenon and a change in the situation.
>
> (Schön, 1983, page 68)

REFERENCING

Teachers will encourage learners to do as much reading around their given subject as possible. This will help to increase the learner's knowledge and understanding of the subject and stimulate independent learning. It also exposes learners to new theories and helps them to formulate new ideas. The learner might then want to include some of the information that they have read about within their own work. However, they will be in danger of plagiarism, passing other people's work off as their own, unless they follow the rules of citation and referencing. When any part of someone else's work is included in an assignment written by a learner then it is vital that the learner makes sure that the reader is aware of this.

Including other people's views and ideas will:

- raise the academic standard of the work
- help present what they want to say in a concise way
- support what they are saying
- demonstrate to the reader that some reading and research has been undertaken.

How to use quotes and references

There are several different ways to include quotes, cite other authors and reference work.

A learner should check with their teacher which style or method is required for the course that they are on. The most common style of referencing is called Harvard APA. All referencing works in a similar way although the way that the information is presented and the format will differ between each style.

A library is a great source of free information

Learners need to consider what is included in their assignment that they did not actually write and how to direct the reader to the original source. There are rules that will need to be followed to achieve this.

Referencing within a text

A learner can read about a given subject and then summarise this in their own words within their assignment. Even if they are using their own words the ideas and theories that have been formulated are from someone else. It is only correct that credit for these ideas should be given to the original author. This can be done within the text of the assignment by stating the surname of the author and the year of the published work along with the page number.

EXAMPLE 1

According to Scales (2010, page 158) questioning techniques are not always fully considered and used by a teacher.

HANDY HINT

Some information will need to be presented inside brackets. This is normally the details of when (the year) it was published and where (the page number) the information can be located. It might help you to think that if information is in brackets it is to identify the source and it doesn't actually form part of the quote.

A learner might find a really good phrase or section that they would like to include within their assignment as a direct quote. This can be done in a similar way if the quote is quite small (under 30 words in length).

EXAMPLE 2

… essay, essay, essay, essay, essay, essay, essay, essay, essay, essay, essay, essay, essay. According to Scales (2010, page 158), 'Questioning in teaching and learning is frequently taken for granted, but it is a skill which needs conscious development if we are to become effective teachers.' Essay, essay, essay, essay, essay, essay, essay, essay, essay, essay, essay, essay, essay, essay, essay, essay …

When using a direct quote it is vital that it is copied exactly as it appeared in the original source. The learner must not alter it in any way. The source of the quote will appear in brackets along with the year and the page number. This will enable the reader to find the original source in case they would like to read further.

When the direct quote is over 30 words then it will need to be presented in a different way. The learner should separate it from the rest of the text by including a line space between the text and the quote. This will help to make the quote stand out from the learner's own words. It should also be indented on both sides.

EXAMPLE 3

… essay, essay, essay, essay, essay, essay, essay, essay, essay, essay, essay, essay, essay, essay, essay, essay …

> 'People unconsciously take messages from the arrangement of furniture, and are annoyed by messages that are contradictory or confusing. People sitting in rows talking to the backs of each other's heads miss subtleties of communication such as facial expressions, eye contact, and humour. How can they see this as a discussion? You have to move people and furniture to create the right environment.'
>
> (Minton, 1987, page 188)

… essay, essay , essay, essay , essay, essay , essay, essay, essay, essay , essay, essay, essay, essay , essay, essay, essay, essay , essay, essay , essay, essay , essay, essay …

HANDY HINT

Quotes are included within the word count of your assignment. You can save on words by removing unwanted words from the start, middle or end of a quote. When this happens you will need to indicate that text has been removed by replacing the missing text with three dots ….

'… the teacher should play to the strengths of the learner when trying to raise enthusiasm in learning.'

(Wilson, 2009, page 181)

The learner might want to summarise something in their own words that they have read in a book where the author is summarising the work of another author. They should start with the person who said it and then state in whose book the quote has been cited.

EXAMPLE 4

Kohler (1950) identified that there was much more to learning than getting an automatic response from learners (cited in Walklin, 1990, page 8).

The same principles apply when learners want to reference a website and there is the name of the author and a date. Sometimes there is not a page number; in this case the paragraph and line number will have to be used.

EXAMPLE 5

All students should have the opportunity to undertake high quality and challenging study programmes tailored to meet their individual needs and ambitions.

(The Department for Education, 2012, para 1:1)

HANDY HINT

Unless you have a lot of time on your hands, don't try to read the textbook from cover to cover. Use the index at the back of the book to locate the topic you want to research and make notes that you can use in your essay. Don't forget to note down the author, year and page number so you can reference it easily when you come to write up your notes.

When a learner wants to summarise in their own words what they have read on a website they might have to reference the title of the website if the author has not been stated. Similarly, there might not be a date. This will need to be referenced as nd (no date).

EXAMPLE 6

The Wolf report suggests that the post-16 funding formula needs to be reviewed if changes are to take place within 16–19 education.

(The Department for Education, 2012, para 2 and 3)

Include a range of quotes within your work but remember not to overload your work with other people's ideas and views. Your teacher wants to know what *you* have learnt and what *you* think so use the quotes to back up what *you* are saying.

Bibliography

The bibliography is a list of all the sources that a learner has used while doing any research for their assignment. It gives evidence that research has been undertaken, in preparing to write the assignment.

The bibliography could consist of books, journals, websites or other sources of information that have been consulted. The learner might not have quoted directly from all of these sources but each source will have contributed to the knowledge and understanding the learner has acquired about that subject. There will be a set format for presenting this information, depending on which style or method is used.

The author's surname should go first followed by their initial; if there is more than one author then they are listed in the same order as the names appear on the book. The year is then included, in brackets followed by the title of the book, which needs to be presented in italics. (Article titles are often presented within quotation marks, and journal titles in italics.) If it is a second or third edition then this should be mentioned next, followed by the name of the places where it was published and then finally the name of the publisher.

This procedure is the same for web references, except the date of retrieval will also need to be included.

EXAMPLE 7: BIBLIOGRAPHY

The Department for Education (2012) *16–19 Funding Formula Review – Funding Full Participation and Study Programmes for Young People.* Accessed 21 March 2013 from: https://www.education.gov.uk/publications/standard/Post16Learning/Page1/EFA-00073-2012.

Minton, D. (2005) *Teaching Skills in Further and Adult Education (3rd edition).* Tunbridge Wells: Gray Publishing.

Petty. G. (2009) *Teaching Today* (4th edition). Cheltenham: Nelson Thornes Ltd.

Scales, P. (2008) *Teaching in the Lifelong Learning Sector.* Maidenhead: Open University Press.

Walklin. L. (2000) *Teaching and Learning in Further and Adult Education* (2nd edition). Cheltenham: Nelson Thornes Ltd.

STUDY SKILLS

Check out online bookshops for second-hand copies of textbooks. They are often in excellent condition and you can always resell them once your course is over.

Reference list

A reference list is a list of all the sources from which a learner has quoted within their work. This can be taken from the bibliography with the page number added after the publisher's name. This will enable the reader to find the quote in its original source more quickly.

EXAMPLE 8: REFERENCE LIST

Minton, D. (2005) *Teaching Skills in Further and Adult Education* (3rd edition). Tunbridge Wells: Gray Publishing. Page 188, 241.

Petty. G. (2009) *Teaching Today* (4th edition). Cheltenham: Nelson Thornes Ltd.

Scales, P. (2008) *Teaching in the Lifelong Learning Sector.* Maidenhead: Open University Press. Page 158.

Walklin. L. (2000) *Teaching and Learning in Further and Adult Education* (2nd edition). Cheltenham: Nelson Thornes Ltd. Page 8.

Wilson. L (2009) *Practical Teaching: A Guide to PTLLS and DTLLS.* Andover: Cenage Learning EMEA. Page 181.

THE MICRO-TEACH

The micro-teach involves delivering the teaching practice session/s, demonstrating a selection of teaching and learning approaches to engage and motivate learners. You need to communicate appropriately and effectively with learners.

A learner includes his peers in a micro-teach session

Micro-teach in action

The micro-teach is an essential part of the course and it will enable a learner to demonstrate some of the skills and techniques that they have learnt. It will also show a teacher that a learner has the ability to put the theory they have learnt into practice. It takes place towards the end of the course and it is normally recorded so that the learner is able to watch it at a later date. This will help them to evaluate, reflect and improve on their own practice.

The micro-teach takes place in front of the rest of the group, who will take on the role of the learners. The teacher will also be present but acting as an independent observer. Once the learner has finished the micro-teach they will be asked to evaluate how they thought it went by writing down their initial thoughts. The rest of the group will also write down what they thought was good about the micro-teach, what they thought needed improving and how they think the improvements could be made. The teacher is required to complete a more detailed form which will include comments on preparation, planning, delivery and monitoring. See below.

Appendix 1   Forms

Form 1   Observation of practice form

Name of candidate		Date	
Aim of session (as on session plan)		Length of session	
A total minimum of 15 minutes of micro-teaching/teaching practice must be observed		Length of observation	

Preparation

Did the candidate	Y/N	Comments
check the environment and resources beforehand?		
take into account any health and safety issues?		
ensure there were enough resources for all learners?		
have a session plan to show: aim/objectives/learning outcomes?		

Delivery

Did the candidate	Y/N	Comments
deliver an introduction, main content and conclusion?		
establish and maintain a rapport with the individual/group?		

Appendix 1   Forms

Form 1   Observation of practice form

demonstrate knowledge of their subject?		
take into account different learning styles, eg VARK?		
use a range of activities as appropriate?		
use relevant resources as appropriate?		
communicate clearly and effectively?		
appear confident and professional?		
take into account entitlement, equality, differentiation, inclusivity and diversity?		
Monitoring **Did the candidate**	**Y/N**	**Comments:**
ask questions and involve the individual/group where appropriate?		
give positive feedback where relevant?		
summarise the session?		

achieve their aim/objective/ learning outcomes?		
clear the area afterwards?		
Identify opportunities for learners to provide feedback?		
evaluate their session?		

Give examples of how learning took place:

Overall feedback:

Observer signature: _____ Name: _____ Date: _____

Once the micro-teach has finished then feedback will normally take place. This part of the session is facilitated by the teacher and it could be completed in several different ways. The most commonly used methods are given as examples on the next page.

EXAMPLE: METHOD 1

Note: The teacher stays at the back of the room throughout this method and facilitates from there.

Once the micro-teach has finished everyone will complete the feedback forms. The learner who did the micro-teach will then briefly feedback their initial thoughts on how they thought it went, to the whole group.

The teacher will then ask all the other learners in turn to state one positive feature of the micro-teach. It is important that everyone feeds back and looks at the person who did the micro-teach, not at the teacher. Once this has been completed they will then have to state one aspect that they feel could be improved and offer a suggestion as to how to do it. One advantage to this method is that that everyone will benefit from the feedback, not just the learner who completed the micro-teach. Giving constructive feedback is a skill that all teachers have to learn and using this method offers learners the opportunity to develop and practise these skills. It also takes some of the pressure away from the person who has just completed their micro-teach. The teacher should then ask if anyone would like to add anything before covering any points that have been missed.

EXAMPLE: METHOD 2

Once the micro-teach has finished everyone will complete the feedback forms. The teacher will then take the learner who completed the micro-teach to another room and give them some feedback while the rest of the group helps set up for the next micro-teach.

This method allows the learner to receive detailed feedback from an experienced teacher in private. However it does not help develop the feedback skills for the rest of the group. The teacher will have to repeat themselves several times if learners are all making the same mistake.

EXAMPLE: METHOD 3

Once the learner has finished their micro-teach they will receive verbal feedback from each member of the group in turn. Their peers will then complete written feedback while the tutor is privately feeding back to the deliverer in another room.

Whichever method is chosen, all of the written feedback from peers and the teacher will be given to the learner who completed the micro-teach to enable them to use it as part of their evaluation and reflection.

Choosing the correct subject for a micro-teach

Learners will be encouraged to choose a topic from the subject area that they intend to teach in the future or from a subject in which they are very interested. A learner should think carefully about what aspect of the chosen subject to deliver. There will be elements within every subject that are easier to deliver as a micro-teach. It will help if there is a practical element as this will enable the rest of the group to get involved by doing something. As the rest of the group will be acting as the learners, it might be necessary to modify the delivery to suit their ability. It is also a good idea to take into account what they might find interesting and fun.

Practical micro-teaches get everyone involved

The teacher should talk with the learner about their choice of subject and how they intend to deliver the micro-teach. This should take place a few weeks before the micro-teach in order for the learner to make any changes to their planning, as suggested by the teacher.

Planning

The learner will be asked to produce a lesson plan for the length of the micro-teach (this might vary a little between each centre but it will be a minimum of 15 minutes). A copy of this lesson plan will be given to the teacher before the start of the micro-teach (see lesson plan template below). Careful consideration will need to be given as to what can actually be achieved within the time available.

HANDY HINT

Don't be too ambitious. Keep it simple. Remember to plan an introduction, main content and a conclusion.

Objectives need to be SMART (see page 86); the smarter the objectives then the easier it will be to check that they have been met. Learners must think about the resources that are available and the type of environment that they will be teaching in. They should consider the best way to set up the room and what classroom layout would best suit what they have planned to teach (see page 69). They will also have to consider which teaching activities will work best and whether there is a good balance of teacher and learner involvement. The different learning styles of the learners will also need to be taken in to account, along with any special considerations that their learners may have. They will also need to consider what assessment methods to use.

Micro-teach tips

- Keep it simple!
- Engage the learners.
- Choose a topic from your subject area.
- Make sure it is something that you know well, so that you will feel confident in your knowledge.
- Make sure that the subject you choose can be taught within the allocated time.
- It can be a good idea to give the learners an activity to do as this will help to make you feel less nervous.
- Use resources, but remember that any giving out of hand-outs during the micro-teach will be counted in the time. It will save time to do this during the set-up/prep time.
- Try out slides or presentations in advance to ensure that everything works. Remember that some PowerPoint versions are not always compatible.
- Run through it at home in front of someone.
- Timing will be strict! Make sure that you practise beforehand.
- Make sure that all resources are ready beforehand.
- Smile (even though your hands are shaking!).

During the micro-teach

The teacher does not expect learners to deliver a perfect micro-teach; however they do expect each learner to deliver a good or satisfactory micro-teach. A learner should think in advance about some of the things their teacher and peers will be looking for during the micro-teach. It is a good idea to run through the micro-teach at home and try to consider the following:

- Am I speaking clearly?
- Can everyone hear me?
- Am I talking too quickly or too slowly?
- What is my body language saying?
- What is the body language of my learners saying?
- Am I using learners' names?
- Do I appear confident?
- Can everyone understand what I am saying?

- Are my questions appropriate and/or challenging?
- Am I including all learners?
- Are these activities appropriate for the learner group?
- Am I using a good variety of activities?
- Are the learners working effectively – either individually or in groups/pairs?
- Is there any reason why I should change my planned teaching activities or resources?
- Am I allowing too much (or too little) time for any activity?
- Have I included some checking questions: for example 'Did everyone see how I did that?'; 'Would you like me to go over those steps again?'
- Have I checked that all of the objectives have been met?

HANDY HINT

Remember: if it goes wrong, don't worry. It is how you react to this that will be the indicator of your teaching skills. Don't panic, stay calm and carry on. Learn from your mistakes.

Afterwards (self-evaluation)

Once the micro-teach has finished the learner must ensure that the room is left clean and tidy. All evaluation paperwork will need to be completed and the feedback process completed. A learner should be encouraged to reflect on their own performance as soon as the session has finished. This reflection will differ from any reflection that they undertake at a later date. Time will change the way that a learner thinks about what they did or how they did it. Learners will also be able to reflect again once they have watched their micro-teach recording.

These are some points to consider for the reflective learning journal:

- How did you feel before you delivered your micro-teach?
- How did you feel straight after it?
- How did you feel when your peers were doing their micro-teach sessions?
- Would you have done anything differently?
- What will you do differently next time?

STUDY SKILLS

❝❞

Writing like everything else in life is a process not a product. You learn to write by writing, and you have to write something over and again, and again, to discover what it is you have to say – and to say it. Writing it once will not do that!

(Minton, 2005, page 342)

A future learner checks the suitability of a course before enrolling

Considerations before enrolling

Before a learner enrols onto a course they should first consider whether it is the right time for them to be undertaking learning. It is wise for them to talk with the teacher before they enrol to ensure that they are fully aware of the course content and how much study time they will need to allow for. Whatever the length of a course, learners will always have other commitments that should be taken into consideration before enrolling.

HANDY HINT

Don't be fooled into thinking that because it is a longer course you will have plenty of time. What it means is that you will have more to do!

Equal consideration should also be given to short courses because if one session is missed there is so little time for a learner to catch up.

Introducing study skills

A teacher should assist learners to use the correct techniques and learning methods to enable them to take ownership of their own leaning. Learners who have a good study plan and recognise their own way of learning (learning styles – see page 52) are more likely to meet their deadlines and succeed on their course.

Northedge (2007, page 13) talks about learners investing in their own development and needing well-developed learning skills. Teachers need to plan some study skills delivery as early as possible on all of their courses to enable their learners to achieve this. This will help to support learners and make them think about when is the best time for them to complete any work outside the delivered session.

This will take some time out of the session but it will be time well spent if a teacher includes some instruction on how to help learners organise their study time and study methods to help maximise the learning that is taking place.

Time management

Managing time can be difficult, especially when a learner has family and work commitments. One of the first things that a learner needs to consider is when they will be able to study outside the classroom. Learners should be encouraged to take responsibility for their own learning and organise their time to enable them to meet every deadline. All learners are different and while some learners will have plenty of time, others, for a variety of reasons, will not. Learners should think about their weekly timetable and make sure that they have allowed enough time to complete all their work.

STUDY SKILLS

It might be tempting to block out a large portion of time to concentrate on your assignment, but it might be better to think about smaller, more frequent study periods. You won't be as effective during a long study period, as you will start to lose concentration. If this is the only option, take regular short breaks.

Weekly plan

This is a good activity that will help learners focus on everything that they have to do in a week and therefore it will highlight what available time they have for any study. It works quite well if this is completed in class (if there is time to do this).

The learner needs to complete a 24/7 grid (see the next page) for a typical week. First learners need to shade in the hours that they normally sleep. They then add their course timetable using a different colour pen. They will also need to shade in travelling time. Next they should use another colour for anything they do on a regular basis that cannot be changed, such as working, an exercise class or taking the children swimming. Another colour should be used for anything they do that they do on a regular basis that could be changed, such as meeting a friend for coffee, food shopping, etc.

Learners are then encouraged to look at the spaces within their 24/7 grid and consider which days and times would be best for them to study. Learners should consider at this point what time of day they prefer to study. Are they a night owl or an early bird? Depending on the time available they might find that they do not have a choice.

This will make the learner realise that they have to manage their time carefully if they are to complete all their work and meet every deadline. They might realise that they will have to make some changes, in which case they should plan to make those changes as soon as possible.

HANDY HINT

It is a good idea for the teacher to keep a copy of this for use during a tutorial.

	6am	7am	8am	9am	10am	11am	12pm	1pm	2pm	3pm	4pm	5pm	6pm	7pm	8pm	9pm	10pm	11am
MON	SLEEP	SLEEP	JOG	TRAVEL	COURSE	COURSE	COURSE	COURSE	COURSE	COURSE	COURSE	COURSE	TRAVEL		GYM	GYM	STUDY	STUDY
TUE	SLEEP	SLEEP		TRAVEL	COURSE	COURSE	COURSE	COURSE	COURSE	COURSE	TRAVEL		HOUSE	WORK	SWIM	STUDY	STUDY	
WED	SLEEP	SLEEP	JOG	TRAVEL		COURSE	COURSE	COURSE	COURSE	COURSE	COURSE	COURSE	COURSE	TRAVEL		STUDY	STUDY	
THUR	SLEEP	SLEEP			HOUSE	WORK		WORK	WORK	WORK	WORK		STUDY	STUDY				
FRI	SLEEP	SLEEP	JOG	TRAVEL	COURSE	COURSE	COURSE	COURSE	COURSE	COURSE	COURSE	COURSE	TRAVEL	FRIENDS	FRIENDS			
SAT	SLEEP	SLEEP	SLEEP	SLEEP	SLEEP	SLEEP		WORK	WORK	WORK	WORK		FOOD	SHOP	STUDY	STUDY		
SUN	SLEEP	SLEEP	SLEEP	SLEEP	SLEEP	SLEEP	STUDY	STUDY		FRIENDS	FRIENDS	FRIENDS	FRIENDS	FRIENDS	HOUSE	WORK	STUDY	

Sleep   ■ Course timetable   Travel   ■ Things that can't be changed

■ Things that can be changed   ☐ Free time   ■ Study time

A weekly plan

Learners should try to be as disciplined as possible with their time and as well as planning on a weekly basis they should also have a study plan for the whole course. Ostler (2009, page 21) suggests that learners use a year planner which they display on a prominent wall in their house as a constant reminder of what they need to do. This way they are able to plan around any weekends away or holidays and still meet deadlines. The teacher will provide the dates that work will be set along with all hand-in dates. A learner should include all this information in their study plan.

	Aug	Sep	Oct	Nov	Dec	Jan	Feb	Mar	Apr	May	Jun	Jul
1			A2 due in	Work							Work	
2												
3			Work									
4					Work							
5							Test 5			Test 8		
6					Test 3				A5 due in			
7			Test 1				Work	Work				Work
8				Work	A3 due in						Work	
9						Away						Test 10
10			Work	Test 2		Away		Test 6	Away		Test 9	Test 12
11						Test 4			Away			
12							A4 due in					
13								Work				
14												
15		A1 due in							Test 7			Work
16			Work		Work	Work					Work	
17					Work					Work		
18									Work			
19								Presen-tation				
20												
21												
22			Work						A6 due in			
23											Work	
24											Work	
25									Work	Work		
26												
27		Away										
28			Presen-tations						Presen-tation			
29			Presen-tations	Work		Work	Work					
30											Work	
31												

▒ Holiday   ░ Course hours

A simple course plan

Course plan

This will allow learners to plan their time over the whole course. It should be thought about in advance to enable a learner to plan ahead. If they know that they have a weekend away then they will add this to their study programme so that they still have enough time to complete all of their coursework. They should also try and allow some time for any unforeseen eventualities as there will be times when things happen that are outside the learner's control. This can be achieved by leaving a few gaps such as free weekends, with nothing planned, just in case this time is required for study.

Using the information from both the week and course plan a learner should be able to plan exactly when they are able to set time aside to study.

Remember that if you *fail to plan then you plan to fail*. Don't feel guilty or beat yourself up if you do not get as much done as you hoped. This could result in you feeling very negative and you might find it difficult to get started again. You might even consider giving up. You need to congratulate yourself on every achievement – however small. Remember, Rome wasn't built in a day and neither was an essay researched and written in 24 hours. Set yourself realistic targets.

The best time to study

The best time to study will vary depending on the learner. Some learners will get up early to complete work as they find that this is the best time for them to think.

Others will prefer to work late into the night. Some learners will do a little bit each day by studying in short bursts while others will prefer to take out a whole morning to immerse themselves in a task.

Things a learner should consider:

- Are you an early bird or a night owl?
- When do you concentrate the best?
- When are there fewer distractions?
- What is your learning style?
- What are your personal strengths?
- How much high-quality study time is available for you in each week? Is this enough?
- Could a partner help with the children or household chores?

HANDY HINT

Try working at different times of the day to see when is the best time for you to study or write. If you are able to choose the time that you study, then you will be more productive and produce better quality work.

Where to study

Learners need to create a learning environment that suits the way that they learn. Some learners will concentrate more if there is some music playing in the background while others will require silence in order to work. When learners are studying in groups some learners might prefer to use a personal music device to enable them to create the correct learning environment without disturbing their peers. The location needs to be quiet, without distractions, comfortable and suitable for all learners to work in.

Some learners prefer to study in a library

Physical comfort is important. The room should be at the correct temperature with good lighting and all resources that might be needed by the learner made available. This will enable the learner to get on with their study without too many interruptions. Some learners might prefer to work in a library away from any possible distractions. Other learners might complete their study in a library to enable them to access resources such as books and computers. It should also allow them access to the internet and any virtual learning environment (VLE) from their own organisation. Although the majority of work that will be handed in will have to be computer generated not all learners have computers at home.

STUDY SKILLS

If you want to do further research but are not sure where to look, use the reference list at the back of the books you are using to find more authors who write about the topics you are interested in.

Who else can help?

When a learner is short of time they might have to enlist the help of their family to assist with children or older relatives. Having a 'study buddy' will also help learners to stay motivated as it will enable them to bounce ideas off each other. A study buddy will be able to collect any handouts from the teacher if a class has been missed. They will also take the time to explain the content of the session to help prevent their buddy from falling behind.

List making

Good time management is a skill that will assist learners in their study. Each day a learner will have different things to achieve and different demands made on them. Making a list will help them to organise and prioritise all the things they need to achieve in a given time span.

Monthly list

This will include all the things that need to be achieved while on the course and the hand-in dates for all work. Learners will be able to plan what has to be completed each month and by when. It is also a good idea that hand-in dates are included in their diaries and on calendars as another reminder.

Weekly list

At the end of each week it is good practice for the learner to consider all the things that they need to do and make a list/plan for the week ahead. It also allows them to check that they have completed everything from the previous week's list so that nothing is missed. As things are completed a learner is able to cross then off the monthly list which is a very satisfying and motivating act. This should help the learner to feel that they are making progress.

Daily list

A learner should spread everything from the weekly list over seven days so that they know what they need to achieve on a daily basis. This method will allow for tasks to be separated into smaller manageable sections that the learner is able to complete.

HANDY HINT

Ask for help. The earlier that a learner informs the teacher that they are not coping with their workload or they don't know what it is they have to do, then the sooner a teacher is able to offer some support.

HANDY HINT

If your mind wanders as you read then make notes as you go along, highlight key words or read aloud.

When learners have a lot of things to do they should switch what they are doing from time to time to give themselves a break. This will also help them to develop a fresh way of looking at things.

Reading skills

A learner makes notes while reading

There are different ways to read and learners can save themselves a lot of time if they learn how to read in an appropriate way to get what they need from the text.

EXAMPLE: METHOD 1

This is when a learner reads every word and totally digests the full meaning of what has been written. It takes time and concentration by the learner but they will have a good understanding of what they have just read.

EXAMPLE: METHOD 2

This is when a learner will has a good look at a piece of written work and *scans* the contents. The learner's eye will be drawn to key phrases and they will read certain parts of the text more than other parts.

EXAMPLE: METHOD 3

This is the quickest way of reading anything. A learner *skims* over most of the content but looks for key headings and words to get a feel for the piece before they decide to give it any further attention.

ACTIVITY

Skim read a small article as quickly as possible. Now write down the key points that you can remember. Now read it again but this time take as much time as possible and read it slowly and carefully. What extra information are you now able to add to your original notes?

Other ways to read

- Audio books are also available from libraries and to download online. These are ideal if a learner struggles with reading or if a learner has an auditory learning style. These can be listened to at any time or in any location to suit individual learners, for example while walking home or waiting for public transport.
- Reading aloud will also help to make sense of a complicated part of the text. By reading aloud to themselves a learner might *hear* and therefore *understand* what they had previously missed by reading quietly to themselves.
- A learner should choose the correct moment to read. Some learners might prefer to read in bed at night while others are happy to read on a noisy bus.

Note taking

It is a good idea for learners to take notes throughout the session, especially if there are no handouts available. But learners should not try to write down everything the teacher says, as this is impossible and they will be too busy concentrating on writing that they might forget to listen!

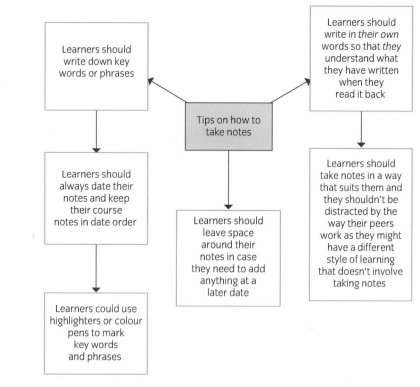

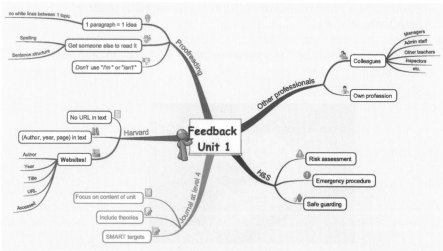

A mind map is a creative way of organising your notes

HANDY HINT

Start the course with a lever-arch folder with dividers in it. Mark each divider with a session date. Be strict with yourself and date all handouts and notes and make sure to file them in the corresponding section. This will save time and reduce stress levels when looking for information.

Barriers to Learning

Ensuring equal opportunities in your centre can begin by turning some of the barriers to learning into positive teaching messages. Communication with your learners is the key.

Past learning experiences

Many adults had a hard time at school and so are wary about re-entering a learning environment, especially if the centre is based in a traditional learning institution.

A high percentage of people have this barrier.

Time

Adults are often restricted to particular times when they can learn. A fixed timetable can effectively prohibit some adults from learning.

Pace

Adults who are returning to learning or who lack confidences in their own abilities may fear that the pace will be too fast for them.

Make sure I don't talk too quickly

Fear

Many people are fearful of using a computer: they might be afraid that they will break it or not understand how to use it.

Not just older people.

Childcare

Many adults will find it too difficult or too expensive to arrange childcare.

Does my organisation help with this?

Costs

Costs are a significant barrier to learning. There may be a number of reasons for this: control over money, access to an income of their own, or having enough money to spare for learning where household needs are the first priority.

FIND OUT COSTS

Literacy, language and accessibility

Learners who need help with literacy or whose first language is not English may need extra support, this may include translation of material and publicity.

An example of a handout on which a learner has added their own notes

Some learners prefer to underline or highlight key words or phrases on handouts or information packs. This will help them to stay focused and it will make the information easier to find in the future. Some learners like to scribble and doodle as it helps them to think. Other learners might prefer to add to the handout using their own words.

Two different methods of taking notes

Some learners prefer to take handwritten notes, others will use a laptop and some might prefer to make an oral recording. Whichever method a learner chooses it should be one that helps them to understand what is being taught and enable them to make sense of their own notes when they read them at a later date

Procrastinate
is to defer, to delay from day
to day

Learners are able to take notes in a variety of ways

ASSIGNMENT WRITING

One of the hardest things about writing any form of essay or assignment is getting started. Some learners will have a tendency to procrastinate and they will do anything rather than start their assignment. Asking them to produce an essay plan which breaks the task into manageable parts will help some learners. Another good tip is to get the learners to start their assignment and then reward themselves once they have achieved their first goal. Once they have planned everything out and written the first page then they reward themselves with a cup of tea and a biscuit or by walking the dog. The assignment tasks are sandwiched between other things, such as more enjoyable tasks that they also have to complete. A teacher could get all their learners to start the assignment in class as this often overcomes that initial hurdle of getting started.

Assignment plan

Learners should organise their assignment plan by using headings, bullet points and the key points that they intend to cover in their assignment. This does not have to be a list but it can take any format that the learner prefers. See the examples below.

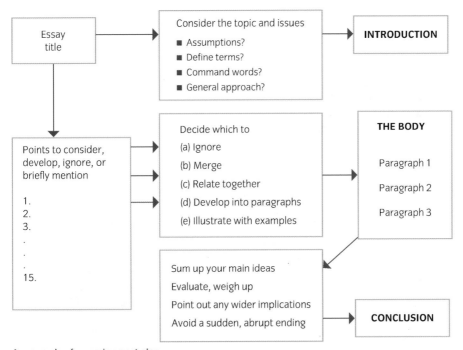

An example of an assignment plan

Paragraph 1

Introduction.

Paragraph 2

Show her opinion of Macbeth by her response to his letter.
Her cruel delight at the King's prospective visit.
Her domination of Macbeth when he enters.

Paragraph 3

She mocks Macbeth for his cowardice.
Shows herself to be without womanly feelings.
Forces him to do her will.
Berates him when he returns with the bloody knives.
Continues to mock him for his fear.

Paragraph 4

Banquet scene.
Reminds Macbeth of his duties.
Covers for him when he sees the ghost.
Berates him in private for his behaviour.

Paragraph 5

Summing up of ways she dominates.
She mocks him.
Her own actions.
Forces him to do her will.

Paragraph 6

Conclusion.

Another example of an assignment plan

Using an assignment plan will allow a learner to breakdown the assignment tasks into manageable sections which they will be able to complete in a logical way. Once they have got the structure of the essay in place, then they will be able to plan in what order to complete it. This will also allow the learner to complete one part at a time, which will make the assignment easier to write, especially if it has to be written over a period of time.

STUDY SKILLS

Don't underestimate how much time you need to take your notes from draft form to a finished piece of work. Allow enough time for formatting and getting your referencing right.

The assignment itself

The most important aspect of assignment writing is that the learner has fully understood the question and therefore answered the question correctly. This means that learners need to fully comprehend the terminology and words that are used.

Term	Definition
Analyse	To break an issue into parts. To look at each part in detail
Assess	To weigh up to what extent something is true. To convince the reader of your argument by citing others. To conclude by stating how much you agree with the original proposition
Clarify	To make something clearer, explain something that is quite complex in simpler terms
Comment upon	To pick out the main points on a subject
Compare	To identify the similarities between two pieces of information
Consider	To say what you think and have observed about something
Contrast	To point out any differences between two pieces of information
Define	To give the meaning of something
Demonstrate	To show how something is done
Describe	To give an account of something, to characterise something
Discuss	To consider all sides and (possibly) make conclusions
Elaborate	To provide more information and details about something
Evaluate	To assess the pros and cons or advantages and limitations about something
Examine	To look at something carefully and establish the key facts about it
Explain	To give the reasons for something
Explore	To look at something from different viewpoints
Give an account of	To give a detailed description of something
Identify	To determine what the key points to be addressed are
Interpret	To demonstrate your understanding of an issue or topic
Justify	To provide evidence to support your ideas and points of view. To consider other people's opinions. To demonstrate purpose

Outline	To convey the main points of something
Prepare	To get something ready
Present	To show something or orally discuss a topic
Reflect	To look back at something
Review	To look thoroughly into a subject. A critical examination
Show how	To present something in a logical order
State	To specify something in clear terms. To present the main features; almost a list but in sentences
Summarise	To give a shortened version of the main points
Use	To put something into action

Presenting assignments

Teachers should make it clear to learners how they would like written work to be presented. There might be requirements from either the awarding organisation or the centre on the type of font or line spacing required, so it is important that learners are fully aware of how to present their work before starting.

All assignments are now expected to be word processed and presented in a professional way. The use of IT has improved the presentation of work from learners and enables them to include the use of colour, along with artwork and diagrams.

All teachers and trainers are expected to be working at level 2 or above in their maths, English and ICT skills (see page 61).

STUDY SKILLS

It might sound obvious, but save your work at regular intervals. One rule of thumb is at least every fifteen minutes. Use a backup device as well, such as a memory stick, just in case your computer breaks down. There is nothing worse than losing lots of work because of a computer malfunction.

General rules

Fonts
Most learners are able to choose the font that they use in their assignment; however some organisations might insist on a particular font so it is up to the learner to check with their teacher. Whatever font is used it should be plain, legible and the font size is normally point 12; for example, Arial 12; Comic Sans 12 and Verdana 12.

Margins

The left- and right-hand margin should be approximately 3cm; the top and bottom margins about 2.5cm. Lines should be spaced at 1.5 line spaced so there is enough space for the teacher to write feedback.

Titles

All assignments should have the full description of the task at the top of the assignment, although this will depend on the organisation.

Header or footer

Each page should have a header or footer with the learner's name, assignment title and date completed.

Page numbering

Pages should be numbered consecutively. Page numbers can be placed centrally or to the right-hand side in the footer. It is good practice to use page X of Y.

Saving trees

Assignments can be printed double sided and the bibliography (if required) can be added at the end of the page. Work can also be submitted directly to the teacher via email.

Word count

When a word count has been set for a written piece of work, learners should indicate the word count at the end, before the bibliography. There is normally a 10% allowance either side of the word count. There may not be a formal word count on assignments or other written work.

Sentences

A learner needs to write in an academic way and include the use of proper punctuation.

Learners should always write in complete sentences and avoid using dashes for punctuation, although acronyms are permitted if a word has first been presented in its entirety and then followed by the acronym in brackets; for example, further education (FE). After that just FE would be acceptable. Long and rambling sentences are often very difficult to read so learners need to be encouraged to try to keep to the point and write in a concise way. Abbreviations such as '&' and 'approx' should be avoided.

Including numbers within the text

When numbers need to be included in any written work they should be spelt out if the number is ten or less. Higher numbers need to be written in numerals; for example, learners need to write 'five', in full, but write '28' numerically. Words will be needed for very large numbers as it makes it easier to understand. For example, learners should write '28 million' instead of '28,000,000.' Sentences should never start with figures such as '28' but spelled out; for example, 'twenty-eight'. Two-digit numbers need to be hyphenated even when they are part of a larger number; for example 'six hundred and twenty-four'. Numerals should be used for statistics and measurements, for example '4%' or '8cm'.

Paragraphs

Paragraphs are collections of ideas, which learners should use to build up their assignment. Each paragraph should follow on from the last and there should be a logical order to the content.

Language

Sexist language should be avoided at all times. This normally includes the use of pronouns (he or she). This can be seen clearly in the following example:

'... it is necessary for the learner to find an appropriate setting when starting an assignment so that he can proceed comfortably and without interruption, thereby increasing his chances of obtaining a good grade.'

An easy way of avoiding sexist language is to write in the third-person gender-neutral singular (eg they, their):

'... it is necessary for the learner to find an appropriate setting when starting their assignments so that they can proceed comfortably and without interruption, thereby increasing their chances of obtaining a good grade.'

Language

Formal language is needed in all written work. The use of slang such as 'phone' and 'telly' should be avoided. Most academic writing requires the learner to write in the third person. However in some assignments it might be appropriate for the learner to write in the first person because they need to state what *they* do. Learners must write in the first person when they are completing any reflective task as they will be discussing what they do and why.

Apostrophes

Apostrophes are used in two different situations in English:

(a) *to indicate a missing part of a word*: I've, don't, can't, it's. These types of apostrophes are known as contractions and they should not be used in formal written work. That means that you should always write these words out in full: I have, do not, cannot, it is.

(b) *to show possession*. In this case, the apostrophe follows the name of the person or thing to which the possession belongs:

The dog's food, the author's paper, the learner's work.

Things can also belong to more than one entity:

The dogs' food (more than one dog); the authors' paper (more than one author); and the learners' work (work of serveral learners).

Spell checking and proofreading

Learners must always spell check their work before handing it in for marking. They will need to ensure that they use the UK spelling checker. Care still needs to be taken as some words are not picked up by the spell checker if they are used out of context; for example 'form' and 'from'. Learners need to take the time to proofread their work carefully before it is submitted.

HANDY HINT

It is a good idea for learners to ask someone else to proofread their work and check it for spellings and grammar before they hand it in. This way mistakes are picked up before it is marked and the learner will be able to make any necessary changes. This will save both the learner and the teacher time. Do not rely on spell check; it does not always choose the correct word for you!

Appendices

Including appendices in written work is a useful way of getting extra information into the assignment without increasing the word count. If an appendix needs to be added it will be mentioned within the text by stating (see Appendix A); the appendix will then be included at the back of the assignment as reference for the reader.

Checklist before submitting work

Have you:

- met *all* the outcomes for this assignment?
- answered *all* the questions?
- presented it in a professional way?

- presented the information in a logical way?
- prepared the assignment in the form required by the teacher?
- proofread everything?
- got someone else to proofread it?
- used appropriate referencing (if required)?
- spell checked it?
- added your name?
- signed to state that the work is your own?
- referenced any quotes correctly (see page 254)?
- made a copy of the assignment?

REFERENCES, FURTHER READING AND OTHER USEFUL SOURCES

REFERENCES AND FURTHER READING FOR UNIT 301

Armitage, A. and Renwick, M. (2008) *Assessment in FE*. New York: Continuum Publishing Group.

Avis, J., Fisher, R. and Thompson, R. (2010) *Teaching in Lifelong Learning*. Maidenhead: Open University Press.

Corder, C. (2008) *Learning to Teach Adults: An Introduction,* 2nd edition. Abingdon: Routledge.

Daines, J. with Daines, C. and Graham, B. (2006) *Adult Learning, Adult Teaching*, 4th edition. Cardiff: Welsh Academic Press.

Francis, M. and Gould, J. (2009) *Achieving your PTLLS Award*, 2nd edition. London: Sage.

Gravells, A. (2008) *Preparing to Teach in the Lifelong Learning Sector,* 5th edition. Exeter: Learning Matters.

Haydn, T. (2008) *Learning to Teach in a Secondary School,* 4th edition. Abingdon: Routledge.

Huddlestone, P. and Unwin, L. (2007*) Teaching and Learning in Further Education Diversity and Change,* 3rd edition. Abingdon: Routledge.

Irons, A. (2007) *Enhancing Learning Through Formative Assessment and Feedback*. London: Routledge.

Jarvis, P., Holford, J. and Griffin, C. (2003) *The Theory and Practice of Learning,* 2nd edition. London: Kogan Page Ltd.

Keeley-Browne, L. (2007) *Training to Teach in the Lifelong Learning Skills Sector.* Harlow: Pearson Education Ltd.

Minton, D. (2005) *Teaching Skills in Further and Adult Education,* 3rd edition. Tinbridge wells: Macmillian Press Ltd.

Petty, G. (2009) *Teaching Today,* 4th edition. Cheltenham: Nelson Thornes Ltd.

Race, P. (2010) *Making Learning Happen*. London: Sage.

Reece, I. and Walker, S. (2004) *Teaching, Training and Learning,* 5th edition. Sunderland: Business Education Publishers Ltd.

Rogers, A. (2003) *Teaching Adults,* 3rd edition. Maidenhead: Open University Press.

Scales, P. (2008) *Teaching in the Lifelong Learning Sector.* Maidenhead: Open University Press.

Walklin, L. (1990) *Teaching and Learning in Further and Adult Education,* 2nd edition. Cheltenham: Nelson Thornes Ltd.

Wilson, L. (2009) *Practical Teaching: A Guide to PTLLS and DTLLS.* Andover: Cengage Learning EMEA.

USEFUL PUBLICATIONS AND WEBSITES

Books

Wertheimer, A. (1997) *Images of Possibility: Creating Learning Opportunities for Adults with Mental Health Difficulties.* NIACE. This book looks at key features and innovative practice in LEA and college provision.

Skill (2002) *Students with Mental Health Difficulties: Your Questions Answered.* This gives an overview of the specific issues related to working with learners with mental health difficulties in a further education context.

Websites

http:/www.archive.excellencegateway.org.uk

http://www.bbc.co.uk/skillswise

http://www.bdadyslexia.org.uk/aboutdyslexia.html

http://www.dfs.gov.uk/

http://www.geoffpetty.com

http://www.hse.gov.uk/education/qca.htm

http://www.ifl.ac.uk

http://www.learningandteaching.info

http://www.teachers.org.uk/resources/pdf/law-and-you.pdf

http://www.tes.co.uk/publications.asp

www.excellencegateway.org.uk

Further sources of help to inclusion

Royal National Institute for the Deaf (RNID)
The RNID runs a telephone/text service, produces information leaflets and fact sheets.

Their publication 'Deaf Students in Further Education' gives a clear account of what learners may need while studying. It is available on their website.
www.rnid.org.uk

Royal National Institute for the Blind (RNIB)
The RNIB produces a wide range of resource materials which will
be useful for learners. It runs a telephone information service and
supports this with a range of fact sheets.
www.rnib.org.uk

Scope (national organisation for people with cerebral palsy)
Scope produces information relevant to people with a physical
disability.

The Scope website offers a large quantity of useful information online
but it also provides an index of additional publications that may be
useful. The publications website is:
http://www.scope.org.uk/action/publications/index.shtm

NIACE (a national organisation that promotes adult learning)
NIACE has published several packs that are accessible to people with
learning difficulties and books on different aspects of education for
adults with learning difficulties.
www.niace.org.uk

BILD (British Institute of Learning Disabilities)
BILD is a not-for-profit organisation which exists to improve the quality
of life for all people with learning disabilities. It provides information,
publications, training and consultancy services.
www.bild.org.uk/about-bild

CHANGE Picture Bank
The CHANGE Picture Bank CD-ROM has pictures to help make
information easier to understand. The pack gives lots of ideas on how
to make information easier to understand, including drawing your own
pictures, using easy words and writing in simple ways.
www.changepeople.co.uk

MIND (the mental health charity)
The aim of this charity is to advance the views, needs and ambitions
of people with experience of mental distress, to promote inclusion by
challenging discrimination, influencing policy through campaigning
and education and inspire the development of quality services which
reflect expressed need and diversity.
www.mind.org.uk

REFERENCES AND FURTHER READING FOR UNIT 302

Fairclough, M. (2008) *Supporting Learners in the Lifelong Learning
Sector.* Maidenhead: Open University Press.

Gould, J. (2012) *Learning Theory and Classroom Practice in the Lifelong
Learning Sector.* Exeter: Learning Matters.

Gravells, A. (2011) *Preparing to Teach in the Lifelong Learning Sector.*
Exeter: Learning Matters.

Kidd, W. and Czerniawski, G. (2011) *Successful Teaching 14–19: Practice and Reflection*. London: Sage.

McGill, R. (2011) *Pose Pause Pounce Bounce*. Available online at www.tes.co.uk. Accessed on 3/01/2013.

Peart, S. and Atkins, L. (2011) *Teaching 14–19 Learners*. Exeter: Learning Matters.

Petty, G. (2004) *Teaching Today*. Cheltenham: Nelson Thornes.

Powell, S. and Tummons, J. (2011) *Inclusive Practice*. Exeter: Learning Matters.

Race, P. (2010) *Making Learning Happen*. London: Sage.

Race, P. and Pickford, R. (2008) *Making Teaching Work*. London: Sage.

Reece, I. and Walker, S. (2003) *Teaching, Training and Learning*. Oxford: Alden Group Limited.

Scales, P. (2008) *Teaching in the Lifelong Learning Sector*. Maidenhead: Open University Press.

QCA (2007) available online at www.excellencegateway.org.uk. Accessed on 08/01/2013.

USEFUL PUBLICATIONS AND WEBSITES

www.incurriculum.org.uk

This is a good website that explains what inclusive practice is and offers useful suggestions when adapting resources, teaching and assessment methods.

REFERENCES AND FURTHER READING FOR UNIT 303

Clutterbuck, D. (2008) *Everyone Needs a Mentor*. London: CIPD.

DCFS (nd) *National Strategy for Individual Tuition*. Available online at www.education.gov.uk. Accessed on 18/12/2012.

Fairclough, M. (2008) *Supporting Learners in the Lifelong Learning Sector*. Maidenhead: Open University Press.

Gibbs, G. (1988) *Learning by Doing: A Guide to Teaching and Learning Methods*. Oxford: Oxford Polytechnic Further Education Unit.

Gould, J. (2012) *Learning Theory and Classroom Practice in the Lifelong Learning Sector*. Exeter: Learning Matters.

Hillier, Y. (2005) *Reflective Teaching in Further and Adult Education*. London: Continuum.

Kidd, W. and Czerniawski, G. (2011) *Successful Teaching 14–19: Practice and Reflection*. London: Sage.

Kolb, D. A. (1984) *Experiential Learning: Experience as the Source of Learning and Development*. Englewood Cliffs, NJ: Prentice Hall.

Megginson, D. and Clutterbuck, D. (2005) *Techniques for Coaching and Mentoring*. Oxford: Elsevier Butterworth-Heinemann.

Moon, J. (2008) *Reflection in Learning and Professional Development*. Abingdon: RoutledgeFalmer.

Peart, S. and Atkins, L. (2011) *Teaching 14–19 Learners*. Exeter: Learning Matters.

Petty, G. (2004) *Teaching Today*. Cheltenham: Nelson Thornes.

Powell, S. and Tummons, J. (2011) *Inclusive Practice*. Exeter: Learning Matters.

Race, P. (2010) *Making Learning Happen*. London: Sage.

Race, P. and Pickford, R. (2008) *Making Teaching Work*. London: Sage.

Rogers, J. (2008) *Coaching Skills: A Handbook*. Maidenhead: Open University Press.

Rolfe, G., Freshwater, D. and Jasper, M. (2001) (eds.) *Critical Reflection for Nursing and the Helping Professions*. Basingstoke: Palgrave.

Scales, P. (2008) *Teaching in the Lifelong Learning Sector*. Maidenhead: Open University Press.

Starr, J. (2003) *The Coaching Manual*. London: Pearson Education Ltd.

Thompson, S. and Thompson, N. (2008) *The Critically Reflective Practitioner*. Basingstoke: Palgrave MacMillan.

Wallace, S. and Gravells, A. (2008) *Mentoring*. Exeter: Learning Matters.

REFERENCES AND FURTHER READING FOR UNIT 304

Gould, J. (2010) *Learning Theory and Classroom Practice*. Exeter: Learning Matters.

Hillier, Y. (2005) *Reflective Teaching in Further and Adult Education*. London: Continuum.

Kidd, W, and Czerniawski, G. (2011) *Successful Teaching 14–19: Practice and Reflection*. London: Sage.

Maslow, A. (1970) *Motivation and Personality,* 3rd edition. New York: Harper Collins.

Moon, J. (2008) *Reflection in Learning and Professional Development*. Abingdon: RoutledgeFalmer.

NCSU (nd) *Tuckman's Group Development Model.* Available Online at www.ncsu.edu. Accessed on 3/9/2012.

Peart, S. and Atkins, L. (2011) *Teaching 14–19 Learners.* Exeter: Learning Matters.

Petty, G. (2004) *Teaching Today.* Cheltenham: Nelson Thornes.

Race, P. and Pickford, R. (2008) *Making Teaching Work.* London: Sage.

Reece, I. and Walker, S. (2003) *Teaching, Training and Learning.* Sunderland: Business Education Publishers.

Rolfe, G., Freshwater, D. and Jasper, M. (2001) *Critical Reflection in Nursing and the Helping Professions: A User's Guide.* Basingstoke: Palgrave Macmillan.

Scales, P. (2008) *Teaching in the Lifelong Learning Sector.* Maidenhead: Open University Press.

Wallace, S. (2011) *Teaching, Tutoring and Training in the Lifelong Learning Sector.* Exeter: Learning Matters.

Warren, K. (nd) *Exploring how Rewards can Raise Learner Motivation and Confidence in Mathematics.* Available Online at www.campaign-for-learning.org.uk. Accessed on 27/3/2013.

USEFUL PUBLICATIONS AND WEBSITES

Websites

www.heacademy.ac.uk (Good for research and hints and tips about teaching in general terms)

www.tes.co.uk (Video clips and resources)

www.teachingideas.co.uk (Good for resources, but may need to be tailored for FE)

www.bbc.co.uk/skillswise (Functional skills and interactive quiz)

www.teachit.co.uk (Teaching English resources)

www.teachersworld.org.uk (New site with strategies and resources, under construction)

www.excellencegateway.org.uk (Good for resources and information about different teaching strategies)

www.prezzi.com (Useful site to help build and create a more interactive version of the PowerPoint presentation)

www.teachers.guardian.co.uk/resources (Good for resources, but may need to be tailored for FE)

REFERENCES AND FURTHER READING FOR UNIT 305/306

Armitage, A. and Renwick, M. (2008) *Assessment in FE*. New York: Continuum Publishing Group.

Avis, J., Fisher, R. and Thompson, R. (2010) *Teaching in Lifelong Learning*. Maidenhead: Open University Press.

Black, P. and William, D. (1998) *Inside the Black Box: Raising Standards through Classroom Assessment*. London: School of Education, King's College.

Corder, C. (2008) *Learning to Teach Adults: An Introduction,* 2nd edition. Abingdon: Routledge.

Francis, M. and Gould, J. (2010) *Achieving your PTLLS Award*. London. Sage Publications Ltd.

Haydn, T. (2008) *Learning to Teach in a Secondary School, A companion to School Exprience,* 4th edition. Abingdon: Routledge.

Huddlestone, P. and Unwin, L. (2008*) Teaching and Learning in Further Education Diversity and Change,* 3rd edition. Abingdon: Routledge.

Irons, A. (2007) *Enhancing Learning Through Formative Assessment and Feedback*. London: Routledge.

Jarvis, P., Holford, J. and Griffin, C. (2003) *The Theory and Practice of Learning,* 2nd edition. London: Kogan Page Ltd.

Keeley-Browne, L. (2007) *Training to Teach in the Lifelong Learning Skills Sector*. Harlow: Pearson Education Ltd.

Petty. G. (2009) *Teaching Today,* 4th edition. Cheltenham: Nelson Thornes.

Pontin, K. (2012) *The City & Guilds Practical Guide to Quality Assurance*. London: City & Guilds.

Read, H. (2004) *Excellence in Assessment and Verification*. Leicester: Read on Publications.

Reece I. and Walker, S. (2007) *Teaching, Training and Learning,* 6th edition. Sunderland: Business Education Publishers Ltd.

Rogers, A. (2003) *Teaching Adults,* 3rd edition. Maidenhead: Open University Press.

Scales, P. (2012) *Teaching in the Lifelong Learning Sector.* Maidenhead: Open University Press.

Steward, A (2006) *A to Z Teaching in FE*. London: Continuum International Publishing Group

Tummons, J. (2005) *Assessing Learning in Further Education*. Exeter: Learning Matters.

Wallace, S. (2007) *Getting the Buggers Motivated in FE*. London: Continuum.

Walklin. L. (2000) *Teaching and Learning in Further and Adult Education*, 2nd edition. Cheltenham: Nelson Thornes Ltd.

USEFUL PUBLICATIONS AND WEBSITES

Websites

Assess to qualifications:

http://wales.gov.uk/topics/educationskills/qualificationsin wales/?lang=en

Assessment guidance booklets:

www.sflip.org.uk/assessment/assessmentguidance.aspx

Assessment methods:

www.brookes.ac.uk/services/ocsld/resources/methods.html

http://www.geoffpetty.com

City & Guilds:

www.cityandguilds.com

Chartered Institute of Education Assessors:

www.ciea.org.uk

Government legislation:

www.legislation.gov.uk

Health and Safety Executive:

http://www.dfs.gov.uk/

www.hse.gov.uk

Initial assessment:

www.excellencgateway.org.uk

Institute for Learning:

www.ifl.ac.uk

Learning and Skills Improvement Service (LSIS):

www.exellence gateway.org.uk/node/57

Peer and self-assessment:

www.ncirc.org/essentials/assessing/peereval.htm

Sector Skills Councils:

www.sscalliance.org

REFERENCES AND FURTHER READING FOR HELPFUL INFORMATION, SUGGESTIONS AND TIPS

Avis, J., Fisher, R. and Thompson, R. (2010) *Teaching in Lifelong Learning*. Maidenhead: Open University Press.

Corder, C. (2008) *Learning to Teach Adults: An Introduction,* 2nd edition. Abingdon: Routledge.

Dawson, C. (2006) *The Mature Student's Guide*, Trowbridge: Cromwell Press Ltd.

Francis, M. and Gould, J. (2010) *Achieving your PTLLS Award*. London: Sage Publications.

Godfry, J. (2010) *Reading and Making Notes*. Basingstoke: Palgrave Macmillan Publishers Limited.

Haydn, T. (2008) *Learning to Teach in a Secondary School,* 4th edition. Abingdon: Routledge

Huddlestone, P. and Unwin, L. (2007) *Teaching and Learning in Further Education: Diversity and Change,* 3rd edition. Abingdon: Routledge.

Irons, A. (2007) *Enhancing Learning through Formative Assessment and Feedback*. London: Routledge.

Jarvis, P., Holford, J. and Griffin, C. (2003) *The Theory and Practice of Learning,* 2nd edition. London: Kogan Page Ltd.

Keeley-Browne, L. (2007) *Training to Teach in the Lifelong Learning Skills Sector.* Harlow: Pearson Education Ltd.

Northedge, A. (2007) *The Good Study Guide*. Maidenhead: Open University Press.

Ostler, C. (2009) *Study Skills, A Pupil's Survival Guide*. Bodmin: MPG Books Ltd

Petty, G. (2009) *Teaching Today,* 4th edition. Cheltenham: Nelson Thornes.

Read, H. (2004) *Excellence in Assessment and Verification*. Leicester. Read On Publications.

Reece I. and Walker, S. (2007) *Teaching, Training and Learning,* 6th edition. Sunderland: Business Education Publishers Ltd.

Rogers, A. (2003) *Teaching Adults,* 3rd edition. Maidenhead: Open University Press.

Scales, P. (2010) *Teaching in the Lifelong Learning Sector.* Maidenhead: Open University Press.

Schön, D. A. (1983) *The Reflective Practitioner in Action.* New York: Basic Books.

Tummons, J. (2005) *Assessing Learning in Further Education.* Exeter: Learning Matters.

Wallace, S. (2007) *Getting the Buggers Motivated in FE.* London: Continuum.

Walklin, L. (2000) *Teaching and Learning in Further and Adult Education,* 2nd edition. Cheltenham: Nelson Thornes.

Wilson, L. (2009) *Practical Teaching: A Guide to PTLLS and DTLLS.* Andover: Cengage Learning EMEA.

Further sources of help for this unit

For more information on spelling, grammar and how to improve your writing, see: www.bbc.co.uk/skillswise

www.brunel.ac.uk/~mastmmg/ssguide/sshome.htm

www.cityandguilds.co/uk-home.hml

www.educationscotland.gov.uk/studyskills/index.asp

www.excellencgateway.org.uk

http://www.geoffpetty.com

www.tes.co.uk/teaching-resource/Study-Skills-6107574/

www.learnhighergroupwork.com/

http://www.bbk.ac.uk/lib/subguides/studyskills/studyskillsweb

http://www.academictips.org/

http://referencing.port.ac.uk/

GLOSSARY

active learning is when a learner takes part in the learning in an involved way. They participate fully and are engaged with the process

affective domain involves learning about beliefs and attitudes; often considered in terms of trying to change a person's beliefs by providing information from a range of viewpoints

andragogy is the term given to teaching adults. It is based on the idea that adults are more motivated and can draw from prior experience and knowledge. Therefore they are self directed as learners

cognitive domain is about learning knowledge and information; often considered in terms of theoretical subjects

deep learning is a type of learning that will last over a period of time because the learner has understood and made sense of the information

diversity is about recognising and celebrating differences between individuals and groups

directive approach is where a teacher takes a proactive and lead role in the session, guiding and instructing the learner

equality is about giving every learner an equal opportunity to succeed. This may include making reasonable adjustments

extrinsic motivation is caused by factors external to the individual learner and unrelated to the task they are performing. Examples include money, good grades, and other rewards

formative assessment is continued checking of learners' progress to help move them towards achieving their individual learning goals

formative feedback is information that is given so that learners can identify what can be further improved as they continue with their studies

Guided learning hours (GLHs) are the number of hours that an awarding body suggests that it takes to deliver a course. This also determines how much funding will be provided per learner

inclusive practice is where a teacher uses a range of strategies and approaches when planning in order to teach everyone regardless of barriers

initial assessment involves checking what has gone on in the past to help improve future learning

intrinsic motivation internal desires to perform a particular task; learners will do certain activities because it gives them pleasure, interests them or develops a particular skill

learning styles are the preferred way that a learner takes on board information. This style can be visual, auditory, read/write or kinaesthetic (practical), otherwise known as VARK

lifelong learning: in 2007 the lifelong learning sector was defined as comprising adult and community learning (ACL), further education (FE), higher education (HE), libraries, archives and information services (LAIS) and work-Based learning (WBL)

non-directive approach is where a teacher takes a back seat during the session, waiting for the learner to take control of their own learning

passive learning is when learning happens to a learner and they are not involved in the process

pedagogy is the term given to teaching children. It is based on the idea that children need to be taught directly and instructed in their learning. They are not very motivated or self directed and do not have very much experience or knowledge to draw from

personalised approach is one in which a teacher plans how they are going to deliver sessions based on individual need. Often used when working with learners who have learning difficulties

procrastinate is to defer, to delay from day to day

reflection-in-action is when you consider what you are doing while you are doing it and make changes along the way. It is 'thinking on your feet' or reactive reflection

roles are 'nouns' (job titles), while responsibilities are what a teacher needs to do to accomplish the role

scaffolded worksheets are a type of worksheet that provides learners with a template as a guide to help give structure to the content. For example, a letter template with headings to work from

SmartScreen is the name of the resources available online from City & Guilds

summative assessment is the proof that learners have learnt

summative feedback is information given so that a learner can see what has been achieved in the work as a final grade and end result

surface learning is when something is learnt by rote resulting in information recall

teaching method is the way in which you deliver a topic to your learners. Also called a teaching strategy

theory is a set of principles or system of ideas designed to explain something; normally developed from research

wiki is a website developed collaboratively by a group of users. It is built by allowing any user to add and edit content. For example, wikipedia

INDEX